DOCKS & PROJECTS

Great Things for the Whole Family
to Make and Do

DOCKS & PROJECTS

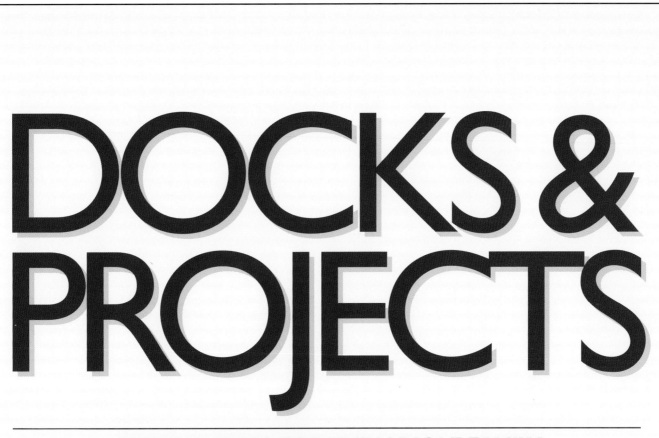

GREAT THINGS FOR THE WHOLE FAMILY

TO MAKE AND DO

EDITED BY ANN VANDERHOOF

Cottage Life BOOKS

TORONTO, CANADA

The information in this book is accurate to the best of our knowledge. Nevertheless, the reader remains responsible for the selection and use of tools and materials. As well, all do-it-yourself activities involve a degree of risk. When working with tools and working – and playing – around water, be sure to observe safety precautions and use care, good judgement, and common sense.

Cataloguing in Publication Data

Main entry under title:
Cottage Life docks & projects: great things for the whole family to make & do

ISBN 0-9696922-1-8

1. Vacation homes – Remodeling.   2. Do-it-yourself work.   I. Vanderhoof, Ann.   II. Title: Docks & projects.

TH4835.C67 1994   643'.2   C94-931996-1

Edited by Ann Vanderhoof
Design by Steve Manley, Overleaf Design Ltd.
Illustrations by Patrick Corrigan

Film by Fieldstone Graphics Inc.

Printed and bound in Canada by
D. W. Friesen & Sons Ltd., Altona, Manitoba

Published by
Cottage Life Books
111 Queen St. E.
Ste. 408
Toronto, Ontario, Canada
M5C 1S2

Published in the United States by
Cottage Life Inc.
Box 1338
Ellicott Station
Buffalo, N.Y. U.S.A.
14205

Trade distribution by
Firefly Books
250 Sparks Avenue
Willowdale, Ontario, Canada
M2H 2S4
and
Firefly Books (U.S.)
Box 1338
Ellicott Station
Buffalo, N.Y., U.S.A.
14205

CONTENTS

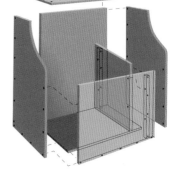

INTRODUCTION

A book for when the urge to make something strikes

If you're like me, your weekend retreat is one of your greatest pleasures. It's the place where you can get away from it all and escape the hectic pace of everyday life. It's often the place that brings you closest to nature. And, most important, a weekend retreat provides the opportunity – and the time – to putter, to build things, and to enjoy activities together as a family.

Docks & Projects is packed full of suggestions for when the urge to make something strikes. Some of our ideas are easy enough for kids (with a little adult supervision); most require only basic do-it-yourself skills, although a few are more appropriate for experienced woodworkers. They are all designed to make your place more comfortable, and more fun.

The projects are collected from the pages of award-winning *Cottage Life* magazine. (See opposite.) Over the years, the magazine's do-it-yourself projects have consistently been one of its most popular features. Readers continually ask to purchase back issues in order to obtain the instructions for a project they have seen in a friend or neighbour's copy of the magazine. Sometimes the project has simply struck their fancy; other times, it has been something they *absolutely needed* to build.

Because doing-it-yourself is not just a pleasure; sometimes it's also a necessity. In out-of-the-way locations, it may be difficult (and expensive!) to hire someone for a building project. And in many cases, a weekend retreat requires you to undertake projects that you've never had to tackle before.

Docks & Projects is here to help.

—*Ann Vanderhoof, Editor*

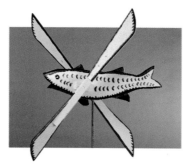

A WORD ABOUT SCREWS

Some of the projects in this book call for Robertson screws and screwdrivers. The square drive of this type of screw provides higher torque and a better grip for the screwdriver, and these screws are less inclined to strip. Readily available in Canada, Robertson screws and screwdrivers can be hard to come by in the U.S. If you can't find Robertson, use Phillips.

HOW TO ENLARGE TEMPLATES

Before you can begin some of these projects, you will need to enlarge our scaled-down templates to full-size patterns. The quickest and easiest way to do this is by using an enlarging photocopier or a pantograph (a tool that is used to copy a design and enlarge or reduce it at the same time). If you don't have access to either, use the following method: Transfer the design onto 1" graph paper, square by square. (One square on our grids equals 1".) Note where the outlines of the pieces intersect our grid and accurately transfer the points to the graph paper. Once the points have been plotted, connect them together for a complete outline.

ABOUT COTTAGE LIFE MAGAZINE

Each issue of *Cottage Life* magazine is packed with informative and entertaining reading to help you enjoy your time at your weekend retreat. Published six times a year, *Cottage Life* contains:
• maintenance and repair tips;
• practical "how-to" advice;
• recipes and entertaining ideas;
• sunny-day and rainy-day activities and games for kids and adults;
• boating, watersports, and fishing advice;
• a real estate section;
• nature, history, and humour;
• and, of course, do-it-yourself projects like the ones in this book.

Since its founding in 1988, *Cottage Life* has twice been chosen "Best Magazine of the Year" by the Canadian Society of Magazine Editors. It has also received Canada's most prestigious magazine award, the Award for Overall Editorial Excellence, given by the National Magazine Awards Foundation.

Enjoyable to read and lavishly illustrated, *Cottage Life* provides essential information for every situation you're likely to encounter at your cottage, cabin, or camp. For information on how to subscribe, contact: *Cottage Life*, 111 Queen St. East, Ste. 408, Toronto, Ontario, Canada M5C 1S2; tel.: (416) 360-6880; fax: (416) 360-6814.

TRADITIONAL COTTAGE CHAIR

With its deep seat, wide arms, and fan back, this chair is perfect for settling into summer. By Jeff Mathers

Some people call it an Adirondack chair. Others call it a Muskoka chair. Whatever name you give it, it can't be beat for reading, snacking, or simply snoozing.

Our version of this classic features a deep, comfy seat with rolled front (so you won't get pinched behind the knees), arms fully 7" wide (perfect for supporting a drink, a plate, or a book), and a fan back – highlighted by a cut-out of a loon. It's made of pine, but cedar is a good alternative. To give the chair a weathered, seen-a-lot-of-summers look, we finished it with Old-Fashioned Milk Paint, which we then rubbed with steel wool to simulate wear. (To order Milk Paint by mail or to find an outlet near you – they are located across Canada and the U.S. – contact the Canadian Old-Fashioned Milk Paint Co., 163 Queen St. E., Toronto, Ont. M5A 1S1, 416-364-1393.)

1. Cut all chair pieces from your pine boards, following the lumber list (at right) and the templates on p. 12.

2. Sand all edges smooth and round all corners with 120-grit sandpaper (or, if you have one, use a router with a ¼" rounding-over bit).

3. Lay one set of parts A, B, and C flat on the ground or work bench, positioning them so part A sits over top of

---

MATERIALS
LUMBER
- **1" x 8" x 16' pine (2 pcs.) to cut:**
  - 2 pcs. ¾" x 7½" x 31½" (part H)
  - 2 pcs. ¾" x 5½" x 38½" (part A)
  - 12 pcs. ¾" x 1¾" x 19½" (part K)
  - 4 pcs. ¾" x 2¾" x 36" (part J)
  - 2 pcs. ¾" x 4" x 37" (part J)
- **1" x 6" x 6' pine (1 pc.) to cut:**
  - 1 pc. ¾" x 4½" x 18½" (part E)
  - 2 pcs. ¾" x 5½" x 5½" (part F)
  - 2 pcs. ¾" x 4" x 21" (part C)
- **1" x 4" x 8' pine (1 pc.) to cut:**
  - 1 pc. ¾" x 3" x 19" (part D)
  - 2 pcs. ¾" x 4" x 26¾" (part B)
  - 2 pcs. ¾" x 1¾" x 3" (part G)

OTHER
4 ⅜" x 2" carriage bolts with nuts and washers
1 box of 100 1¼" Robertson flathead screws
Paint and urethane, or stain to finish

TOOLS
Table or radial-arm saw
Jigsaw
Router (optional)
Crescent wrench (for carriage bolts)
120-grit garnet sandpaper
Electric drill (⅜" and ⅛" bits)
Robertson screwdriver

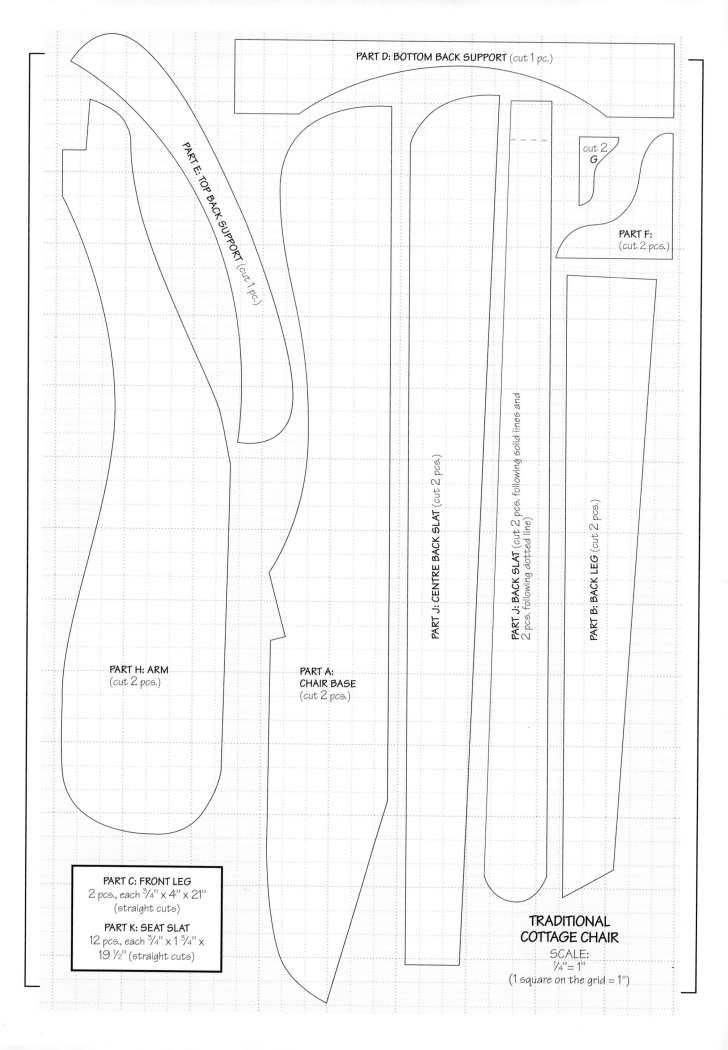

PART D: BOTTOM BACK SUPPORT (cut 1 pc.)

PART E: TOP BACK SUPPORT (cut 1 pc.)

cut 2
G

PART F:
(cut 2 pcs.)

PART J: CENTRE BACK SLAT (cut 2 pcs.)

PART J: BACK SLAT (cut 2 pcs. following solid lines and 2 pcs. following dotted line)

PART B: BACK LEG (cut 2 pcs.)

PART H: ARM
(cut 2 pcs.)

PART A:
CHAIR BASE
(cut 2 pcs.)

PART C: FRONT LEG
2 pcs., each ¾" x 4" x 21"
(straight cuts)

PART K: SEAT SLAT
12 pcs., each ¾" x 1 ¾" x
19 ½" (straight cuts)

TRADITIONAL
COTTAGE CHAIR

SCALE:
¼"= 1"
(1 square on the grid = 1")

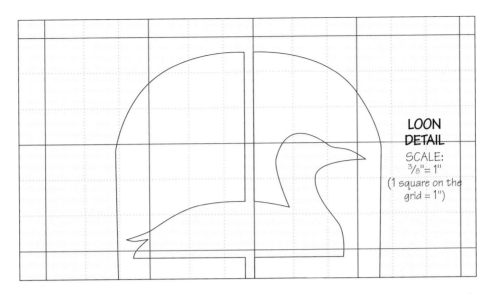

LOON DETAIL
SCALE:
³⁄₈" = 1"
(1 square on the grid = 1")

part B, and part C sits over top of part A. Also make sure parts B and C are parallel to each other. See Diagram 1, next page.

4. Using a ³⁄₈" drill bit and an electric drill, drill four holes – two through parts A and B and two through parts A and C. The position of these holes is not critical, as long as they are approximately diagonal to each other. See Diagram 1.

5. Repeat steps 3 and 4 for the other side of the chair.

6. Bolt parts A, B, and C together with ³⁄₈" x 2" carriage bolts.

7. Screw part D into notch on both parts A, using two 1¼" flathead screws per side, making sure you hang part D over sides of part A by ¼" on both sides. See Diagram 2.

8. Fasten part E to the tops of parts B, also using two 1¼" flathead screws per side. The distance between the tops of parts B should be the same as the distance at the bottoms. See Diagram 2.

9. Screw support brackets F to parts C, so they are flush with the tops of parts C and centred, using two 1¼" screws per side. See Diagram 1.

10. Screw support brackets G to parts B, flush with the fronts of parts B and 21" up from the bottom, using two 1¼" flathead screws per side. See Diagram 1.

11. Set arms H onto support brackets and screw them down with two 1¼" flathead screws into support bracket F and one screw into support bracket G. Also use two 1¼" screws per side to fasten the arm to part B.

DIAGRAM 1

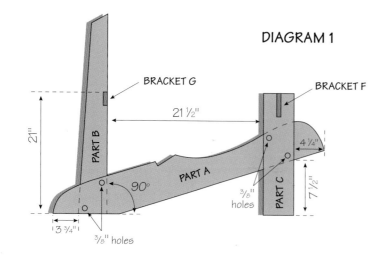

12. Screw back slats J onto chair one at a time, keeping the slats flush with the bottom of part D. These slats should be spaced ¼" apart, with the two large slats in the centre and the shorter ones on the outside. If you want your chair to have a loon cutout, use the template on p. 13 to cut the two large slats before attaching.

13. Screw seat slats K into place using 1¼" screws, keeping the slats ¼" apart and starting at the rear of the seat and working your way forward. Hang the slats over the edges of parts A ¼" on either side. The three slats that fit between the front legs C will have to be trimmed down ½" and a third one notched, so they will fit between the legs.

14. If you choose to finish the chair with Milk Paint, apply two coats, followed by a coat of satin-finish urethane to weatherproof it. Alternatively, apply an exterior penetrating stain or an oil finish that will preserve the natural colour of the pine.

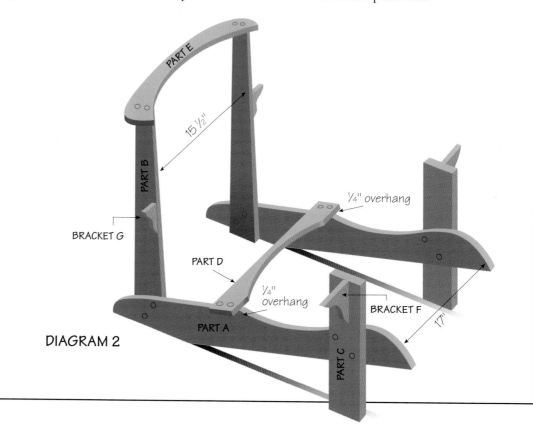

DIAGRAM 2

RUSTIC ROPE OCEAN MAT

Our version of this shipboard mat is designed to sit in front of fireplace or door. By Bruce Macdonald

The name for this mat design is said to derive from its swirling folds, which resemble ocean waves. Sailors used to while away the hours at sea by making these from old rope, and smaller sizes were used aboard ship as "thump mats" to stop blocks from banging themselves to pieces on the deck.

FIG. 1
Find the middle of the rope and form a loop, making sure the right end crosses over the left.

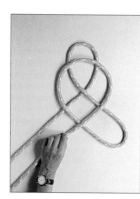

FIG. 2
Leaving a bight (oblong loop) in the line, make a second loop with the right end, crossing back over the first loop.

FIG. 3
Make another bight in the line using the left end, and run it under the bight made in Figure 2.

FIG. 4
Start the weave by threading the rope – over and under – through the loops previously constructed.

This mat may be woven inside of an hour without difficulty. It's a good idea to practise with some short lengths of old cord first, however, just to get the hang of it. For the large floor mat (18" x 30"), we used 100 ft. of ⅝" Manila rope. For a smaller mat (11" x 17"), a nice size for a hot-pad or table centrepiece, you will need 65 ft. of ⅜" white dacron or coloured nylon line. New Manila is available at most hardware or marine stores. It's less expensive than synthetic line and has a pleasantly rustic appearance. If you are going to use the rope in a hearth mat, make sure it's

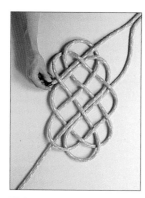

FIG. 9
Continue around the mat course, snugging up rope loops evenly. If at this point you've made a loop or two too large, it's simple enough to go in and even them up.

FIG. 10
Once you have doubled the course (when two rope widths have been completely woven), double it again by repeating the same process with the other end of the rope.

FIG. 11
You may take as many turns around the mat course as you like. Traditionally, three is the minimum, and five is about the maximum; more than that and you start to see some buckling of the line at the intersections. (Our Manila floor mat has four courses; the smaller yellow mat, five.)

FIG. 12
Finish the mat by trimming the rope and sewing the short ends under the mat with a darning needle and whipping twine. To reinforce the mat, you can sew side-by-side strands together where they intersect on the mat's outside edges. Mats that are left outdoors will shrink slightly, which makes them tighter and stronger.

FIG. 5
Continue the weave as shown...

FIG. 6
...to complete one full course of the mat.

FIG. 7
After the basic weave has been established you can begin to double the course...

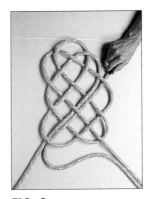

FIG. 8
...by threading the right end through the same pattern, simply retracing the weave.

not the tarred kind. (If you opt for a floor mat of synthetic line, avoid white rope, which will soon look grubby.) I once had a mat made from the worn-out mainsheet of an old sailboat. The rope was full of small chafes and raggedy splices, and the mat looked well used from day one.

A knife, a darning needle, whipping twine, and some patience are the only tools you'll need. If you start off with new rope, whip the ends before you begin. (See box at right.) The first steps establish the overall size and shape of the mat, so make the pattern as neat and even as possible. At every step, check the picture to ensure your rope crosses as illustrated and the size of your loops approximates the size of those shown.

WHIPPING THE LOOSE ENDS

Make a loop in an end of whipping twine, leaving a tail of several inches. Lay the looped section along the unfinished free end of the rope, with the loop's head at the raw end of the rope. Hold the loop in place and, starting about ¾" away from the rope end, begin to wrap the twine smoothly and tautly around the rope, moving towards the raw end.

When you get near the end, cut the twine and slip the cut end through the loop you left. Now grasp the tail at the other end and pull until the loop disappears below the upper edge of the wrap.

Cut off both leftover ends close to the whipping.

PADDLE & ROD RACKS

These holders give canoe paddles and fishing rods a place of honour on the cabin wall. By Ron Frenette

A certain amount of cheerful clutter is acceptable – even traditional – at a cottage or cabin. Some favourite possessions, however, like fishing rods and canoe paddles, don't take well to being piled in a heap along with life jackets, tarpaulins, and sodden water toys. Besides, they look so great hung on a wall, it seems a shame to relegate them to the rafters or a dark corner of the shed.

To help you give your paddles and rods a place of honour, we've created two simple racks. One is a variation of the other; some of the same templates and essentially the same techniques are used to make both.

MATERIALS

LUMBER

You can use cherry, ash, white pine, white cedar, or even exterior-grade plywood for the rack, and any contrasting (or complementary) wood for the decorative plaque.

Paddle rack:
1 piece ¾" x 8½" x 25" (for vertical backboard)
1 piece ¾" x 5" x 22" (for horizontal shelf)
1 piece ¼" x 2" x 7" (for decorative plaque)

Fishing rod rack (upper section):
1 piece ¾" x 8½" x 25" (for vertical backboard)
1 piece ¾" x 5" x 22" (for horizontal shelf)

1–4 pieces ³⁄₁₆" x ⅝" x 2" (optional; for rod-tip gates)

Fishing rod rack (lower section):
1 piece ¾" x 5" x 25" (for vertical backboard)
1 piece ¾" x 5" x 22" (for horizontal shelf)

HARDWARE

Paddle rack:
4 1½" #8 wood screws (for joining parts)
2 1½" or 2" #8 wood screws (for mounting)

Fishing rod rack:
8 1½" #8 wood screws (for joining parts)
4 1½" or 2" #8 wood screws (for mounting)
1–4 ¾" #5 brass screws (optional; for attaching rod-tip gates)

1–4 brass washers (optional; for rod-tip gates)

FINISHING
80–120-grit sandpaper
Tack cloth
Spar varnish
⅜" wooden plugs or maple "button" plugs

TOOLS
Jigsaw or band saw
Portable drill or drill press
¾" and 1½" spade or Forstner bits; assorted twist bits
Router with ¼" or ½" rounding-over bit (optional)
Hand plane
Rat-tail file
Carpenter's glue

FOR BOTH RACKS

Enlarge the templates (pp. 20 and 22) and copy them onto stiff cardboard. (To create full-size versions of the templates, copy the 1:3 scale outlines onto 1" graph paper. Note where the project outlines intersect the grid on our templates and transfer the points onto the 1" graph paper. Once the points have been plotted, connect them together for a complete outline.) The backboard is the same for both the paddle rack and the upper section of the fishing rod rack.

Because the horizontal shelf piece meets the vertical backboard at a 90° angle, it's important that the horizontal piece be planed smooth and true, so the two pieces meet cleanly from end to end. The bottom edge of the backboard should also be planed true.

It's much easier to do all the preliminary sanding, drilling, countersinking, and counterboring before any assembly.

THE PADDLE RACK

1. Backboard: Trace the template onto the wood, aligning the bottom edge with a straight, smooth edge of the board. Using a band saw or jigsaw, cut just outside the line.

2. Horizontal shelf: Trace the template onto the wood. Using a band saw or jigsaw, cut out the shelf, staying just outside the line. To create the paddle slots, drill ¾" holes using the drill marks provided on the tem-

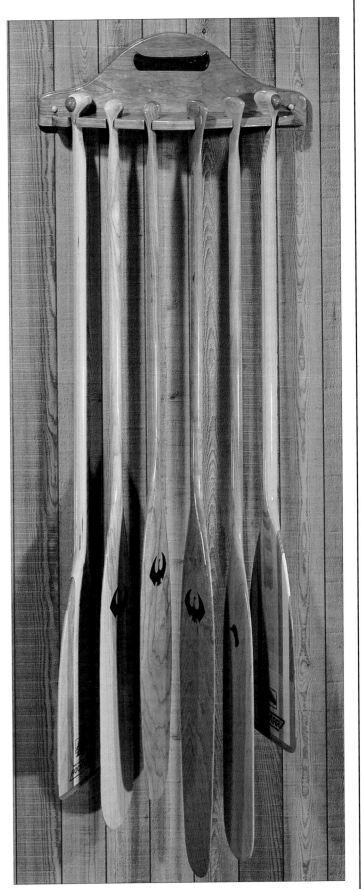

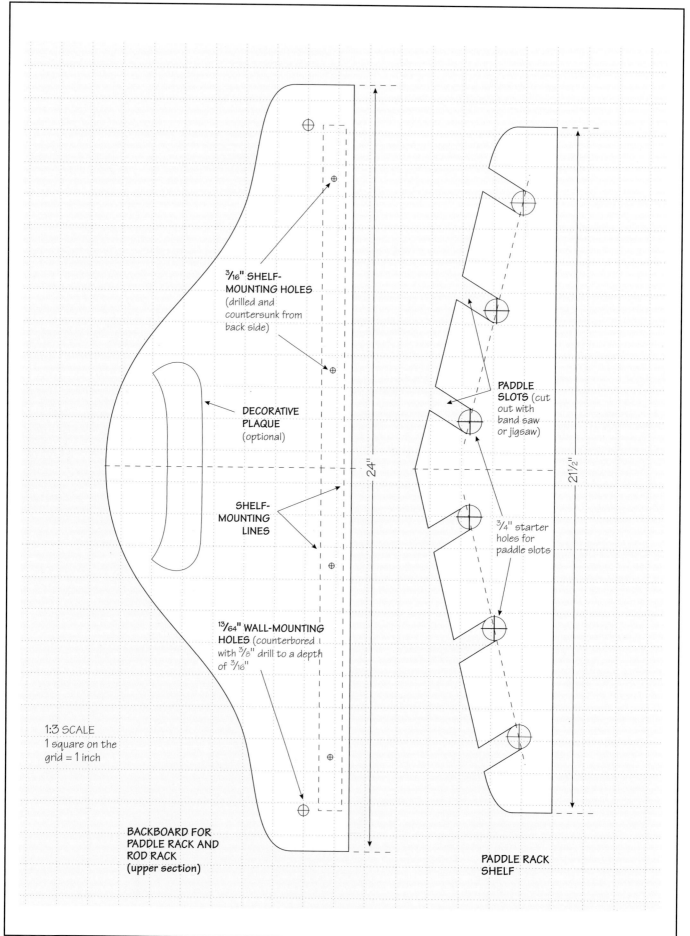

³⁄₁₆" SHELF-
MOUNTING HOLES
(drilled and
countersunk from
back side)

DECORATIVE
PLAQUE
(optional)

24"

PADDLE
SLOTS (cut
out with
band saw
or jigsaw)

SHELF-
MOUNTING
LINES

21½"

³⁄₄" starter
holes for
paddle slots

¹³⁄₆₄" WALL-MOUNTING
HOLES (counterbored
with ³⁄₈" drill to a depth
of ³⁄₁₆")

1:3 SCALE
1 square on the
grid = 1 inch

BACKBOARD FOR
PADDLE RACK AND
ROD RACK
(upper section)

PADDLE RACK
SHELF

plate, and then draw the angled, parallel lines from the holes to the front edge of the piece. Cut along the lines with a band saw or jigsaw to create the slots, and clean them up with a rat-tail file and sandpaper. Before cutting the slots, it's a good idea to make some test cuts on scrap lumber and make sure all your paddles will fit the standard slot. To accommodate fatter paddles, just cut the slots a little wider.

3. If you have a router, make a smooth edge on the backboard and shelf with a ¼" or ½" rounding-over bit. Round only the front edges, not the back edges that go flat against the wall. (If you don't have a router, round the edges with 80-grit sandpaper.) Sand both pieces with 80-grit, then 120-grit sandpaper. Varnish flows over curves but doesn't finish off square edges very well.

4. Next, using a $^{13}\!/_{64}$" bit, drill wall-mounting holes in the backboard using the drilling marks on the template. The screws may be left flush with the backboard or, for a more professional finish, counterbored with a ⅜" drill to a depth of $^{3}\!/_{16}$". If you choose to counterbore them, the holes can be plugged with decorative maple "button" plugs that will hide the screws once you've secured the rack to the wall.

5. Finally, using the lines on the template, draw shelf-mounting lines on the backboard. From the back side, drill and countersink four $^{3}\!/_{16}$" holes. Then, in the back edge of the shelf,

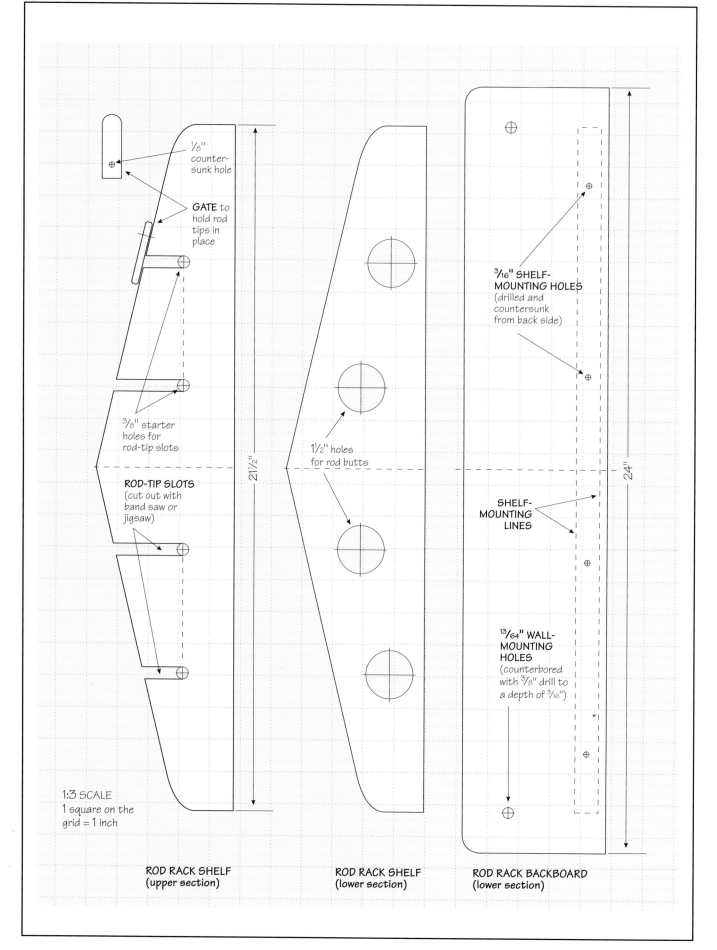

⅛" counter-sunk hole

GATE to hold rod tips in place

⅜" starter holes for rod-tip slots

ROD-TIP SLOTS (cut out with band saw or jigsaw)

21½"

1:3 SCALE
1 square on the grid = 1 inch

ROD RACK SHELF (upper section)

1½" holes for rod butts

ROD RACK SHELF (lower section)

³⁄₁₆" SHELF-MOUNTING HOLES (drilled and countersunk from back side)

SHELF-MOUNTING LINES

¹³⁄₆₄" WALL-MOUNTING HOLES (counterbored with ⅜" drill to a depth of ³⁄₁₆")

24"

ROD RACK BACKBOARD (lower section)

drill four ⁹⁄₆₄" holes to mate with the larger ones you just drilled in the backboard. Attach the pieces with glue and four 1½" #8 screws. (The shelf is narrower than the backboard by 1¼" on each end, so be sure it's centred before assembly.)

6. Finishing: Make the canoe decorative plaque, if desired, using the template provided. Cut it out of ¼" wood, preferably a type that goes nicely with the backboard. Attach it with glue. Sand the rack with 120-grit sandpaper, clean with a tack cloth, and apply 4–5 coats of spar varnish.

7. Mounting: Remember that the finished rack has to be high enough to hold your longest paddles off the floor. If you're fastening the rack directly onto wood (such as studs or tongue-in-groove panelling), predrill two ⁹⁄₆₄" pilot holes in the wall and fasten with 1½" #8 screws. If you're mounting the rack on plaster lath or drywall, we strongly recommend that you use plastic or metal wall anchors and 2" #8 screws.

THE FISHING ROD RACK

This rack was designed to hold four fishing rods with reels attached, so it has two sections, an upper and a lower. The upper section is much the same as the paddle rack: Use the backboard template (p. 20) and the upper-section shelf template (opposite). Drill four ⅜" holes in the shelf using the drill marks provided. Using a band saw or jigsaw, cut narrow slots as indicated on the template. The four slots are narrower than those on the paddle rack, to accommodate the tips of the fishing rods without letting them fall out. Assemble the upper section, following steps 3, 4, and 5 as above.

The lower section is also constructed from two pieces, but the horizontal shelf has holes to accommodate fishing rod butts. After cutting out the pieces from the templates (opposite), use a 1½" spade or Forstner bit to drill the four holes as marked. We tried nine different rods and all of them fit; those who have rods with different-sized butts could adjust the size of the holes. Drill mounting holes in both pieces as in steps 4 and 5, above. Assembly and finishing are the same as for the paddle rack.

When you hang the racks, the distance between the two sections will vary depending on the length of your fishing rods.

If there is any danger of the rods falling out of the rack, the tips can be locked in place with simple wooden "gates." Following the template, cut ³⁄₁₆" x ⅝" x 2" pieces from scrap wood, drill a ⅛" shank hole in each piece, and countersink. Next, drill ⁷⁄₆₄" pilot holes in the front edge of the rod rack's top section (see template) and attach the gates with ¾" #5 brass screws with brass washers between the two wooden surfaces. The washers will allow the gate to open and close easily without coming loose.

ROPE HAMMOCK

Roomy, comfortable, and the perfect place to settle in for a snooze. By Suzanne Kingsmill

Nothing is more relaxing than swinging gently in a hammock on a lazy summer's day. Blissful summer memories are made of moments like these – but they're not so blissful when the kids descend on you as you peacefully snooze in the only hammock in sight. Fight back! Let them use the ratty old relic from days gone by and make a brand-new, deliciously comfortable, roomy rope hammock of your own.

1. Choosing the rope: For strength and years of carefree swinging, use only high-quality hammock cord, not macramé cord or thin braided rope. (See "A Line on Rope," p. 29.)

2. Building the loom and shuttle: Clamp the two dowels upright, about 70" apart. They should be parallel to each other, leaving the top 18" free, with enough room on all sides to move the shuttle of rope around each dowel. Make your shuttle using the plans on p. 26.

After cutting the rope you need for the braids and harnesses (see below), tape one end of the remaining rope to your shuttle and wind it all on in one piece. To do this, turn the *shuttle*, keeping the rope under gentle pressure. Don't wind the cord around the shuttle or

---

MATERIALS AND TOOLS

5 lbs (about 975') ⁵⁄₁₆", soft polypropylene hammock cord

2 dowels, 1" in diameter by 4' long (old broom handles will do)

2 pieces 1" x 1" x 60" oak, ash, maple (or any hardwood) for spreader bars

2 metal hammock rings, 2" diameter

1 piece plywood, ¼" x 5" x 24" (for shuttle)

Clothespins, safety pins or paper clips, pushpins, masking tape

3 2"–3" nails

Hammer, jigsaw, drill, clamps as necessary

Candle or lighter

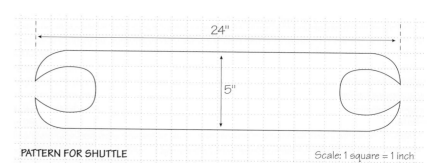

Photo A: Spreader bar

you'll end up with twisty rope that will drive you crazy. If it tangles don't pull; just fluff it up and it should sort itself out.

PATTERN FOR SHUTTLE   Scale: 1 square = 1 inch

24"

5"

3. Braiding the edges:

For each braid cut two (yes, two) 220" lengths of cord. Tie both lengths around one loom pole with a reef knot so you have two equal strands of rope on either side of the knot, four strands in all. See Photo B. Melt the cut ends with a lighter or candle to keep them from unravelling. Take the far-right strand and draw it over the one to its left, then take the far-left strand and draw it over the two to its right. Repeat the above sequence and continue until the chain is 80" long. Tie it to the other dowel with a reef knot. Repeat the whole process for the second braid and push the lower braid well down the dowels.

Photo B: Starting the braid

4. The harnesses:
Hang one metal hammock ring on a 2"–3" nail, and hammer in two more nails, one on either side, at least 5" away. For the first harness, cut 10 114" lengths of rope and melt all cut ends. Loop them through the hammock ring so that the ropes are of equal length on either side. (Each doubled rope will fall naturally into a front and back row.) Now, starting at the far right-hand back strand, bring it forward; then push the far right-hand front strand back. Do the same with each rope in turn, being careful to keep them in order so that each strand moving forward is part of the same piece as the strand you are moving back.

Photo C: Tightening the braid

When you have all 20 strands in their new locations, take the far right-hand strand, bring it through between the front and back rows, and hang it on the nail to the left. Bring the far left-hand strand back through between the rows, and hang it on the nail to the right. Now repeat the entire process of moving the front strands to the back and the back strands to the front, again starting at the far right-hand side. Once again, move the far right-hand strand between the rows and onto the left-hand nail, then the far left-hand strand between the rows and onto the right-hand nail.

Repeat the above steps, creating the pattern shown in Photo D. Firm and

20 ⁵⁄₁₆"-diameter holes countersunk to avoid wear on the harnesses

3" 1½"

tighten the pattern as you go. When two strands are left, tie them in a reef knot. Make the second harness in the same manner.

5. The weave: Go back to the top braid on your loom, and mark the loops for weaving the first row of the hammock body. Make your first mark at one end in the loop nearest the dowel, then fasten safety pins or paper clips as markers at approximately 5¼" intervals. End with your last mark at the other dowel. You should have made 16 marks, dividing your braid into 15 equal sections.

Now, unwind about 9' of rope from the shuttle. Standing in front of the right-hand dowel, thread the rope *down* through the first marked loop of the braid from *front to back*. Continue to thread from front to back through each of the 16 marked loops. See Photo E. Tie off the rope around the left dowel with a reef knot, and then go back to the right dowel and pull this threaded rope through the loops until it is taut, but not so taut as to strain the dowels. Since your dowels are 70" apart, this threaded rope will be approximately 70" in length. (The 80" braid will be slack at this point.) Next, measure out an additional 19" of the rope and mark it with a safety pin. The object is to keep the rope in each row approximately 89" long. Use a cloth measuring tape, or cut a 19" piece of string or yarn, sling it around your neck, and use it as a measure at the end of each row.

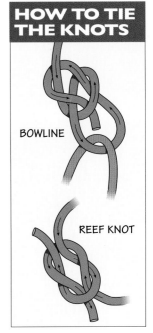

HOW TO TIE THE KNOTS

BOWLINE

REEF KNOT

Once you've marked your 89" spot with a safety pin, stick a pushpin into the dowel at the level of the row you're working on and hang the safety pin on it. Bring the shuttle around the outside of the right dowel (*counterclockwise*) and under the upper braid. Pull some slack into the first loop of your last row to make it easier and stuff the shuttle *down* through the loop from *front to back*. Hang in there! The first few rows are the hardest.

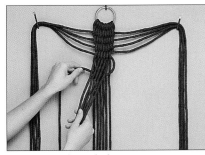

Photo D: Making the harnesses

Photo E: The first row of loops

Continue pushing the shuttle *down* and from *front to back* through each successive loop until you have made 15 passes. Make sure you count. If you don't get 15, undo the row and do it again. At the left dowel, pull on your newly completed row until it's taut, measure out the additional 19", mark it with a safety pin, and hang it on a pushpin. Even out the slack. Bring the shuttle *clockwise* around the outside of the left dowel and under the top braid and find the first loop. Test your choice by tugging on the loop. It should form a diamond shape, with your hand at the lowest corner, and it will put tension on the rope hanging on the pushpin. See Photo F. Stuff the shuttle *up* through this and subsequent loops from *back to front*, and count your passes until you reach 15 at the right dowel. Pull the rope taut and measure to the 89" mark, remove the safety pin from the row above, and use it to mark your new 89" length. Hang it on the pushpin. Even out the slack of the previous row and then weave back to the left dowel (testing your first loop in the same manner as above). Go *down* and from *front to back*, as you did for the first row. Continue until you have 38 loops on each dowel, including the loop of the top braid. Every fourth or fifth row, push all but the last couple of loops up the dowel and out of the way, securing with masking tape, twist ties, or extra pushpins.

6. Connecting hammock to bottom braid: Mark the bottom braid in the same way as you did the top braid. You should be starting at the left dowel. Bring the rope clockwise around the dowel and thread it *up* through the first marked braid loop

Photo F: Finding the "diamond"

from *back to front*. Now pass it *up* through the first loop of your last row from *back to front*, exactly as you did for every other row. Now thread it up through the braid at the second mark, and continue to alternate between the loops of your last row and the braid until you have completed 15 passes and threaded it through all 16 marks. Measure out 19" as usual, and secure at the right dowel with a reef knot.

7. The spreader bars: Make the spreader bars according to Photo A on pp. 26–27.

8. Attaching harnesses to spreader bars:
Hang a harness on a nail and thread the far-left and far-right ropes through one spreader bar so that at least 10" of cord hangs free. Tie a simple knot below each hole so the spreader bar hangs parallel to the floor. Thread remaining ropes through and tie simple knots so each rope is under slight but similar tension and the bar stays level. Repeat with the other harness and bar.

Harness and spreader bar

*Photo H:
Attaching body
to harness*

9. Attaching hammock body to harnesses: Before taking the hammock off the loom, thread a length of string or yarn through all the loops on each dowel and tie to itself. This prevents your loops from getting lost – once lost they are almost impossible to find again. After removing the hammock from the loom, lay it on the ground. Take the loop of the braid and the one next to it and tie the 10" length of rope at one end of a spreader bar to these two loops using a bowline. See Photo H. Make your bowline as close to the simple knot as possible.

Continue tying two loops of the hammock proper to one rope from the spreader bar until they are all tied on. Do the same for the other harness and, bingo, you have your hammock. Some fiddling may be required to correct the tension on the harness ropes; to do so, adjust either the simple knot or the bowline. When you're sure the tension is right, cut off the loose ends and melt them.

Now pick two healthy trees (they should have a diameter of at least 14") far enough apart to let your hammock hang almost at full stretch. Screw threaded hooks into each tree – your attachment points should be 4½'–5' above ground level – and hang your hammock. Back in gently, lie down, and enjoy!

A LINE ON ROPE

The fibres in good polypropylene hammock cord are much thinner – and therefore softer and more pliable – than the coarse polypropylene fibres used in traditional rope. Your best bet is to use 5/16" polypropylene braided cord. Dacron cord is stronger and more durable, but it's nearly twice as expensive, can be difficult to work with, and only comes in natural colour. There may be a manufacturer of high-quality hammock cord in your area; ours came from Kingcord Industries Inc., Reynold's Rd. #1, Lansdowne, Ont. K0E 1L0, (613) 659-2448. Polypropylene cord comes in beige and brown. Dozens of colours are available if you order 10 lbs. – enough for two hammocks. Kingcord accepts mail orders from anywhere in Canada and the U.S.

PINE BOX FOR FIREWOOD

This fireside companion keeps your logs neat, dry – and close to where you need them. By John Everett

On cool evenings or stay-indoors days, nothing is more comforting than the sight, smell, and warmth of the fireplace or woodstove. And nothing is more convenient than a fully stocked wood box at its side, so no one has to worry about heading out in the rain or chill (or bugs) when the fire burns low.

The "bin-style" front opening of this box allows it to be filled – and emptied – easily, while still providing a top surface for resting mugs or matches on. There's a separate area inside for storing kindling and newspaper.

The box is made of glued-up pine boards using simple butt joints. All screw holes are plugged, and all grains (except those on top) run vertically. We used a clear finish, but the box could also be stained. If your lumberyard allows you to pick and choose, bring along a square and select boards that are straight and pleasing to the eye. Place them side by side to determine whether they will glue up flush and achieve a good joint with a minimum of pressure. My preference runs to boards with small, tight knots. The rays around the knots provide a pleasing visual effect known as "chatoyancy," for its gem-like resemblance to a cat's eye.

MATERIALS

We made our wood box out of pine because it's easy to work with and relatively inexpensive. For an even simpler version made of plywood, see "The Easier Option" on p. 34.

LUMBER

3 pieces 1" x 8" x 6'
3 pieces 1" x 6" x 6'
1 piece 1" x 6" x 8'
1 piece 1" x 12", to yield one 9¾" x 27¾" piece for the top
1 piece ¾" wood-core plywood, to yield one 15½" x 24¾" piece for the base

OTHER

1 box 1½" #8 Robertson wood screws
12 1¼" #8 Robertson wood screws
Carpenter's glue
Sandpaper – 60 or 80, 100, 150, and 220 grit
Urethane
⅜" pine plugs or decorative wooden buttons
Tack cloth
Hangers (optional)
Steel wool (0000 grade)

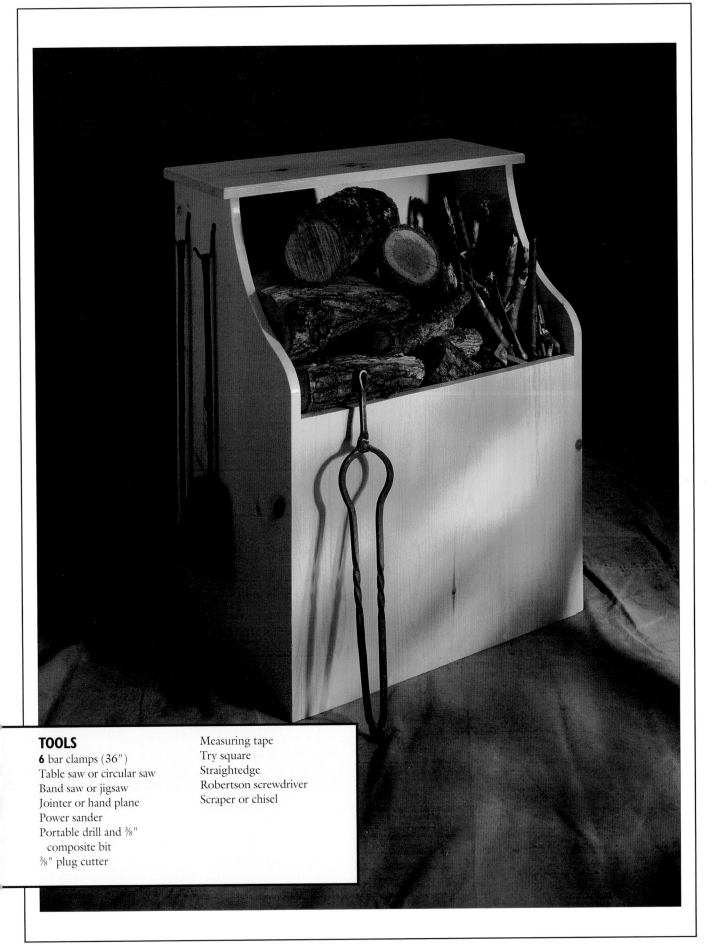

TOOLS

6 bar clamps (36")
Table saw or circular saw
Band saw or jigsaw
Jointer or hand plane
Power sander
Portable drill and ⅜"
  composite bit
⅜" plug cutter

Measuring tape
Try square
Straightedge
Robertson screwdriver
Scraper or chisel

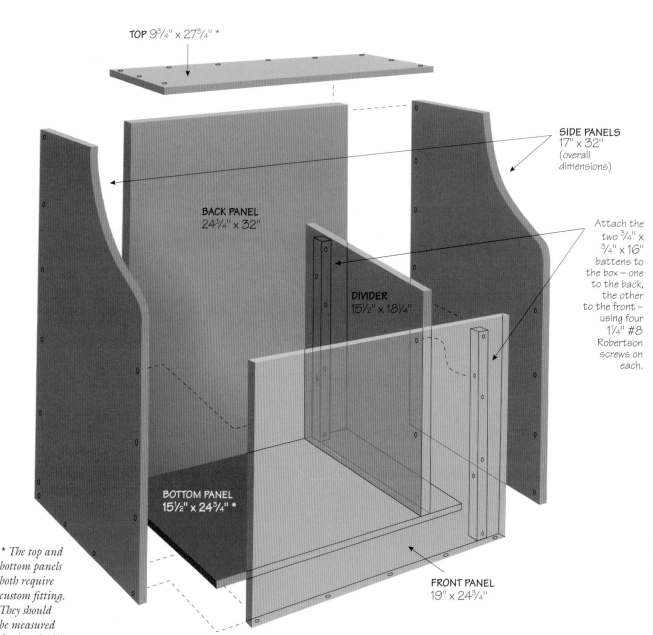

TOP 9¾" x 27¾" *

SIDE PANELS
17" x 32"
(overall
dimensions)

BACK PANEL
24¾" x 32"

Attach the
two ¾" x
¾" x 16"
battens to
the box – one
to the back,
the other
to the front –
using four
1¼" #8
Robertson
screws on
each.

DIVIDER
15½" x 18¼"

BOTTOM PANEL
15½" x 24¾" *

FRONT PANEL
19" x 24¾"

*The top and
bottom panels
both require
custom fitting.
They should
be measured
during the "dry
run" and then
cut to final
size just before
assembly.

GETTING STARTED

These instructions will make oversize panels that can be squared and cut to finished size after they have been scraped and sanded.

1. Take two of the 1" x 8" boards and the three 1" x 6" x 6' boards, and cut two 34" lengths from each. Use two 1" x 8" x 34"s and two 1" x 6" x 34"s for the back. For each side, use one 1" x 8" x 34" piece and two 1" x 6" x 34" pieces. It's helpful to label the pieces so they don't get mixed up.

2. From the remaining 1" x 8" piece, cut two 22" lengths and two 20" lengths. From the 1" x 6" x 8' cut two 22" lengths and one 20" length. The four 22" lengths will be glued up for the front of the wood box, and three 20" lengths will make up the divider.

GLUING UP

This is a major step in the process, and should be done in a relaxed, unhurried manner. It is, in effect, a one-shot deal, so dry clamping before the glue is applied is critical. Dry clamping will show you the tightness of the joints, and how much truing will be required. If you've chosen your boards carefully, you might not have to true the edges at all. However, if they're really out of alignment you'll have to straighten the edges with a jointer or hand plane.

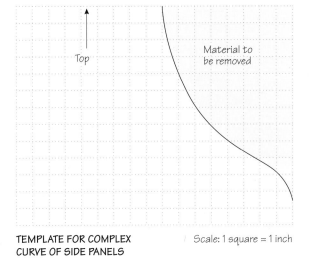

Top

Material to be removed

TEMPLATE FOR COMPLEX CURVE OF SIDE PANELS   Scale: 1 square = 1 inch

When clamping the side panels, use six clamps, three on top and three underneath, spaced alternately. (See diagram, below.) Shorter panels should only require three or four clamps. The boards will want to bow when the clamps are tightened, so keep the bars tight against the wood to stop the pieces from shifting. Whether you're wet or dry clamping, always remember to use wood blocks to protect the edges of the boards.

BONDING SESSION:

When gluing up the back and side panels, use six clamps, three on top and three on the bottom, spaced alternately. Shorter panels should only require three or four clamps.

1. Place the boards to be glued on top of one row of bar clamps, and use a roller, a brush, or your finger to coat each edge with glue. Make sure each edge is evenly and uniformly covered.

2. Line the boards up and evenly tighten the clamps just a little. Check to make sure all the boards are flush and haven't shifted. Make any necessary adjustments by pressing or lifting the boards.

3. When everything's lined up, put the top clamps in place and tighten them with moderate-to-firm pressure. Go back and tighten the bottom clamps to this pressure as well. Glue beads rising up along the joints – easily removed with a scraper when dry – indicate a good glue-up.

4. Let the panel dry overnight to ensure a lasting bond.

5. Repeat this process for the rest of the panels.

6. After each panel has dried sufficiently,

the surface can be smoothed. Remove the glue beads with a sharp chisel or scraper and sand the panel with progressively finer grades of sandpaper to remove any ridges or bumps. Be sure to sand both sides of the panels, as all surfaces – except for the bottom – are "show" sides.

PLYWOOD: THE EASIER OPTION

A simpler construction alternative to the solid-pine wood box is to use ¾" fir plywood and assemble the box with glue and nails. It can then be painted and decorated with coloured stencils. The use of plywood eliminates the challenge of gluing up boards, and the project can be completed in significantly less time.

To ensure accurate cuts, attach a reliable straightedge to the plywood sheet with the C-clamps and use this edge as a saw guide. From the single 4' x 8' sheet of plywood, cut one 17" x 8' strip, and one 24¾" x 8' strip using a circular saw with a sharp plywood blade.

Then, from the 17" x 8' strip, cut two 32" lengths for the sides, and one 9¾" x 27¾" piece for the top.

Next, from the 24¾" piece, cut one 32" length for the back, one 19" piece for the front, and one 15½" piece for the base. Finally, cut an 18½" length for the divider. (You may wish to cut the pieces for the base and divider after the sides and back are assembled – as you would for solid-wood construction.) Enlarge the template on p. 33, mark the curved details on each of the side pieces, and cut using a band saw or a jigsaw with a plywood blade.

Once the pieces are cut to size, apply a coat or two of sanding sealer and lightly sand all the components until they're smooth. The sanding sealer will ensure that subsequent coats of paint will cover evenly. Follow the same assembly instructions as for the solid-wood version, but use wood glue and nails to fasten the pieces together.

Paint the box and, if you desire, use stencils to apply some decorative details to the front and sides.

MATERIALS
LUMBER
1 4' x 8' sheet of ¾" fir plywood

OTHER
Carpenter's glue
1 box 2" spiral nails
Sandpaper (100, 150, and 220 grit)
Sanding sealer and paint
Tack cloth
Hangers (optional)

TOOLS
Circular saw
Jigsaw or band saw
Measuring tape
Try square and straightedge
Hammer
C-clamps (2)

PREPARING THE PANELS FOR ASSEMBLY

1. Square one end of each of the panels and then cut them to length: sides and back to 32", front to 19", and divider to 18¼". Rip the sides to 17" in width, and the front and back to 24¾". At this time the plywood bottom can be cut to a rough size of 15½" x 24¾". The bottom and the divider will receive their final sizing partway through the assembly of the box; the top will be cut to size after all other pieces have been assembled.

2. Enlarge the template on p. 33, and mark and cut the curve on each of the side pieces. Try to include any interesting knots, swirls, or grain details in the panels, but keep in mind that these features are very hard and shouldn't fall across lines to be sawed.

3. Predrill holes for screws and plugs. (See plans, p. 32.) I used a composite bit (available at hardware stores) that cuts a pilot and shank hole, countersinks, and cuts a ⅜" hole for the wooden plug all at once.

Because these bits can damage the surface of the wood if they're pushed in too far (which is quite easy to do), I used a 2" x 3" piece of plastic cut from an empty windshield-washer fluid bottle as a "panel protecter." The idea is to make a hole in the plastic with the composite bit, then hold the plastic sheet in position while you're drilling the panels. That way, if the drill pulls, or you drill too deep, the plastic will act as a shield against marring the surface. If you decide to use wooden buttons instead of plugs, check the diameter and drill accordingly.

ASSEMBLING THE PANELS

Assemble the panels using 1½" #8 Robertson screws. Before final assembly, it's a good idea to do a trial run using just enough screws to hold the panels in place. Two pairs of hands will make this exercise much easier. Once you're sure everything will fit together, it's time for the final assembly.

1. Carefully align one side with the back, and moderately tighten the top screw. Next, do the bottom screw, and then another near the centre. Tighten the screws, then repeat the process with the second side.

2. Slide the base into place. Position the front on top of the base and flush with the edges of the sides. Mark the base and cut to size so that it fits *inside* the box. Now, screw the sides, the back, and the front to the base.

3. Check the depth of the box for the divider to fit inside. From a piece of scrap – like the one produced when the divider was ripped to width – cut two ¾" x ¾" x 16" battens. Use 4" wood blocks to accurately position the divider 4" from the right side of the box and mark a vertical line on the inside of both the front and back panels. Attach the battens to the box – one to the back, the other to the front – using four 1¼" #8 Robertson screws on each. Then attach the divider to the battens with two more 1¼" screws on each batten. To make life easier, you might want to finish the divider before screwing it in place. (See below.)

4. Cut the top of the box to size, leaving a ¾" overhang on the front and sides. There was some very slight bowing in my back panel, so I elected to have the top stand proud ⅛" in the back. Therefore, I cut the top to 9⅞" x 27¾". Sand the top to the same smoothness as the other panels, round the edges slightly, and attach.

5. Use ⅜" pine plugs to fill the counterbored screw holes. These can be cut from a matching piece of scrap pine using a drill and a plug-cutting bit. Simply drill out the plugs and then pop them out of the scrap board with a screwdriver. When the box is assembled, put a drop of glue on each wood plug and tap them into place. Let the glue dry, cut away the tops of the plugs with a chisel, and sand them flush.

FINISHING

Because all the panels (except the bottom) were sanded before assembly, the only sanding you have to do at this point is around the wood plugs.

Finish all surfaces – inside and out – with three or four coats of urethane or, for easier brush cleanup, six coats of water-based urethane acrylic. In between coats, give all surfaces a *light* rub with 220-grit sandpaper or 0000-grade steel wool, removing the dust with a tack cloth. When the last coat has dried, add some decorative hooks to the side of the box so you can hang fireplace tools.

DECK CHAIR & FOOTSTOOL

This set lets you lounge around in comfort – then folds up for easy storage. By the Kleinburg Craft Cooperative

This handsome chair and matching footstool not only are extremely comfortable, but they're also portable and store away compactly. The chair comes apart in two sections that slide into one another (making for easy carrying, too), and the footstool folds up.

Designed by the Kleinburg Craft Cooperative in Toronto, Ontario, this furniture is based on a 1920s chair design by Bauhaus architect Ludwig Mies van der Rohe. The set pictured here is made of oak with a golden stain that allows the beauty of the grain to show through; however, you could build it in another hardwood if you like.

For those who want to save some time, the chair and footstool are available in kit form – with the lumber pre-cut – from the Kleinburg Craft Cooperative, 158 Eastern Ave., Toronto, Ont. M5A 4C4, (416) 603-0855. (Finished furniture is also available for sale.)

MATERIALS
LUMBER
(all oak, thickness planed and sawn to these dimensions):
Chair:
1 piece 1³⁄₁₆" x 7" x 84"
(for 2 back rails and 2 seat rails)
28 lineal feet of ½" x 2⅝"
(for 12 slats and 2 handle boards)

Footstool:
1 piece ¾" x 3" x 3' (for 2 top rails)
1 piece ¾" x 4" x 4' (for 4 legs)
13 lineal feet of ½" x 2⅝"
(for 6 slats and 3 leg braces)

OTHER
56 1¼" #8 flathead Robertson screws, brass or stainless steel (for chair)
28 1¼" #8 flathead Robertson screws, brass or stainless steel (for footstool)
4 ¼" x 1½" zinc-plated or stainless-steel hexagon-head bolts with locking nuts and washers (for footstool)
Sandpaper – 50 grit for rough sanding; 80–120 grit for finish sanding
1 1½" hook and eye
Stain suitable for outdoor use

TOOLS
Thickness planer, or have lumber thickness planed at lumberyard
Table saw and band saw
Electric drill
#8 combination countersink drill bit (or ⅛" bit for pilot hole, ³⁄₁₆" bit for shank hole, and countersink)
⅝" Forstner bit
¼" and ⅛" drill bits
Sander
Router with ⅛" rounding-over bit for slats and ⅛" or ¼" rounding-over bit for rails
#8 Robertson screwdriver
Clamps

MAKING THE CHAIR

1. Cut all pieces from oak boards, following the lumber list opposite and the plans on pp. 38–39:

– Cut 12 slats for seat and back (Part A).
– Cut two handle boards (Part B).
– Cut two seat rails (Part C) and two back rails (Part D).

2. Using a disk or belt sander or a rasp, round the top and bottom of each rail to form a smooth curve with a radius of ⅞".

3. Using a router with a ⅛" rounding bit, round off the edges of the slats; round off the edges of the rails with a ⅛" or ¼" bit. Sand all surfaces.

4. To assemble the chair seat, carefully mark the positions of the slats on the seat rails, following the plans. Set the two seat rails approximately 15¾" apart on centre,

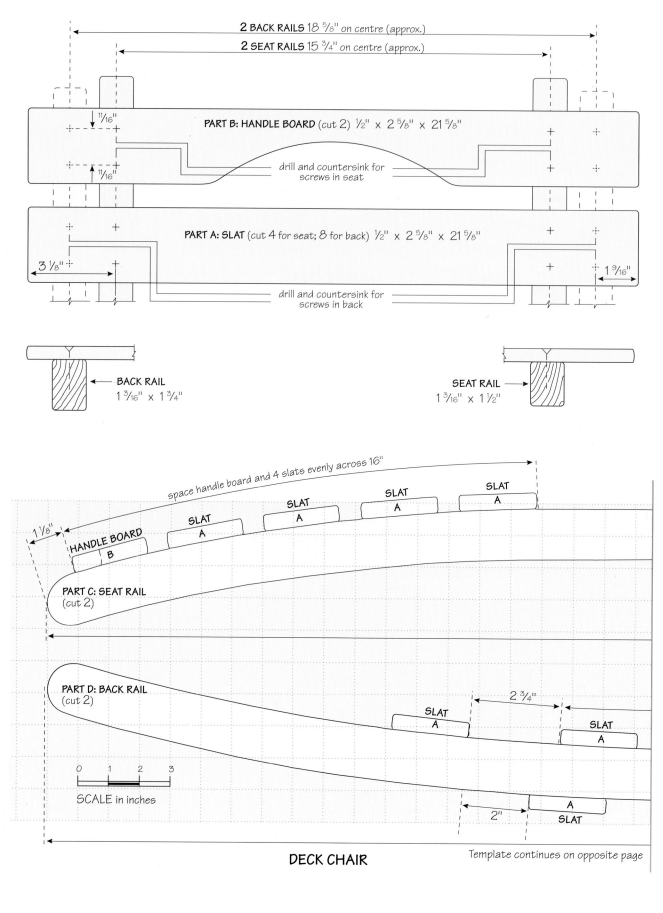

2 BACK RAILS 18 ⅝" on centre (approx.)

2 SEAT RAILS 15 ¾" on centre (approx.)

11⁄16"

11⁄16"

PART B: HANDLE BOARD (cut 2) ½" × 2 ⅝" × 21 ⅝"

drill and countersink for
screws in seat

PART A: SLAT (cut 4 for seat; 8 for back) ½" × 2 ⅝" × 21 ⅝"

3 ⅛"

1 9⁄16"

drill and countersink for
screws in back

BACK RAIL
1 3⁄16" × 1 ¾"

SEAT RAIL
1 3⁄16" × 1 ½"

space handle board and 4 slats evenly across 16"

1 ⅛"

SLAT
A

SLAT
A

SLAT
A

SLAT
A

HANDLE BOARD
B

PART C: SEAT RAIL
(cut 2)

PART D: BACK RAIL
(cut 2)

2 ¾"

SLAT
A

SLAT
A

0 1 2 3

SCALE in inches

A
SLAT

2"

DECK CHAIR

Template continues on opposite page

and position the handle board and the end slat on the rails. Clamp in place, then drill and countersink two holes on each end of the slats using the #8 combination bit; insert screws. (To make fastening easier, rub soap or wax on the threads of the screws.) Repeat procedure with the remaining three slats, spacing them evenly.

5. Assemble the chair back using the same procedure: Mark the positions of the slats on the back rails, following the plans. Set the two back rails approximately 18⅝" apart on centre, as shown, and position the two lowest slats on the top sides of the rails. Clamp in place, then drill and countersink two holes in each end as above. Repeat procedure, doing the handle board next, then fastening the five other slats on the top side, spacing them evenly. Position the remaining slat on the *underside* of the back rails; measure very carefully, as proper positioning of this slat is critical for the chair to rest at the correct height when set up, and there is no tolerance for error.

6. To finish the chair, sand with 80–120-grit paper and then stain as you like. Our chair is finished with three coats of Sikkens Cetol #1 (in Golden Oak), which the woodworkers at Kleinburg Craft Cooperative recommend as excellent for outdoor use.

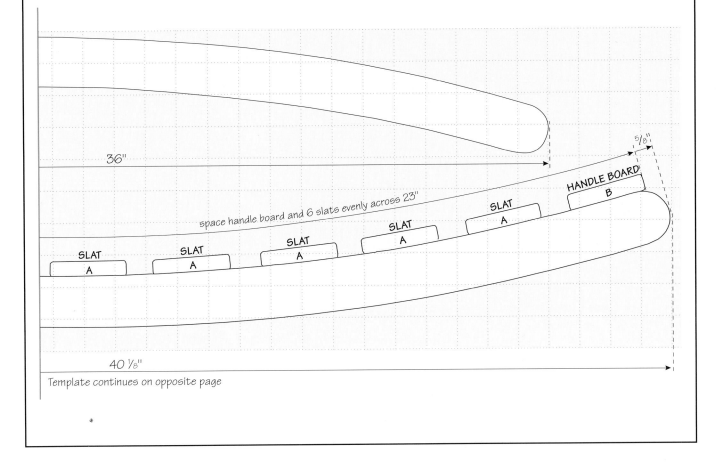

36"

5⁄8"

HANDLE BOARD
B

SLAT
A

SLAT
A

SLAT
A

SLAT
A

SLAT
A

SLAT
A

space handle board and 6 slats evenly across 23"

40 ⅛"

Template continues on opposite page

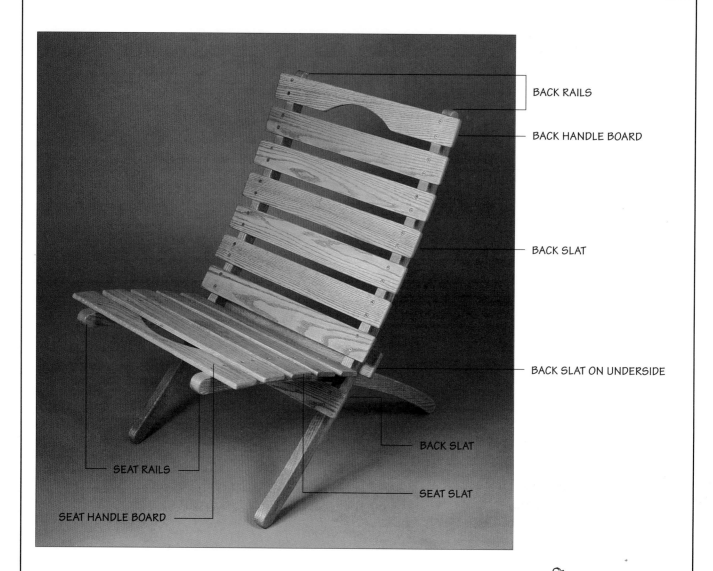

BACK RAILS

BACK HANDLE BOARD

BACK SLAT

BACK SLAT ON UNDERSIDE

BACK SLAT

SEAT SLAT

SEAT RAILS

SEAT HANDLE BOARD

SPACE-SAVING STYLE:

Insert the seat section through the slat on the underside of the back section (curves going the same way) to make a single unit that's easy to carry and store. When it's time to put the chair together, just separate the two sections and insert the legs of the seat section through the space between the bottom two slats of the back.

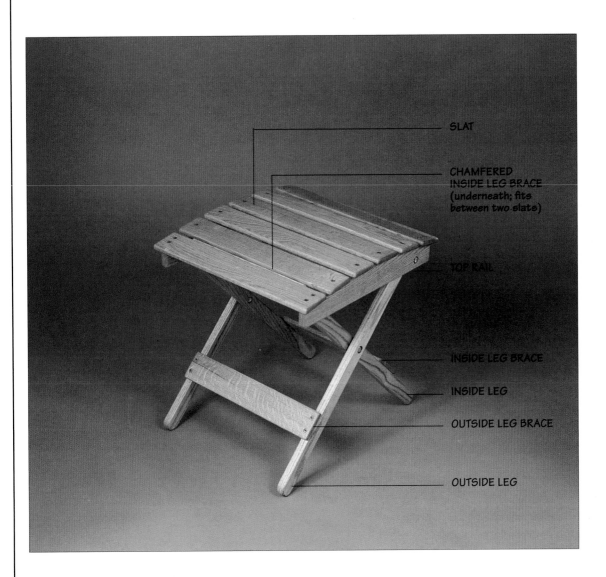

SLAT

CHAMFERED
INSIDE LEG BRACE
(underneath; fits
between two slats)

TOP RAIL

INSIDE LEG BRACE

INSIDE LEG

OUTSIDE LEG BRACE

OUTSIDE LEG

MAKING THE FOOTSTOOL

1. Follow steps #1, #2, and #3 as for the chair, using the plans on pp. 42–44. Cut six slats (Part E), two outside legs (Part F), two inside legs (Part G), two top rails (Part H), two inside leg braces (Part I) , and one outside leg brace (Part J).

2. Before sanding, cut a 35° chamfer on one edge of one inside leg brace.

3. To assemble the top, mark the position of the slats on the top rails as indicated on plans. Clamp the outside slats in position, and drill and countersink two holes in each end of both these slats using the #8 combination bit; fasten with screws. Fill in the rest of the slats, spacing them evenly, and put one screw in each end.

4. Mark positions of bolt holes in the legs and top rails. (Note that the top rails are not symmetrical; the bolt hole goes in the wider end.) Using the ⅝" Forstner bit, counterbore the bolt holes on one side to recess the bolt heads and nuts. (On the outside legs, the top bolt hole is counterbored on one side, and the middle bolt hole is counterbored on the other.) Then, using the ¼" drill bit, drill out the bolt holes.

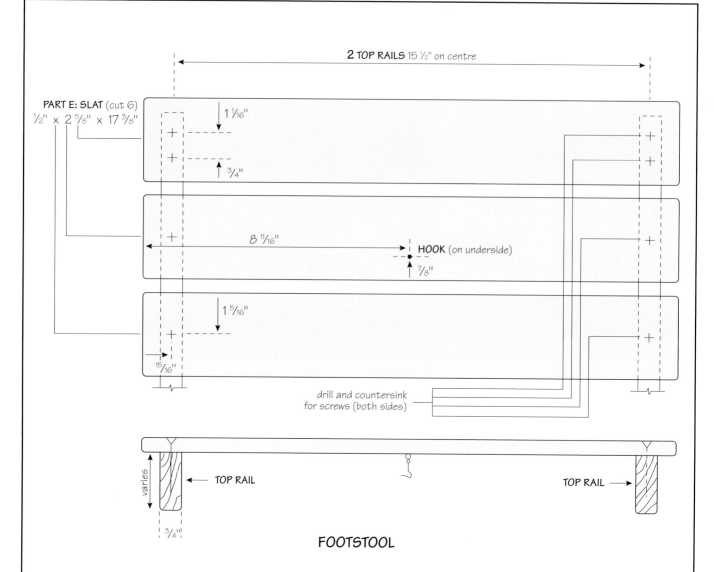

2 TOP RAILS 15 ½" on centre

PART E: SLAT (cut 6)
½" x 2 ⅝" x 17 ⅜"

1 ¹/₁₆"

¾"

8 ¹¹/₁₆"

HOOK (on underside)

⅞"

1 ⁵/₁₆"

¹⁵/₁₆"

drill and countersink
for screws (both sides)

varies

TOP RAIL

TOP RAIL

¾"

FOOTSTOOL

5. To assemble the inside set of legs, position the two inside legs 12³/₁₆" on centre, with the counterbored sides facing in. Clamp the two inside leg braces in place, being sure to place the brace with the 35° chamfer at the top, with the angle facing down. (See plans; this bevelled edge will fit between two of the slats in the top and hold the footstool open.) Drill and countersink holes as above, putting two screws in each end of the braces.

6. To assemble the outside set of legs, position the remaining two legs 13⅞" on centre, with the counterbored sides of the middle bolt holes facing out. Clamp the outside leg brace in place and drill and countersink holes, putting two screws in each end.

7. Insert bolts to connect inside leg assembly to outside leg assembly, using washers as spacers as required.

8. Lay top upside down on table; fold out leg assembly to form an "X," and then bolt leg assembly to top, again using washers as spacers as required.

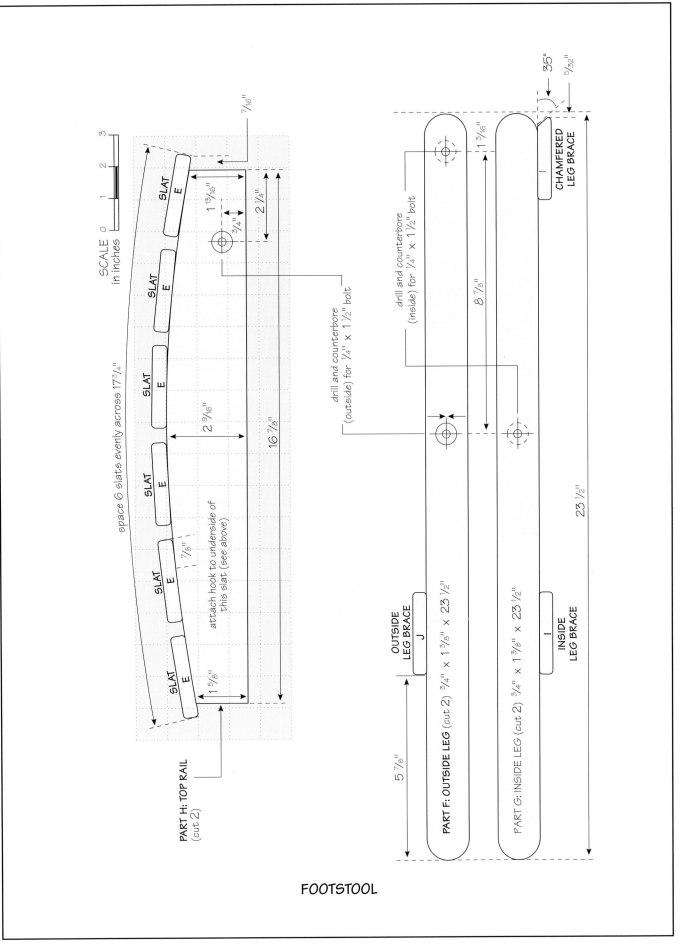

SCALE in inches

0 1 2 3

space 6 slats evenly across 17 3/4"

SLAT E

SLAT E

SLAT E

SLAT E

SLAT E

SLAT E

7/16"

1 13/16"

3/4"

2 1/4"

2 9/16"

16 7/8"

1 5/8"

7/8"

attach hook to underside of this slat (see above)

drill and counterbore (outside) for 1/4" x 1 1/2" bolt

PART H: TOP RAIL (cut 2)

35°

5/32"

1 3/16"

8 7/8"

drill and counterbore (inside) for 1/4" x 1 1/2" bolt

CHAMFERED LEG BRACE

23 1/2"

5 7/8"

OUTSIDE LEG BRACE

J

PART F: OUTSIDE LEG (cut 2) 3/4" x 1 3/8" x 23 1/2"

INSIDE LEG BRACE

I

PART G: INSIDE LEG (cut 2) 3/4" x 1 3/8" x 23 1/2"

FOOTSTOOL

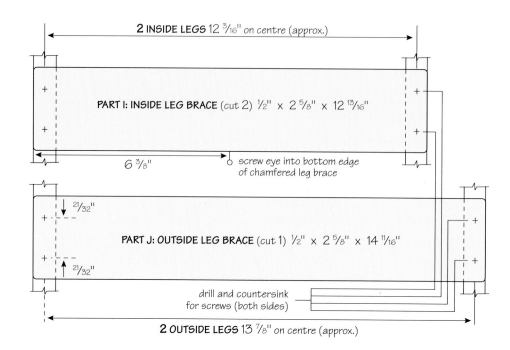

2 INSIDE LEGS 12 ³/₁₆" on centre (approx.)

PART I: INSIDE LEG BRACE (cut 2) ½" x 2 ⁵/₈" x 12 ¹³/₁₆"

6 ³/₈"

screw eye into bottom edge
of chamfered leg brace

21/₃₂"

PART J: OUTSIDE LEG BRACE (cut 1) ½" x 2 ⁵/₈" x 14 ¹¹/₁₆"

21/₃₂"

drill and countersink
for screws (both sides)

2 OUTSIDE LEGS 13 ⁷/₈" on centre (approx.)

FOOTSTOOL

FULL COLLAPSE:

The bolted, X-shaped leg assembly allows the footstool to fold. To set it up, open the legs so that the top leg brace fits between the first and second slats. Secure with hook.

9. Using ⅛" bit, drill pilot hole for hook no more than ⅜" deep into the underside of the footstool top, as marked on plans. Screw in hook. Centre eye in bottom edge of chamfered leg brace; drill pilot hole as above and insert eye, screwing it in until catch is snug.

10. Finish the footstool as you did the chair.

With thanks to woodworkers George Kovacs and Lorrie Matchett of the Kleinburg Craft Cooperative.

MAKE A COTTAGE BOOK

No cottage, cabin, camp, or chalet should be without an operating manual. By Ann Vanderhoof

A "cottage book" hanging in a highly visible spot can spare your guests the effort of trying to figure out the complexities of how your place works – and it can spare *you* the results of their misguided efforts. It's also great for jogging your own memory when it comes to opening up at the start of the season and closing up at the end. And, in an emergency or when things break, a cottage book puts needed information readily at hand.

A brightly coloured, three-ring binder is a handy format since you can add or delete pages as your cottage procedures change. The book should contain:

• instruction manuals for pumps, motors, water purifiers, and other crucial equipment

• septic system maintenance records

• detailed opening and closing procedures for water, electrical, and septic systems; boat and equipment storage and start-up; dock assembly and disassembly

• day-to-day operating instructions for your place, such as how to get the old outboard going, the combinations for the locks on the dock box or the shed, location of keys for the boathouse and guest cabin, directions for garbage disposal

• emergency information: names and phone numbers of doctors, helpful neighbours, relatives, police, and ambulance; location of the nearest hospital and directions there by car and/or boat; location of the first aid kit

• the lot and concession numbers for your property, plus careful directions to it by road and water (in case someone has to give directions on the phone in an emergency)

• instructions for summoning help if your place is not equipped with a telephone: how to operate the CB radio, the nearest neighbour with a phone, or the closest pay phone (tape some change in your cottage book)

• name, phone number, and location of the nearest veterinarian

• maps of the lake and surrounding area showing marinas, stores, hospitals, and points of interest (your favourite fishing spot, perhaps?)

• list of any boating regulations governing the lake, as well as unwritten rules regarding noise, neighbourly courtesy, etc.

• blank pages for your guests' anecdotes and lists of depleted supplies.

THE DOCK OF YOUR DREAMS

Everything you need to know to build a first-class floating dock. By Max Burns

Reduced to absolute basics, a floating dock consists of a platform, or deck, to hold humans and park boats next to, with some sort of flotation to keep that platform from sinking. Floating docks won't work everywhere – for instance, you need about 3 ft. of water, measured at the low-water mark, in order for a floater to function. But floating docks do suit a large number of waterfront properties, especially those with deep water right offshore or with fluctuating water levels. Floating docks also exert modest impact on the lake, river, or ocean bed below, thus leaving fish habitat and spawning areas largely undisturbed. For this reason, government agencies in charge of granting approvals and permits for shoreline work generally favour floating docks, which in turn usually means less pre-construction red tape and fewer delays.

Floating docks also have the advantage of versatility. They can be adapted to most sites and in some cases can be used as barges to transport all sorts of stuff to island locations. Perhaps the most appreciated advantage the typical floater offers, however, is the way it lends itself to both closet carpenters and experienced handy-folks. This builder-friendly nature can also be a disadvantage, accounting for most of the floating frights that haunt the world's shorelines. Bureaucrats may govern the location and type of dock, but there are rarely regulations or even official guidelines to assist eager-beaver builders in the actual construction.

To fill this void, I hounded some of the best dock builders for their secrets, tossed in a few of my own prejudices, and put together the following guide to floating docks that work.

BASIC DESIGN CONSIDERATIONS

The theory of flotation applies to any object placed in water, be it a floating dock, a boat, a rubber duck, or the noisy kids next door. Any object will float if the weight of the water it displaces (that is, the water it pushes aside) is greater than the total weight of that object, such as your dock fully loaded with sunbathers, for instance. The weight of any floating object exerts a downward force on the water that is met by an equal and opposite upward force known as buoyancy. Buoyancy acts on the centre of gravity of the displaced volume of water – that theoretical space where the water would reside if your dock wasn't sitting there. Ideally, this centre of gravity should coincide with the horizontal centre of the dock. If everyone moves with drinks, magazines, and deck chairs to one side of the dock, the upward force is now pushing more on one side of the dock – the unoccupied side – than the other. If it pushes up hard enough, the dock will tilt, perhaps enough to even dump its load, after which the dock will be in balance once again (although the dumped load might be a bit upset).

WHAT MAKES A FLOATING DOCK STABLE

This leads us to the most common criticism of the floater – it works just fine until someone steps onto it. But a floating dock doesn't have to be a terror to traverse. The golden rule for building a stable floater is to keep it long, wide, low, and heavy. A consensus among dock builders points to a 6' wide x 20' long dock as the

minimum size needed for a stable floater. When you step onto a dock, you not only sink the end you're stepping on, but you also raise the opposite end (just as the movement of humans, drinks, and deck chairs did above). The farther away that opposite end is and the more heft it has, the greater the odds that the dock won't even acknowledge your intrusion. On the other hand, your presence on a 2' wide x 6' long floater with a high centre of gravity is immediately acknowledged – much as it is when you stand at one end or to one side of a canoe. Having a brave volunteer present at the other end of the diminutive dock (or canoe) can help, adding heft at the opposite corner to partly offset your arrival – but it's better to count on a well-designed dock than on the generosity of others.

So long, wide, and heavy are good. But keep that weight low in order to maintain a low centre of gravity for the dock. Lowering the centre of gravity has the same effect as widening the dock: It becomes more difficult for humanity or nature to upset the floating object's balance (much as sitting down in a canoe makes the canoe less prone to capsizing). The benefits of a heavy dock may seem debatable to those of us in the sometimes-frozen north who must remove that weight from the water in the fall and return it in the spring; but such laborious activities only put a strain on the joys of two weekends. For the remainder of the season (or all year long if you're in an area immune to winter's freeze-up), you will give silent praise to that weight every time you step onto your dock.

WHERE TO PLACE THE FLOTATION

Flotation is the stuff that keeps the floating dock from sinking. There are various types (more on that in a minute), but whichever type you choose, its placement is also a key factor in the dock's stability. If a dock is going to rock and roll, this action will be most pronounced at the edges. (The centre of a dock is never the first part to dip into the water.) Any force applied to the edge of a dock – like diving off the end – will en-

MAKING IT LEGAL: SUPPORTING YOUR DOCK WITH PAPERWORK

Part of a good dock builder's job is to ensure that all the necessary permits and approvals have been taken care of; if they're not, you may be subject to some heavy-duty fines and possible imprisonment; to add insult to injury, you may also be required to remove the dock at your expense, restore the shoreline to its previous state, and pay for any downstream shoreline damage. Ouch.

Why all the fuss? When working on or near the shoreline, you are dealing with the most biologically productive part of any body of water. The main function of the various levels of government that regulate shoreline alterations is to protect that sensitive area – for you, for your neighbours, and for the future.

Unfortunately, there is little consensus among the various government agencies that oversee shoreline work as to what constitutes reasonable use of, or alterations to, shorelines. Approvals may have to come from several government agencies and levels of government, such as those responsible for the environment, natural resources, conservation, navigation of waterways, the welfare of fish, and building and electrical codes. This could mean contacting federal and provincial or state governments, local municipalities, conservation authorities, state or local commissions – and, in some cases, even your neighbours. Hard to believe this many people could be so interested in where you park the family skiff. But don't despair; my experience in contacting such agencies throughout North America is that the majority of government bureaucrats tend to be helpful to those appreciative of their efforts. Still, it's wise to plan at least a season before you want to build.

A good way to speed up the approval process is to keep the project simple. The amount of time you spend dealing with bureaucrats is usually in direct proportion to the degree of work you plan to do to that shoreline area – the more work, the more bureaucracy. And aside from decreasing the bureaucratic entanglement, a minimalist approach to shoreline alterations also reduces costs and the resulting impact on the environment. It's one of those rare situations where everybody wins.

courage the dock to rotate on its "roll axis" (also referred to as the "rotational axis"), a theoretical point located roughly in the centre of the dock where the horizontal and vertical centres of gravity intersect. Flotation distributed equally across the underside adds buoyancy (the force that keeps things afloat) to the centre of the dock, raising the height of the roll axis, which *increases* a dock's tendency to rotate. It follows that maximum stability is achieved when the flotation is placed around the perimeter of the dock, the area with the greatest tendency to react to any external force. Additional flotation should be installed at points of extraordinary loads – such as under a diving board or where a ramp joins the floating portion of a dock, since both can act like levers on the dock, encouraging it to roll.

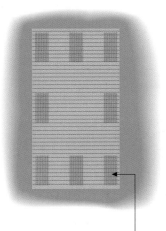

For maximum stability, arrange your flotation around the perimeter of the dock.

There is no set industry standard for determining the amount of flotation required to keep you and your dock afloat. Estimates vary from 20 to 35 lbs. of buoyancy per square foot of dock decking, depending on the type of flotation you choose and the weight of the dock. The low end of this scale often takes into consideration the amount of buoyancy provided by any wood in contact with the water. At the upper end, it is not a simple matter of the more the merrier; too much buoyancy will result in an unstable dock with an excessive amount of freeboard (the amount of the dock above the waterline). Choose your preferred flotation system and ask the manufacturer or dealer about the quantities needed for your particular dock.

TYPES OF FLOTATION

FOAM: *All foam billets are not created equal*

One popular form of flotation is the expanded polystyrene (EPS) foam billet. EPS is made by introducing a foaming agent into molten polystyrene. The foaming agent expands as the plastic cools, creating little pockets or bubbles in the plastic. Variations in the formula and manufacturing process result in closed-cell or open-cell EPS – and, in dock flotation, the distinction is critical. Closed-cell EPS is more rigid and has lower air and water permeability, making it the foam of choice for dock flotation. The foam coffee cup you see blowing across the street is of closed-cell construction; otherwise, it would not have held liquid prior to being tossed away. Open-cell EPS lets air and water pass through, and has a much higher absorbency rate than its closed-cell cousin. So-called "beadboard", usually white and sometimes found in residential construction, is open-cell foam; it should never be used for dock flotation.

Styrofoam billet

Another distinction can be made between moulded and extruded closed-cell EPS. The extrusion process orients the polystyrene molecules in one direction, creating a stronger, less permeable material. Styrofoam, the blue stuff made by Dow, is an extruded, closed-cell EPS foam. In comparison, moulded billets (usually white) are more fragile and will take on water, increasing their weight dramatically. If the contained water freezes, the billet can break apart.

One of the advantages of EPS foam is that, even when punctured, it will not sink. But this also means that should ice or nasty weather break up an EPS billet, the remnants will bob about the lake and shoreline for a very long time. (Styrofoam tends to break into chunks; the white stuff, however, will crumble.) All forms of EPS are susceptible to damage from sun, oils and gases, and abrasion. If you decide to float your dock on foam, it must be encased in a subframe below the decking of the dock, both to protect it from direct contact with anything but water, and to secure the billet in place. (See plans, p. 58.) Although this is rarely done, each billet should also be wrapped in black 6-mil (or thicker) polyethylene sheeting to protect it from ultraviolet (UV) rays and gas and oil spills, followed by a galvanized chicken-wire cage to protect it from gnawing varmints. The subframe, if designed correctly, can also act as a skid to support the dock if it is dragged onto land for seasonal storage.

FOAM-FILLED FLOAT DRUMS: *Enclosing the foam in plastic*

Because of the risk of littering the water and shoreline with bits of foam, EPS is not approved as dock flotation in an increasing number of jurisdictions (check with your local authorities) unless it is enclosed in a hard, protective container, such as the dedicated plastic float drum. These drums are specifically made as dock floats, usually from high-density polyethylene (the same stuff your red plastic gas can for the lawn mower or outboard motor is made from). Each drum possesses reasonably high impact strength, especially when filled with EPS foam. The foam also prevents the drum from sinking if it is punctured, although it could lose some of its buoyancy if the foam is of an open-cell type. If the foam is closed-cell, you probably won't even know the drum has been hit.

Foam-filled polyethylene float drum

Foam-filled float drums are available from numerous manufacturers in a variety of shapes and sizes. They bolt directly to the upper frame of the dock, usually through preformed holes in the upper perimeter ridge, although some floats have slots moulded into them for two-by-whatever lumber to slip into. In either case, a subframe is unnecessary. While eliminating the subframe partly offsets the additional cost of the float drums, it also reduces weight where it is needed most – down low.

Some manufacturers mould the perimeter ridge with its attachment holes about two-thirds of the way up the drum's height. By using one or the other side up, dock builders can easily achieve more or less freeboard for their dock. But, remember, any increase in freeboard without a proportionate increase in weight and flotation will result in a decrease in stability.

Topper foam-filled recycled-tire float

Another means of enclosing EPS foam is in a recycled car tire. Topper Floating Structures, the leading manufacturer of such floats, fills each tire with foam, then places a pressure-treated wood disc on either side of the hole where the wheel would reside. These "hubcaps" are secured in place with bolts that also serve as attachment points to the dock.

As with the float drum, no subframe is needed, but Topper floats are sufficiently heavy to compensate for the loss of weight. They're also reasonably durable. An unexpected bonus is that the pattern and shapes produced by the tires underneath the dock work to dampen wave action. The Topper floats remain visible from the side, however, and while it can be argued that a new tire mounted on a vehicle looks pretty good, a used one on your dock may eliminate it from the local Decorator Dock contest.

HOLLOW FLOAT DRUMS: *Filled with air instead of foam*

Plastic float drums are also available without the foam filler. These hollow floats are much the same as their foam-filled siblings, except that they are a little more susceptible to damage (the foam acts as a shock absorber) and they will take on water and sink when punctured. There is also a risk of one of these floats collapsing under the weight of the dock if it is dragged onto land for seasonal storage. However, punctured polyethylene can be easily repaired by plastic welding the broken pieces together. (I use an old soldering iron for this, and an expensive air mask to filter out the nasty fumes. Not an inside job.)

Pop-bottle-filled Enviro Float

One of the most innovative plastic float drums produced to date is the Enviro Float. From the outside, it looks like an ordinary float drum with the mumps. That's because inside there are 80 individual "plastic pressure vessels," a wonderful euphemism for clear plastic two-litre pop bottles, all pressure-tested, sealed, and stacked within the outer shell like wine in a wine cellar. The hard plastic outer shell is made from the polyethylene leftovers of industry. The beauty of the secondary flotation system on the inside is not just that it consists of recycled plastic, but that it actually reuses containers – no reprocessing of material required.

STEEL TUBES: *When a strong, heavy dock is called for*

Another alternative for floating a dock is the steel-tube float. These are awkward and heavy to handle on shore, but are without doubt the most durable flotation devices, and certainly the best suited to coping with the rigours of ice. In common with concrete floats (see below), steel-tube floats are best suited to mooring boats that verge on floating cottages, since they make for a big, heavy dock.

The steel tubes should be specifically designed for application as floats, although a reputable dock builder can modify lengths of steel pipe for the task.

THE FLOATING WORLD

TYPE OF FLOTATION	DESCRIPTION	QUANTITY NEEDED FOR A 6' X 20' DOCK AND APPROXIMATE COST*	APPROXIMATE BUOYANCY PER FLOAT**
Styrofoam Buoyancy Billet	Blue polystyrene extruded foam billet, closed-cell construction	4½ billets @ $45–$50 apiece	425 lbs.
Moulded EPS billet	Expanded polystyrene foam billet, moulded and cut to size; usually white	4½ billets @ $40 apiece	425 lbs.
Polyethylene dedicated float drum, foam-filled	Polyethylene shell, usually black, filled with either open or closed-cell foam	Varies greatly, depending on size and manufacturer; approximately 6 floats @ $80–$200 each	Varies greatly, depending on size and manufacturer; ranges from 20 to 1,000 lbs.
Polyethylene dedicated float drum, air-filled	Same as above, but without the foam filler	Varies greatly, depending on size and manufacturer; approx. 6 floats @ $80–$150 each	Varies greatly, depending on size and manufacturer; ranges from 300 to 750 lbs.
Enviro Float	Recycled polyethylene shell filled with reused pressure-tested and sealed plastic 2-litre pop bottles	5–6 floats @ $120–$150 each	625 lbs.
Steel tube	Long steel tubes, either custom-made or new pressure-tested pipe modified for dock applications; sometimes foam-filled	2 19"-diameter pipes @ $30–$45 per linear foot of float	125 lbs. per linear foot of float
Polyethylene dedicated float tube, foam or air-filled	High-density polyethylene (HDPE) pipes, linked together to form a large gridwork; longitudinal (float) pipes usually foam-filled	3 float pipes and 3 coupling pipes, 10"-diameter, @ average of $70 per linear foot of assembled float gridwork	18 lbs. per square foot of assembled float gridwork
Recycled-tire float	Recycled tires, EPS-filled; capped at both ends with pressure-treated plywood discs	16 floats @ $25–$35 each	150 lbs.
Recycled industrial drum	Steel or plastic, used and abused, hollow except for whatever nasty residues remain from their previous life	5 45-gallon drums; free and up	450 lbs.

*Cost is in Canadian dollars
**There is no industry standard for the amount of buoyancy required to keep a dock afloat. Estimates vary from 20 to 35 lbs. per square foot. If the dock has a wood substructure in the water, this wood provides buoyancy, so less buoyancy is required in the flotation itself. Some manufacturers sell floats in larger sizes with greater buoyancy, which provide options for larger, heavier docks. Keep in mind that the cost of the surrounding dock structure required by the flotation may offset any theoretical cost savings.

APPROXIMATE SIZE AND WEIGHT OF A TYPICAL UNIT	AVAILABILITY	THE QUICK REVIEW
7" x 20" x 96", 14 lbs.+	Building-supply stores and dock builders	Light, reasonably strong when handled, easy but messy to cut. Extruded closed-cell construction ensures that it retains most of its buoyancy. Can be damaged by abrasion, chemicals, and fuels. Not approved for use as dock flotation in all jurisdictions.
7" x 20" x 96", 7.7 lbs.+	Building-supply stores and dock builders	Cheap, but very fragile; highly susceptible to damage by weather, abrasion, freezing, chemicals, fuels, and darn near everything else; messy to work with. Although light to begin with, will absorb water, decreasing its buoyancy. Not approved for use as dock flotation in all jurisdictions.
Varies greatly, depending on size and manufacturer; typical: 12" x 24" x 48", 15 lbs.+	Building-supply stores, dock builders, and direct from the manufacturer	Available in a variety of shapes and sizes; quite durable. Attachment holes usually provided for easy bolting of floats to the bottom of the decking frame, making a subframe unnecessary, which partially offsets the added expense of these floats.
Varies greatly, depending on size and manufacturer; typical: 12" x 24" x 48", 30 lbs.+	Building-supply stores, dock builders, and direct from the manufacturer	Much the same as its foam-filled sibling, only a little more susceptible to damage. (The foam acts as a shock absorber.) When a puncture occurs, this float will take in water and sink.
16" x 27½" x 50", 35 lbs.	Dock builders and direct from the manufacturer (based in Winnipeg, MB)	Similar in use to a foam-filled dedicated float drum. Should a puncture occur, the odds of more than one "plastic pressure vessel" being affected are slim, leaving 79 other vessels to carry the load; use of recycled pop bottles gives this float high marks for environmental friendliness.
Typical: 19" diameter x 24' long, 25 lbs. per linear foot	Direct from the manufacturer	Heavy, awkward to handle, and expensive, but gets top marks for durability. No subframe is required or needed structurally or for stability. Overkill for those mooring only small boats.
Varies: 12" x 6' x 20' for our sample dock, 35 lbs. per linear foot of assembled gridwork	Dock builders and direct from the manufacturer	The gridwork of pipes provides all the strength, so no framework is required. A light-duty dock for small boats; modest weight compromises stability.
25" diameter x 10½" high, 35 lbs.	Dock builders and direct from the manufacturer	Reasonably durable, easily bolted to dock, no subframe required; combined weight of floats should compensate for any loss in stability attributable to the missing frame's weight.
22" diameter x 33" long, 48 lbs.	The dump, industrial and farm-supply warehouses, a friend who works at the factory	Ugly, difficult to secure to the frame, not particularly durable, will sink when punctured; light weight compromises stability; real risk of pollution from remnants of previous contents. Not approved for use as dock flotation in all jurisdictions.

Steel will rust and, after about 25 years, this can lead to leaks, although some dock builders are galvanizing the tubes and brackets. In some cases, the tubes are also filled with foam.

THE PLASTIC PIPE GRID: *Suitable for light duty*
A relatively new idea for flotation is a grid made from high-density polyethylene (HDPE) pipe. In a typical set-up, three 10"-diameter pipes are run longitudinally, one at each side and one down the centre. These pipes, known as the float pipes, are often foam filled, and are linked together using three or more coupling pipes, also made from 10"-diameter HDPE. (Picture an H with additional lines closing in the open ends, top and bottom.) Where the float pipes intersect the coupling pipes, short sections of 12"-diameter HDPE are installed on the coupling pipes, which act as sleeves for the float pipes. The pipe ends are sealed and mounting tabs for the decking are installed on the coupling units. All joints are plastic welded.

What results is a very strong, relatively lightweight gridwork of sealed pipes – no wooden framework is required. Although similar in concept to the steel-tube float, HDPE pipe floats are at the opposite end of the dock spectrum, stability being compromised by modest weight and modest buoyancy. They make for a light-duty dock suitable for small boats and limited exposure to nature's wrath. Not recommended for loungers who don't want to risk spilled lemonade when the neighbour's boat goes by or someone dives off the end of the dock.

CONCRETE FLOATS: *Not for the do-it-yourselfer*
Okay, so concrete float sounds like an oxymoron. But so does "army intelligence," and we still use that. Remember, any object will float if the weight of the water it displaces exceeds the total weight of that object. So, yes, we could end up with the peculiar dockside arrangement of concrete floats held in place with concrete anchors.

Concrete floats are foam-filled and form the entire dock; both framework and decking are unnecessary. What you get instead is a ready-made floating concrete sidewalk, delivered to your shore. Concrete floats are expensive and very heavy (they usually require launching by crane), but offer strength and stability about on a par with a sidewalk. They are especially well suited to oceanfront locations where fluctuating tides and high waves often play havoc with residential floating docks. Like steel tubes, they are overkill for small boats.

Concrete floats are not suited to the do-it-yourselfer (unless, of course, writing a cheque is your idea of active involvement), and therefore they are not included in the how-to charts and notes.

INDUSTRIAL DRUMS: *Not a flotation option*
An unacceptable type of flotation is the recycled industrial drum. When the drum reaches your dock, there is a high probability that it still holds vestiges of the sub-

THE PLANNING COMMITTEE

Good planning is paramount. A dock that can't handle the various tasks expected of it risks becoming a berth of the blues. And the best place to start planning your dock is with your family.

How big is the family, extended to all potential dock users? What are their ages? Are there special considerations to take into account, such as elderly or disabled family members?

List the activities of each family member – water-skiing, fishing, sailboarding, whatever. One preferred sport may dictate a dock's shape or required accessories. But allow some flexibility for future uses. A designated swim area, without cleats or other toe-jammers, is always a dandy idea, and there should be space for people just to sit and think about absolutely nothing if they choose.

How big is the boat? What, you've got more than one? List the types, and the various mooring requirements.

How much, or how little, do you want to spend? Small budgets can often be accommodated by doing the work in stages, building one section this year, then adding sections as finances permit.

Next, look at the site itself. You need to evaluate its exposure to nature's capricious ways. Wind, open water, and ice can all unbuild what you have built if you don't respect the forces at work. If you're new to the area and unfamiliar with what nature could have in

store for you, ask the neighbours. They usually have some good horror stories to relate.

And don't forget the shoreline, both above and below the waterline. Is it bedrock, a pile of stones, sandy, muddy, or you name it? A high cliff rising out of the water may demand an extra-large dock to compensate for the loss of activity space at water's edge. What is the depth of water out to 12, 24, and 36 feet from shore? How much does the water level fluctuate?

For simplicity's sake, we have chosen to build a basic rectangle (see plans, pp. 58–61), but it can be adapted and expanded to suit your needs. Maybe a T-shape, for instance – or an L or a U – would work better to solve your traffic congestion and provide the mooring space you need. A dock section run out at an angle works especially well if the shoreline runs out at an angle too, and may even open an area for docking a boat that would otherwise be too shallow. As a bonus, variations on the traditional rectangle usually lead to a more stable dock, both nature and humanity having to exert a greater force on it to make it move.

Perhaps the most important lesson we can learn from professional dock builders is that no two sites or situations are the same. What works, or doesn't work, for your neighbour won't necessarily have the same effect for you. It is your family's needs and desires, and what nature lent you for a waterfront, that will dictate the design of your dock.

stances transported in it – toxic chemicals, for instance. Even in areas where these barrels are not banned as dock flotation, why would anyone take a chance on letting the kids swim around them? Or drink water from the lake they temporarily float on, and often eventually sink in?

CHOOSING THE WOOD

Framing is what lies under the decking; it supports the deck and keeps the flotation in place. The design of the framework will vary with the type of flotation you've chosen (see plans, pp. 58 and 60) but, regardless of the design, hefty framing members like 2" x 8"s and 2" x 10"s are needed.

For the decking planks, either 2" x 4"s or 2" x 6"s work best. Wider boards have more wood per plank to shrink and expand, putting more strain on the hardware that holds the dock together.

What's the best wood to use? In the framework, it's tough to beat Douglas fir for strength. It also has reasonable natural resistance to rot. But lumberyards often don't stock fir in the sizes needed for dock building and it must be specially ordered. If you can't get fir, try to find hemlock or tamarack – both also very rot resistant.

Otherwise, use the same wood for the framework as for the decking and be sure to accompany it with good hardware. (More on this in a minute.) For the decking, western red cedar, redwood, cypress, and eastern white cedar (in that order) all offer reasonable longevity and beauty.

Some plastic alternatives are also now on the market. (See "A Plastic Dock," below.) Then there's pressure-treated wood, with its supposed longer life – some companies offer lifetime warranties – and lower cost. Unfortunately, these long-term benefits can be difficult to take advantage of. (How long do you hold onto your receipts, necessary for making claim against a warranty?) Working with pressure-treated wood also exposes you to toxic dust and to the chemicals needed to treat cut ends, and recent government investigations have discovered that industry standards for quality are sometimes not adhered to (both the grade of the wood and the degree of preservative absorption being substandard). Pressure-treated wood is also prone to warping and cracking when exposed to weather.

The preferred decking woods come with their own natural decay-resistant resins, good for 18–22 years, no nasty chemicals or warranties needed. They also stain well should you want to alter, or preserve, the original colour. Left to their own devices, however, they will all weather to a mellow, soft grey and you won't have to refinish the dock every couple of years.

When it comes to getting quality wood, the do-it-yourselfer is always at a disadvantage because of the minimal quantities needed for one project. Understandably, the choice goods usually go to the account with the biggest order, and lumberyards don't like you picking through their stocks for the better pieces, as it leaves them with a lot of junk. Budget for a minimum 20% rejection rate.

When your wood arrives, stack it and let it sit in the shade for a couple of days to dry and shrink prior to installation.

A PLASTIC DOCK

If you're looking for a dock whose decking will last for generations, consider plastic.

Plastic decking is very durable, with a lifespan of at least 100 years, likely much longer. There are basically two types: one that is made from recycled materials and comes in standard lumber dimensions, and another that is a fabricated extrusion made from new plastic and is usually sold in lengths that are some variation on a squared-off "U"-shape. Neither type is suitable for structural applications, such as dock stringers, because they lack the necessary strength.

Several manufacturers of "plastic lumber" have come and gone. One of the more interesting versions still with us is Trex, made by the Mobil Chemical Company. It is a composite made from reclaimed plastic and waste wood. Like other plastic lumbers, Trex is heavy, more like oak than cedar, which can be an advantage in dock building. Unlike the others, Trex can be painted or stained because it contains some wood. This is not necessary, though; left untreated, the "natural" shade of Trex will weather to a light grey. Mobil also produces Trex in a colourfast dark brown. (When choosing plastic lumber, keep in mind that dark-coloured plastics can get hot in the sun.)

Plastic lumber tends to sag, so the decking must be supported in more places than wood decking would need to be.

In the second category of plastic decking is Brock Dock's extruded "plank" made out of PVC, which boasts a non-slip surface. These planks attach to the dock framework using special clips screwed to the stringers below, so no fasteners stick out above the surface.

Standard home power and hand tools can be used on both types of plastic decking.

The durability of plastic decking is its strong point – but it is also a drawback. Real untreated wood rots; the sawdust and scrap you create when cutting it can be burned in the fireplace. The same cannot be said for plastic lumber.

And, finally, examined up close, plastic lumber neither looks like wood nor feels like wood; it looks, feels, and smells like plastic. But before you dismiss it solely on that basis, remember that the same can be said for most pleasure boats.

PUTTING THE DOCK TOGETHER
THE IMPORTANCE OF GOOD HARDWARE

Perhaps the most overlooked ingredient in good dock design is the construction hardware, the stuff that holds a dock together. Good hardware will outlast any wooden framework or decking. The beauty of good hardware – strong and carefully thought out – becomes apparent the moment you start putting your dock together, and that beauty continues to shine as you use the dock and service it in the ensuing years.

Dock hardware is available in steel, aluminum, and stainless steel. Steel without any protective coating is going to rust and look ugly, and likely corrode away before you do. Therefore, look for galvanized steel. Larger pieces should be hot-dipped galvanized, as opposed to plated. Hot-dipped galvanizing produces a gloppy, thick dull silver finish. Plating produces a smooth sheen and is much thinner, and is thus appropriate only for smaller items such as screws.

Aluminum hardware can also work well. Lighter than steel, aluminum must be of thicker stock to duplicate the strength of steel. It is also about three times more expensive than hot-dipped galvanized steel plate. Stainless steel is very strong, won't rust, and will likely last generations longer than the wood around it. Count on the finished product to cost at least five times more than anything made from hot-dipped galvanized steel. Use aluminum and stainless steel only where the hardware will show; otherwise, no one will know you've spent the extra money.

There are many manufacturers of good dock hardware. Generally, it's best to stick with one brand of hardware where the pieces have been designed to work together and are readily available. Ideally, each piece should be predrilled using the same bolt pattern, allowing structures to be assembled like Lego.

USE SCREWS AND BOLTS, NOT NAILS

No matter whose hardware you use (or even if you decide to skimp on such necessities), screws and bolts work better than nails in almost all situations. As wood expands and shrinks with the weather, nails can pull out and sit proud above the surface, looking for toes to attack. Screws and bolts draw the pieces of wood together and can be retightened as the wood moves. (Nails also make it difficult to take pieces apart if you make a mistake during construction. Not that you would, of course; I only mention it here in passing.)

ASSEMBLING THE FRAMEWORK WITH BRACKETS AND BRACES

For attaching longitudinal framing members (called stringers) to the crossers and end plates (called headers), use galvanized brackets designed specifically for this use on docks. (Do not use joist hangers designed for residential construction, as they are not intended to withstand the rigours your dock will face.) Virtually all dock hardware manufacturers make such brackets; they can be used with or without backup

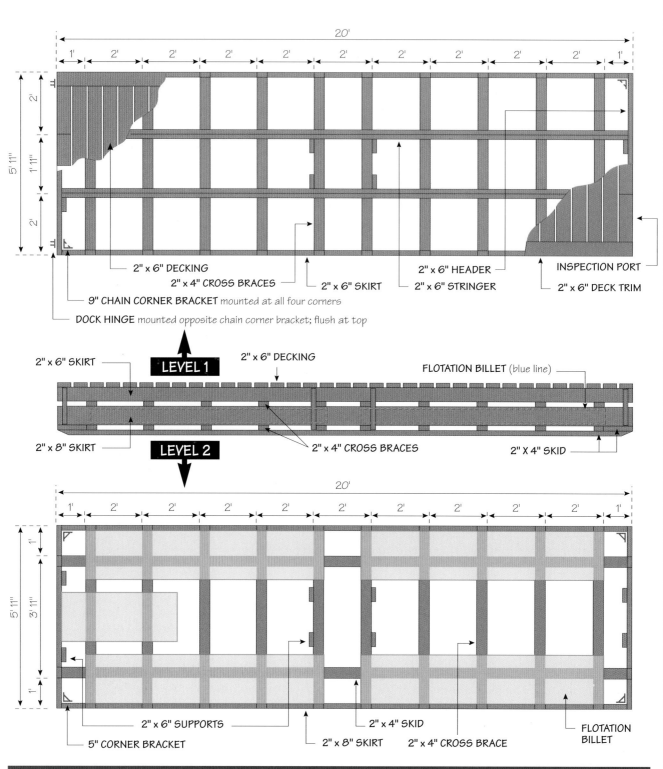

20'

1' 2' 2' 2' 2' 2' 2' 2' 2' 2' 1'

5' 11"
2'
1' 11"
2'

2" x 6" DECKING
2" x 4" CROSS BRACES
2" x 6" SKIRT
2" x 6" HEADER
2" x 6" STRINGER
INSPECTION PORT
2" x 6" DECK TRIM

9" CHAIN CORNER BRACKET mounted at all four corners

DOCK HINGE mounted opposite chain corner bracket; flush at top

2" x 6" SKIRT
2" x 6" DECKING
FLOTATION BILLET (blue line)

LEVEL 1

2" x 8" SKIRT
LEVEL 2
2" x 4" CROSS BRACES
2" X 4" SKID

20'

1' 2' 2' 2' 2' 2' 2' 2' 2' 2' 1'

5' 11"
1'
3' 11"
1'

2" x 6" SUPPORTS
5" CORNER BRACKET
2" x 8" SKIRT
2" x 4" SKID
2" x 4" CROSS BRACE
FLOTATION BILLET

6' X 20' DOCK USING STYROFOAM BUOYANCY BILLETS FOR FLOTATION

Both this dock and the one on p. 60 offer 12"–15" of freeboard. Freeboard can be increased by increasing the size of the framing lumber (installed on edge) lying above the flotation. For example, with the dock using Styrofoam billets, replace the upper deck 2" x 6" skirt and stringers with 2" x 8" lumber; on the float-drum dock, replace the 2" x 6" cross braces with 2" x 8"s, and the skirt with 2" x 10"s. However, keep in mind that by increasing freeboard, you are also raising the centre of gravity, which will result in a corresponding decrease in stability.

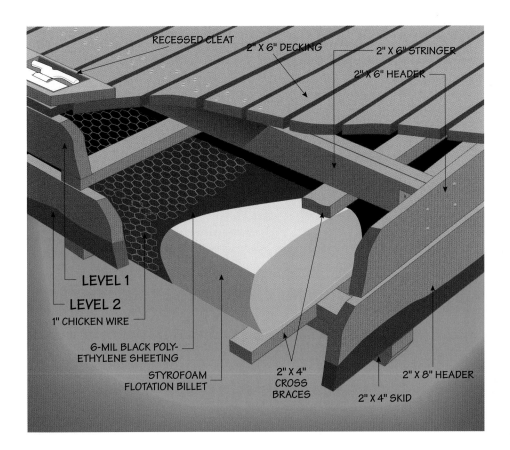

RECESSED CLEAT
2" X 6" DECKING
2" X 6" STRINGER
2" X 6" HEADER
LEVEL 1
LEVEL 2
1" CHICKEN WIRE
6-MIL BLACK POLY-ETHYLENE SHEETING
STYROFOAM FLOTATION BILLET
2" X 4" CROSS BRACES
2" X 4" SKID
2" X 8" HEADER

MATERIALS

WOOD *(all cedar)*

For Level 1 (frame and decking):

20 2" x 6" x 12'   **1** 2" x 6" x 18'
8 2" x 6" x 20'   **5** 2" x 4" x 12'

For Level 2 (substructure):

2 2" x 8" x 20'   **1** 2" x 8" x 12'
1 2" x 6" x 12'   **2** 2" x 4" x 20'
5 2" x 4" x 12'   **1** 2" x 4" x 8'

HARDWARE

2½" plated or ceramic baked flathead or
   buglehead screws*
5"–6" plated or ceramic baked flathead
   or buglehead screws*
3" carriage or machine bolts
4" carriage or machine bolts
6" carriage or machine bolts
8 dock joist hangers or corner brackets
   for attaching headers to stringers
4 9" corner brackets with slat for chain
4 5" corner brackets
2 dock-to-ramp hinges

FLOTATION

4½ Styrofoam billets, 7" x 20" x 8'
115 sq. ft. 6-mil black polyethylene
   sheeting
115 sq. ft. galvanized 1" chicken wire

plates, which spread the load over a larger surface area.

Should stringers need to be spliced, overlap the joints with a wood backup plate of the same dimension as the stringer, the overlap extending a minimum of 2' on either side of the joint.

Under stress, a rectangle wants to become a parallelogram. To curtail this unruly behaviour, the corners of your dock should be braced in such a manner as to create a triangle in each corner. One of the best and easiest ways to do this is to install braced metal inside corner brackets. (See drawing, p. 61.) Some manufacturers also offer an outside corner bracket to be used in conjunction with the inside bracket for particularly heavy-duty applications.

I favour the convenience of corner brackets that include built-in slats for the anchor chain. (When such brackets are used, the dock should be designed with a short section of removable decking at the corners, to allow easy access to the chain for adjustment. See plans, p. 58.) But there are also anchor brackets available for applications that call for anchor chains to be located on the sides of the dock.

* Robertson-type screws are preferred for this application; Phillips-type are a good second choice

8' X 16' FLOATING DOCK SECTION USING FOAM-FILLED DEDICATED FLOAT DRUMS

Float drums come in a great many shapes and sizes, and alterations to the plans may be necessary to accommodate your choice of float. Some floats even provide moulded channels for the framing, which dictate the location of structural lumber. Check with the float manufacturer.

MATERIALS

WOOD (all cedar)
3 2" x 4" x 16'
3 2" x 10" x 16'
40 2" x 6" x 8'
2 2" x 6" x 16'

HARDWARE
2½" plated or ceramic baked flathead or bugle-head screws*

5"–6" plated or ceramic baked flathead or bugle-head screws*

3" carriage or machine bolts

4" carriage or machine bolts

4" lag bolts (for attaching flotation to frame)

12 5" corner brackets for attaching cross braces to outer frame (2 per brace)

4 5" corner brackets with slat for chain

2 dock-to-ramp hinges

optional: outside corner brackets and/or backing plates, depending on brand of hardware used; would then require 4" carriage or machine bolts instead of 3" ones

FLOTATION
8 foam-filled dedicated plastic float drums

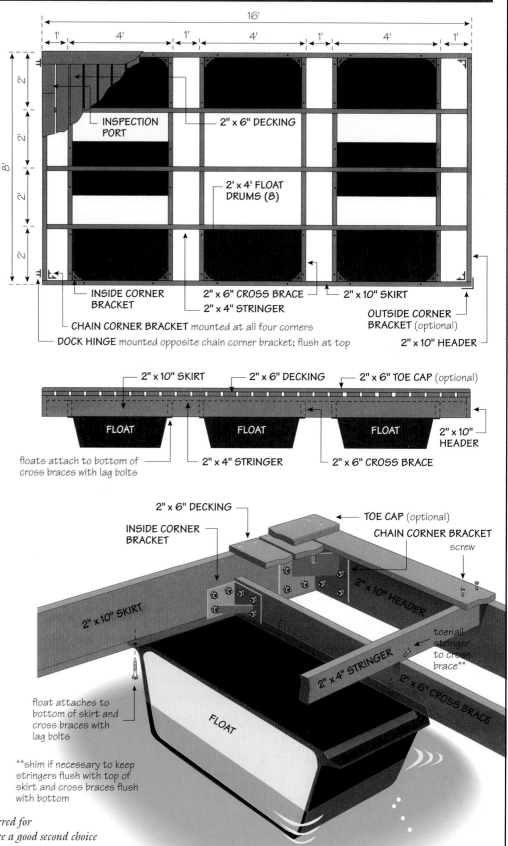

16'
1' — 4' — 1' — 4' — 1' — 4' — 1'
8'
2' 2' 2' 2'

INSPECTION PORT
2" x 6" DECKING
2' x 4' FLOAT DRUMS (8)
INSIDE CORNER BRACKET
2" x 6" CROSS BRACE
2" x 4" STRINGER
2" x 10" SKIRT
OUTSIDE CORNER BRACKET (optional)
2" x 10" HEADER
CHAIN CORNER BRACKET mounted at all four corners
DOCK HINGE mounted opposite chain corner bracket; flush at top

2" x 10" SKIRT
2" x 6" DECKING
2" x 6" TOE CAP (optional)
FLOAT   FLOAT   FLOAT
2" x 10" HEADER
floats attach to bottom of cross braces with lag bolts
2" x 4" STRINGER
2" x 6" CROSS BRACE

2" x 6" DECKING
TOE CAP (optional)
INSIDE CORNER BRACKET
CHAIN CORNER BRACKET
screw
2" x 10" SKIRT
2" x 10" HEADER
toenail stringer to cross brace**
2" x 4" STRINGER
2" x 6" CROSS BRACE
float attaches to bottom of skirt and cross braces with lag bolts
FLOAT
**shim if necessary to keep stringers flush with top of skirt and cross braces flush with bottom

* Robertson-type screws are preferred for this application; Phillips-type are a good second choice

PUTTING ON THE DECKING

For maximum strength, arrange the decking so the planks cross the principal framing members at a 45°–90° angle. Perpendicular decking creates less waste; angled decking creates more visual interest. Avoid butt ends (a place for rot to begin) by using decking long enough to cover the span in one go (for example, an 8'-long 2" x 6" for an 8'-wide dock).

If possible, decking should be installed with the end growth rings curving downward (convex, or bark side up) to prevent the edges from cupping above the deck surface over time. Fasten the decking to the framing members using two screws per deck board at each intersection, leaving about a ⅜" gap between planks if using untreated wood, ⅛" if using pressure-treated. (The gaps will get larger as the pressure-treated wood shrinks.)

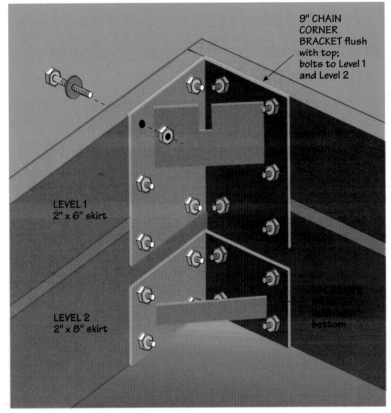

9" CHAIN CORNER BRACKET flush with top; bolts to Level 1 and Level 2

LEVEL 1 2" x 6" skirt

LEVEL 2 2" x 8" skirt

bottom

CORNER DETAIL OF FLOATING DOCK, p.58

CONNECTING SECTIONS

One area that trips up do-it-yourselfers is the method of connecting the sections of floating dock together. The usual practice is to employ some variation on a hinged mechanism, from steel rods to barn-door hinges. This permits free up-and-down movement at the ends of each section, setting the stage for the infamous roller-coaster effect as each section attempts to rotate about its own roll axis as you travel from one end of the dock to the other. The solution is to use a dock connector that is not a standard hinge but ties the sections rigidly together top and bottom, while still allowing for easy disconnection and reconnection for seasonal service. With this type of connector (available from most manufacturers of good dock hardware), the load applied to one section is shared by all the sections, greatly increasing stability and thwarting the tendency for the sections to rotate on their individual axes. The sections in effect act as one.

RULES ABOUT RAMPS

No floating dock exists in isolation; you've got to get to it, after all. The best means of connecting that dock to land will differ for virtually every site, but usually the solution involves a ramp between land and dock. For those who haven't yet experienced one, a ramp in the 2'-wide category is like a gangplank: It needs railings on both sides, unless of course you are blindfolded, walking it to your demise. A ramp the same width as the dock – in other words, at least 6' wide – makes for a much nicer entrance. You can transport a canoe over it, or a motor, chairs, lunch – and even walk by someone doing the same thing, without fear of falling into the drink. Essentially, the ramp is constructed in the same manner as the decking and decking subframe, only without the floats.

Unlike the connections between sections of floating dock, those between ramp and dock must allow for independent vertical movement of the two in response to changes in water depth and surface conditions. At land's end, the ramp must be hinged for free movement, ideally to a stationary platform such as a crib, retaining wall, or some other immobile structure. Expandable rock pins – usually available at places that rent rock drills – are the ticket for bolting the hinges at the land end of a ramp, or any platform the ramp will be attached to, into bedrock. Special T-bolts are available for imbedding into concrete, and galvanized heavy-duty nuts and bolts are dandy for attaching ramps to cribwork. Comfy chairs work well for attaching humans to the deck.

Typical hinge for connecting dock section to ramp

A nifty solution to the problem of attaching a ramp to bedrock (regrettably I can't claim credit for inventing this) is to use a $2\frac{5}{16}$" ball and trailer hitch. The ball is embedded (using a suitable glue – again, usually available at places that rent rock drills) into a hole drilled into the bedrock, and the hitch is mounted to the pointed end of an A-frame. The ramp is then constructed on this frame. With the ramp hinged at the dock (preferably at the ends of the A-frame) and the trailer hitch securing the ramp to the shore, this system allows for ample vertical and lateral movement where water levels don't fluctuate much. Come winter, the ramp can easily be unhooked from terra firma and folded up onto the dock.

Where ramp meets dock, hinges work well, locking the dock and ramp together horizontally but not vertically, so it can move as the water level changes. Because these hinges are subject to high lateral loads, use only top-notch hardware (which you should do in any event). One high-end dock hinge places the hinge pin bolts in nylon bushings, thereby reducing pin wear while eliminating metal-to-metal squeaking as the hinge works in response to dock and ramp movement.

Another method of mating ramp to dock is to allow the end of the ramp that leads to the dock to ride free. The ramp rests on the dock decking, and moves along the dock on wheels as the water level varies. Unlike the direct connection of a hinge, however, some wheeled-ramp designs may allow side-to-side movement of the dock in relation to the ramp. And be forewarned that the resulting step created by the ramp at the point where it rests on the dock can be a hazard. Any exterior step should be at least 5″ high, preferably 6″–8″, if the eyes are to readily perceive it as a change in elevation. If the step is smaller than 5″, extend the decking boards on the ramp to meet the dock, perhaps hinging this overlap so it can automatically adjust for changes in the ramp angle.

Speaking of which, if water levels change dramatically along your waterfront over the course of the season, the ramp can become exceedingly steep. A ramp angle steeper than 30° can be dangerous to negotiate, especially if you use cedar decking, which gets a bit slippery when wet. For a ramp that currently angles down 30° to the dock, each 1′ drop in water height will require an additional 2′ of ramp to maintain this 30° maximum. In other words, if the 10′ ramp used on our 6′ x 20′ sample dock is level when your lake or river is at high water, it can tolerate a 5′ drop in water height before exceeding the allowable 30° angle. In areas where water levels vary greatly, design the ramp so it is almost level when the water is high. Should this not be possible, or should the change in water level be so great that the ramp still becomes impossibly steep, alternative solutions include installing a longer ramp, lengthening the existing ramp with an additional section, lowering the shoreline mounting point as the water level drops, and raising the dock mounting point by installing bolt-on steps.

Because a long ramp weighs more than a short one, more flotation may be required in the dock (or in some cases, the ramp end) to offset the additional weight. This extra flotation is best placed at the juncture of ramp and dock.

Also keep in mind that as the ramp tilts from 0° to 30°, the distance its far end is from shore decreases by 3″ for every 2′ of ramp (15″ in the case of our 10′ ramp). Therefore, the length of ramp must also take into consideration the distance away from shore the floating dock must be in order to maintain a minimum of 3′ of water below it.

If the point where the ramp is secured to land is much higher than the water level, steps can be erected on the dock to raise the end of the ramp permanently. The rise (height) of each step should be 6″–8″, and the run or tread (the part you step on), 9¼″–14″, not including any nosing (the optional 1″ tread overhang). Vary from these measurements only if you enjoy tripping over bad designs. It's also wise to install a sturdy handrail if the total rise of all the steps exceeds 24″.

DO IT WITH A KIT

Those uneasy about designing and building their own docks from scratch may want to consider dock kits. Available direct from the manufacturer in many cases as well as from dealers, the kits usually include hardware, plans, and a bill of materials to build a dock using the manufacturer's preferred flotation; some kits even include all the framing and decking materials required.

Some of the kits, however, produce a short dock section, which means you would have to buy at least two kits in order to meet the standards of stability set out here (securing the sections together with connectors, not hinges, of course; see p. 61). As well, be forewarned that the plans issued by some companies do not meet even minimum standards for what constitutes a stable and long-lasting floating dock. Armed with the information contained in these pages, however, you should be able to recognize and avoid any kit-astrophes.

ANCHORING YOUR DOCK

Aside from a few industrial-strength floaters, residential-type floating docks need more than that ramp connection to keep them from drifting away in a storm. That's why it's wise to sink a few additional dollars into anchors.

You'll need about twice the weight of the dock in anchors. (A 6' x 20' or an 8' x 16' floating dock section with a wooden frame will weigh in at 1,000–2,000 lbs.) Don't skimp, because each submerged anchor loses weight equal to the water it displaces, and don't use old engine parts or other carcinogen-coated rejects. Five-gallon pails of cement are not the ticket either, as they lack surface area and tend to roll. Fortunately, it's not very difficult to make a good anchor.

Build a simple wooden mould to hold about 1 cubic foot of concrete (2' long x 1' wide x 6" high makes a nice size), insert a 6-mil polyethylene liner, mix the concrete right in the mould (being careful not to tear the plastic liner), add some reinforcing rods, then set a galvanized steel ring into the concrete while it's still wet. After it sets, turn the mould over and dump out your anchor, then make another and another until you've got enough to equal twice the weight of your dock. Each anchor will weigh about 150 lbs., but before panic strikes, remember that moving the anchors about gets easier once they are in water, and even easier if you've got a friend helping.

Gang several of these anchors together at each corner of the dock to make up the required weight. Grouping smaller anchors together like this often provides a toehold that can otherwise be hard to find on rocky bottoms. On very smooth rock, underwater rock pins may be necessary – or you could just use a lot more weight.

The heavier the anchors you use, the less scope you need, scope being the length of anchor chain.

The end of the dock farthest from shore should have two anchors (or two groups of anchors if you are ganging them together) cross-chained with ⅜" (min-

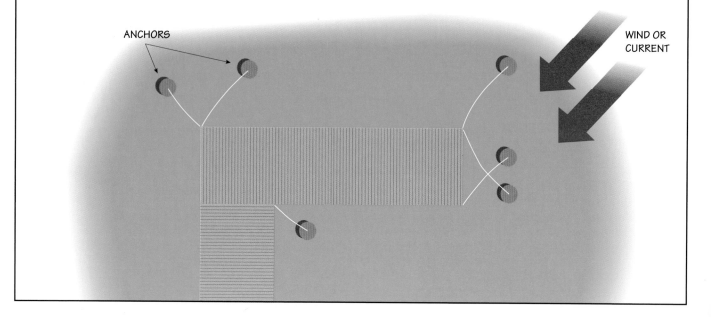

ANCHORS

WIND OR CURRENT

imum) galvanized chain. In cross-chaining, the left corner of the dock is linked to the right anchor and the right corner of the dock is linked to the left anchor, the chains running at approximately 45° to the dock.

If prevailing winds regularly twist the dock to one side, what is known as a long or storm anchor may solve the problem. It consists of a length of chain run out from the corner that faces into the prevailing wind. The guiding rule is that the length of this chain should equal about three times the depth of the water at the front of the dock. Allow the weight of the chain to hang straight down from the corner and then out along the bottom into the wind. Attach a heavy anchor at the end. The chain itself could weigh 150 lbs. or more, and will usually snag onto rock or dead trees, or bury itself in the mud or sand. What you get is a wind shock absorber.

As an alternative to anchors, it is possible in some cases to keep the ramp and dock in place using cables, pinned to the dock at one end and to dry land at the other. The cables are kept under tension, preventing the dock from moving laterally, while still allowing for some vertical movement. However, such trick stuff is beyond most dock-it-yourself builders, and many professionals for that matter.

Regardless of the project, the do-it-yourself route almost invariably saves money. But there is a cost. Even the most handy of cottagers is not going to build a dock as nicely put together as that of an experienced dock builder. Yet it's still possible, by taking time and using quality materials, for the most hammer-handicapped among us to put together a reasonable dock he or she can be proud of. In fact, when it comes to pride, nothing purchased will ever surpass that which we have built with our own hands – and who dares put a price on that?

GOOD LOOKIN': TEN HIGHLY SUBJECTIVE TIPS FOR A GREAT DOCK

1. Cover the structural framework of the dock along the sides and ends: 2" x 10" to 2" x 12" skirts along the lower edge of the dock work well for this, and also provide a smooth, strong surface to attach bumpers for boats to snuggle up against.

2. Don't load the dock with excess trim. Wood pressed on wood holds water and is likely to be the first place to rot. Let the wood breathe, physically and visually.

3. Round over all exposed edges with a router or file. Not only does this look neat, but the elimination of square edges also makes contact with body parts less painful.

4. Avoid used car tires for dock bumpers. They're acceptable as dock floats because few but the fish see them. But the only place they should be on public display is on used cars.

5. Many people choose to stain their docks. Stain looks great – until it starts to fade and peel. Once committed to stain, you're in it for the long haul and will have to recoat the dock every few years. This is obviously too much work when you could be swimming or boating. So pass on the stain and let the wood go grey naturally. It looks fine, trust me.

6. Ban all 200-watt intrusions. Loud music is ugly.

7. Do not feel restricted to conventional dock design. Run the decking diagonally. Create a cedar sunburst. Make an octagonal dock. An elongated diamond shape, the points at the far ends lopped off, creates four roomy spaces to tie boats up to, while the truncated ends provide space for the ramp at the shore and a dedicated swim area at the opposite end.

8. Integrate the shoreline with the dock. For example, cover multiple rock pins with a 6" x 6" bolted down, then cover the bolts and 6" x 6" with decking. Any concrete shoreline structure should also be covered, preferably with the same material as the dock decking. And if your dock incorporates steps, the runners should also be of the same material as the dock decking.

9. Hold off on the patio lanterns.

10. And finally, for the ultimate in dock beautification, invite me over for a dockside lunch.

DOCKSIDE STORAGE BOX

A place at the water's edge to store everything from paddles to life jackets, fishing tackle to towels. By Jeff Mathers

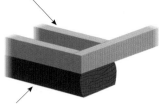

2"x4" pressure-treated floor frame

railway tie or 2' x 2' patio stones

FLOOR & GROUND DETAIL
Embed railway tie in ground; make sure tie doesn't hang past floor frame

A dock box near the water's edge is a guaranteed problem-solver. It offers an attractive storage space for all the accoutrements of waterfront life. A well-designed dock box means fewer trips to tote things from cottage to lake and back again, and a corresponding decline in dockside clutter. (Need for a dock box seems to increase in direct proportion to the number of steps the cottage is from the water.)

This model features tongue-and-groove pine on the outside. It has doors at the front that swing open, as well as a lift-up lid, which is fitted with brackets on the inside to hold paddles or oars. Ventilation holes along both sides allow air circulation when the box is closed, so towels and life jackets can dry.

BUILDING THE DOCK BOX

1. Level the ground where you want the box to sit, and embed railway ties or patio stones to set the box on. Backfill leaving only a couple of inches of the foundation exposed, so you don't see it when the box is on top.

2. To make the floor, assemble a 2" x 4" pressure-treated frame with 3½" ardox nails, running the 2" x 4"s on 18" centres. Make the frame 34½" wide x 70½" long. Nail on

MATERIALS
LUMBER
160 ft. 1" x 6" tongue-and-groove pine
60 ft. 2" x 3" spruce studs
30 ft. 2" x 4" pressure-treated studs
1 sheet ¾"x 4' x 8' pressure-treated plywood
50 ft. 1" x 4" pine
3 ft. 1" x 2" pine
8 ft. 1" x 1" pine
2 hardwood dowels, 1½" x 34½"
1 hardwood dowel, ¾" x 36"
2 pieces ¼" plywood, 2⅞" x 26"
2 railway ties or **6** 2' x 2' patio stones
Wood scraps for paddle brackets

OTHER
3 large strap hinges
4 medium strap hinges
4 ft. brass chain
1 4½" hasp
3½" ardox nails
2½" ardox nails
2½" flathead screws
1¼" flathead screws
Outdoor penetrating stain or oil finish
1 piece screening, 8" x 24"

TOOLS
Circular saw or table saw
Hammer and screwdrivers
Drill and 1½" spade bit
Stapler

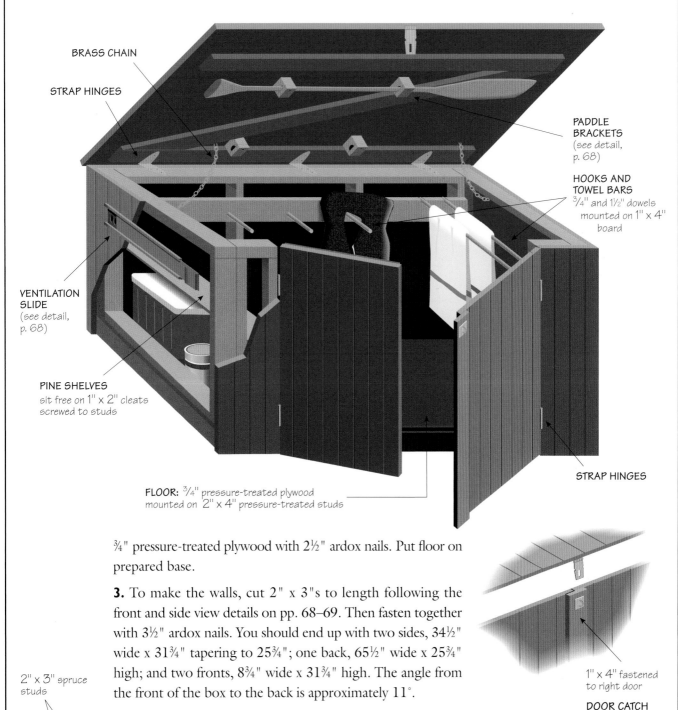

BRASS CHAIN

STRAP HINGES

PADDLE
BRACKETS
(see detail,
p. 68)

HOOKS AND
TOWEL BARS
¾" and 1½" dowels
mounted on 1" x 4"
board

VENTILATION
SLIDE
(see detail,
p. 68)

PINE SHELVES
sit free on 1" x 2" cleats
screwed to studs

STRAP HINGES

FLOOR: ¾" pressure-treated plywood
mounted on 2" x 4" pressure-treated studs

2" x 3" spruce
studs

TOP CORNER
CUTAWAY DETAIL

tongue-and-
groove pine

1" x 4" fastened
to right door

DOOR CATCH
DETAIL

¾" pressure-treated plywood with 2½" ardox nails. Put floor on prepared base.

3. To make the walls, cut 2" x 3"s to length following the front and side view details on pp. 68–69. Then fasten together with 3½" ardox nails. You should end up with two sides, 34½" wide x 31¾" tapering to 25¾"; one back, 65½" wide x 25¾" high; and two fronts, 8¾" wide x 31¾" high. The angle from the front of the box to the back is approximately 11°.

4. Fasten walls to floor and to each other with 3½" ardox nails. Cover the outside with 1" x 6" tongue-and-groove pine.

5. Construct the lid and doors using tongue-and-groove pine, following the diagrams on p. 69, making sure you fasten the 1" x 4" cross braces with 1¼" flathead screws. Screw a 1" x 4" to the front of the right door, leaving a 1¾" lip to overlap the left door. See detail above.

6. Fabricate ventilation brackets (one for each side) out of pine

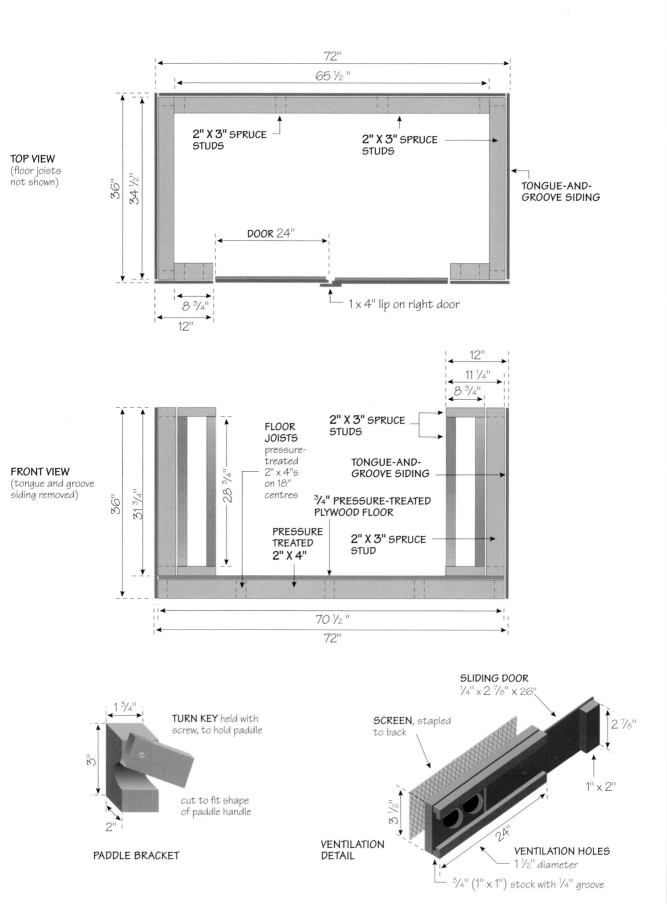

TOP VIEW
(floor joists not shown)

72"

65 ½"

2" X 3" SPRUCE STUDS

2" X 3" SPRUCE STUDS

TONGUE-AND-GROOVE SIDING

36"

34 ½"

DOOR 24"

8 ¾"

12"

1 x 4" lip on right door

FRONT VIEW
(tongue and groove siding removed)

12"

11 ¼"

8 ¾"

2" X 3" SPRUCE STUDS

FLOOR JOISTS pressure-treated 2" x 4"s on 18" centres

TONGUE-AND-GROOVE SIDING

¾" PRESSURE-TREATED PLYWOOD FLOOR

PRESSURE TREATED 2" X 4"

2" X 3" SPRUCE STUD

36"

31 ¾"

28 ¾"

70 ½"

72"

1 ¾"

TURN KEY held with screw, to hold paddle

3"

cut to fit shape of paddle handle

2"

PADDLE BRACKET

SLIDING DOOR
¼" x 2 ⅞" x 26"

SCREEN, stapled to back

2 ⅞"

1" x 2"

3 ½"

24"

VENTILATION DETAIL

VENTILATION HOLES
1 ½" diameter

¾" (1" x 1") stock with ¼" groove

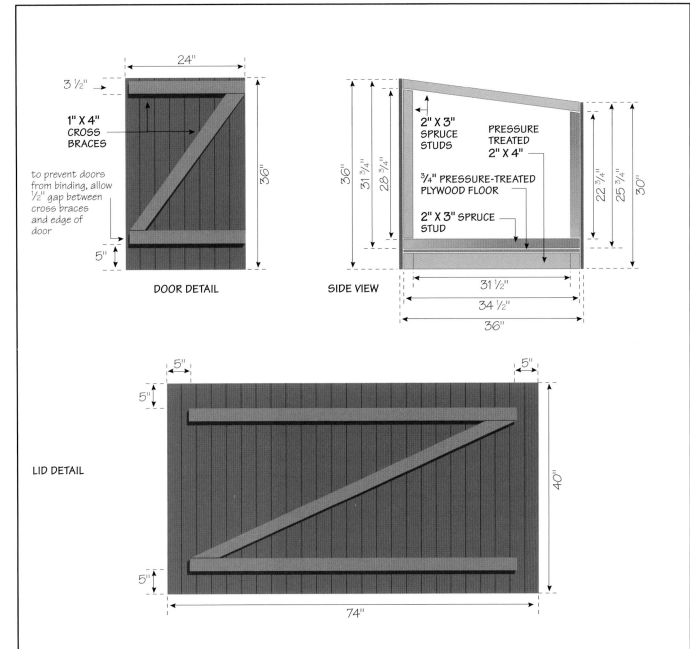

24"

3 ½"

1" X 4" CROSS BRACES

to prevent doors from binding, allow ½" gap between cross braces and edge of door

36"

5"

DOOR DETAIL

2" X 3" SPRUCE STUDS

PRESSURE TREATED 2" X 4"

¾" PRESSURE-TREATED PLYWOOD FLOOR

2" X 3" SPRUCE STUD

36" **31 ¾"** **28 ¾"**

22 ¾" **25 ¾"** **30"**

SIDE VIEW

31 ½"

34 ½"

36"

5" **5"**

5"

40"

LID DETAIL

5"

74"

A NOTE ABOUT DIMENSIONS:
2" x 3" spruce studs have a nominal dimension of 1½" x 2½". Similarly, 2" x 4"s are 1½" x 3½".

according to the diagram opposite. Screw to side of box before you fasten screening material. Then continue to drill 1½" hole all the way through sides of box. Remove bracket, fasten screening, and mount back onto box.

7. To make hooks for life jackets, mount ¾" dowel pegs on a 1" x 4" board. Cut notches in one end of the board to support 1½" dowels for towel bars. Nail the 1" x 4" to the back studs. Attach a piece of similarly cut 1" x 4" to the front. Make paddle brackets following diagram opposite; screw to lid using 2½" flathead screws.

8. Fasten lid and doors with hinges. Screw heavy-duty brass chain to the lid and underside of studs so that the lid will stay open but not fall all the way back. Also screw a hasp to the lid and right door, to lock the lid to the doors.

9. Apply an exterior penetrating stain or an oil finish.

CANOE & SAILBOARD RACK

A simple system that frees up space and keeps your watercraft out of harm's way. By Ron Frenette

Canoes and sailboards littered about the waterfront aren't just hazardous and unsightly; they take up valuable relaxation space, too. More importantly, haphazard storage is bad for watercraft: Fibreglass and Kevlar canoes get scored and scraped, and the varnish gets worn off wooden canoes – or those with wood trim – by repeated contact with the ground. The good earth then provides moisture and cellulose-loving bacteria that combine to cause the wood to rot. Another drawback to leaving watercraft on the ground is that they get just plain dirty – full of sand and spider webs.

This tidy storage rack can accommodate one canoe (15–17 ft. long) and one sailboard (ours was 12 ft. long), keeping your dock or beach clutter-free while extending the life of your favourite watercraft. The rack could also hold two canoes or three sailboards, depending on your needs; simply substitute the appropriate arms. By adjusting some of the measurements, especially the vertical pieces, an enterprising builder could adapt the rack to hold three ca-

Horizontal end piece
$^{17}/_{64}$" drill holes
2"
2 ½" 1 ½" drill holes
2"
Front toe board 2" x 8" x 96"

DIAGRAM A

MATERIALS

LUMBER
3 pieces spruce 2" x 8" x 16'
3 pieces spruce 2" x 4" x 8'
1 sheet ¾" fir plywood, good one side (G1S)

HARDWARE
26 carriage bolts with nuts and washers, ¼" x 3½"
12 carriage bolts with nuts and washers, ¼" x 4"
16 2" #8 Robertson flathead wood screws

FINISHING
Scrap carpeting
250 ml of wood stain and 2 L of spar varnish *or* 2 L of exterior enamel

TOOLS
Table saw, radial arm saw, or circular saw
Drill press or portable drill
Band saw or jigsaw
Level and combination square
$^{17}/_{64}$" twist bit and 1½" spade bit or Forstner bit
$^{7}/_{16}$" open-end wrench
C-clamps
Paint brushes

noes, four sailboards, or a combination.

The rack can be constructed in approximately 14 hours and can be easily dismantled for transportation and storage. (Because the rack is not fully enclosed, it isn't suitable for winter storage. During the winter, keep your watercraft indoors.)

Set the rack up in a shady area to protect the contents from UV radiation. If you can't find a shady spot, or if falling pine needles and tree sap pose a problem, keep your craft covered with a tarpaulin.

THE BASIC FRAME

1. From the 2" x 8"s, cut the following pieces: two pieces 60" long (the vertical supports); two pieces 41" long (the horizontal end pieces); two toe boards 96" long (one front and one back, which will run between the end pieces).

2. In each 96" toe board, drill four holes (two at each end) as shown in Diagram A, using a 1½" spade or Forstner bit. These large holes will be where the bolt and nut from the end pieces will meet. Drill the holes carefully so your rack will be easy to set up and take apart.

3. Next, cut a smooth curve at one end of each horizontal end piece. (The edge of a dinner plate makes a good curve.) Then, on both end pieces, lay out and drill eight ¹⁷⁄₆₄" holes, positioning them as indicated in Diagram B. Use an adjustable com-

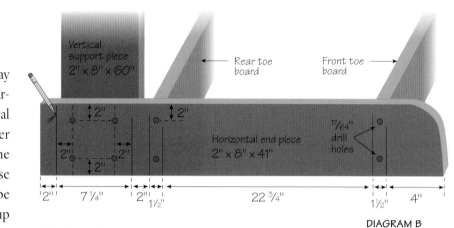

bination square to lay out all your lines, carrying the six vertical reference lines over to the inside of the base boards. These benchmarks will be helpful for lining up the pieces when you assemble the rack.

DIAGRAM B

4. Cut a smooth, round curve at one end of each vertical support piece: This rounded end will be the top. Then lay out and drill two 1½" clearance holes, one 9½" from the bottom and one 48" from the bottom. See Diagram C.

5. On the back edge of the verticals – the edge closest to the 1½" holes – mark a centre line. Mark two lines across the back edge, one 9½" from the bottom and one 48" from the bottom. Where these lines intersect with the centre line, drill a ¹⁷/₆₄" hole as shown in Diagram C. This is where the carriage bolts for the back support pieces will slide through later. The 1½" hole allows you to put the nut on the bolt.

6. Now it's time to assemble the frame. Recruit a helper and set up the two toe boards and horizontal base boards on a flat surface. Use a square to be sure the alignment is correct. Next, with the ¹⁷/₆₄" drill bit, follow the holes you drilled earlier in the end pieces, continuing them through the end grain of the toe boards. Your drill should emerge in the centre of the 1½" hole drilled in the side of the toe boards. Insert a 4" carriage bolt, attaching a washer and nut in the 1½" hole.

Repeat this process for all eight holes (four per toe board) and tighten the nuts firmly with an open-end wrench. See Diagram D.

7. Stand the 60" verticals in place, near the back of the rack, with the 1½" holes towards the rear of the rack. Place the verticals on the *inside* of the horizontal boards and hold them temporarily with C-clamps.

8. Use a level to make sure the verticals are perfectly upright. Following the ¹⁷/₆₄" holes you drilled in the end pieces earlier, continue the holes through the vertical. Insert 3½" carriage bolts (four on each vertical), attach washers and nuts, then tighten them down.

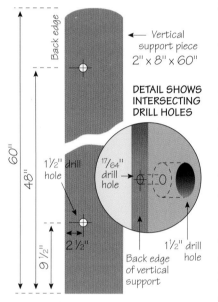

DETAIL SHOWS
INTERSECTING
DRILL HOLES

DIAGRAM C

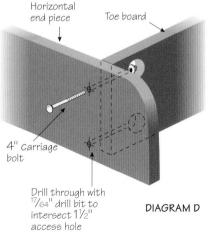

DIAGRAM D

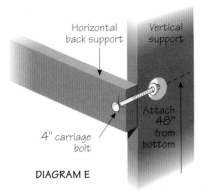

DIAGRAM E

9. The next step is to create the horizontal back support. On a straight 2" x 4" x 8', mark and drill a $^{17}/_{64}$" hole at each end as shown in Diagram E, so it will line up with the $^{17}/_{64}$" holes you drilled in the back edge of the vertical, 48" from the bottom. Fasten in place with 4" carriage bolts.

10. Now go on to the angled back supports. These crucial 2" x 4" support pieces run from the centre of the horizontal back support to the back edge of the 60" vertical. They attach to the vertical 9½" from the bottom, in the holes you drilled earlier. An easy way to complete these diagonal pieces is to clamp a length of 2" x 4" in place, scribe the angles, then cut the wood to fit. Drill $^{17}/_{64}$" holes at the top and bottom of each support piece as shown in Diagram F. Through-bolt the top holes with 3½" carriage bolts, and use 4" carriage bolts on the bottom, threading on the nut and washer through the 1½" access hole.

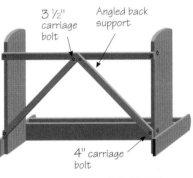

DIAGRAM F

THE CANOE SUPPORT ARMS

11. Using a table saw, radial arm saw, or circular saw, rip four 8" x 96" lengths of the ¾" G1S fir plywood. Make a tracing template from the scaled-down diagram on p. 74. Using a band saw or jigsaw, cut out four identical pieces, two for each arm. Sand the rough edges all around.

12. Next, drill the four carriage-bolt holes with a $^{17}/_{64}$" bit, referring to the template. It's a good idea to clamp the boards in pairs and drill them together. Stain and finish the arms now; you'll find that after assembly there won't be enough room for a brush.

13. Cut two pieces of scrap 2" x 4" x 4½" as spacers. Attach one between the two halves of each support arm with 2" wood screws as shown on the template.

14. To assemble, slide one arm onto the 60" vertical so one plywood piece is on either side of the vertical 2" x 8". Slip 3½" carriage bolts through the holes you predrilled, running the bolt from the outside in. Add on washers and nuts, and tighten, making sure the arm is horizontal. Repeat on the other vertical.

15. To adjust the height of the arms, loosen the carriage bolts and slide the arms up or down. On this particular rack, the canoe arm is 14" off

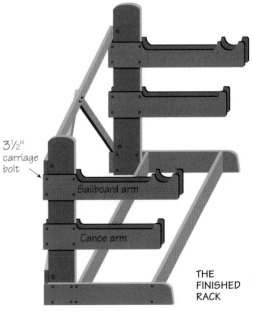

THE FINISHED RACK

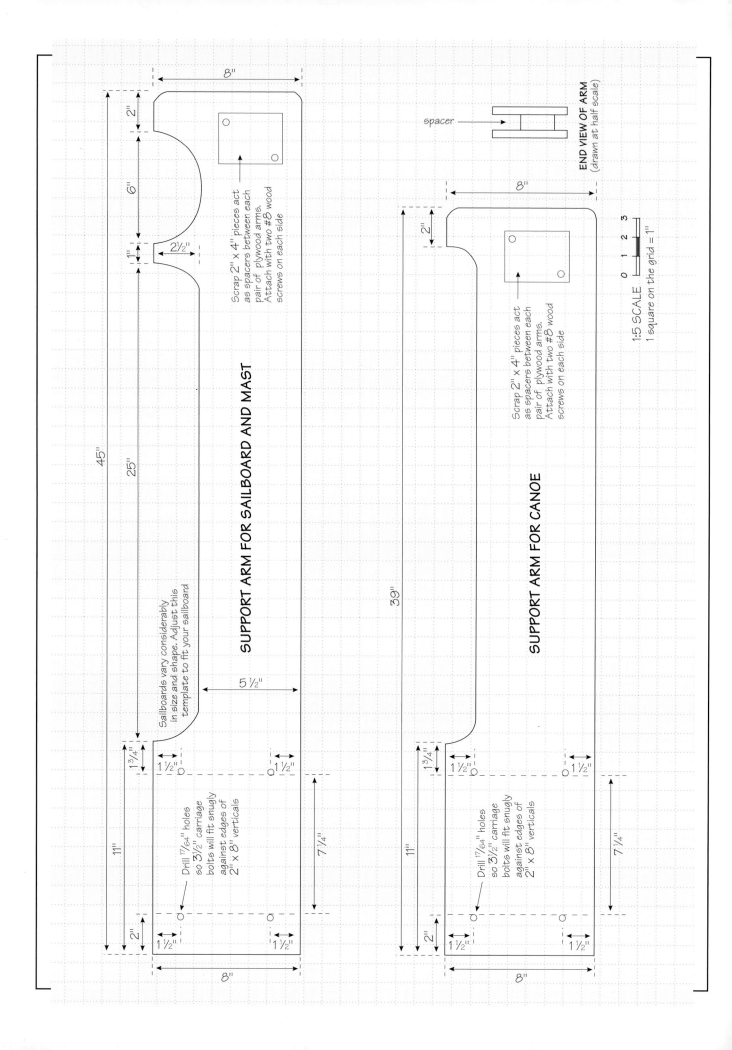

SUPPORT ARM FOR SAILBOARD AND MAST

8"

2"

6"

1"

2½"

45"

25"

Sailboards vary considerably
in size and shape. Adjust this
template to fit your sailboard

5½"

Scrap 2" x 4" pieces act
as spacers between each
pair of plywood arms.
Attach with two #8 wood
screws on each side

1¾"

1½"

1½"

11"

7¼"

Drill ¹⁷/₆₄" holes
so 3½" carriage
bolts will fit snugly
against edges of
2" x 8" verticals

2"

1½"

1½"

8"

SUPPORT ARM FOR CANOE

8"

2"

39"

Scrap 2" x 4" pieces act
as spacers between each
pair of plywood arms.
Attach with two #8 wood
screws on each side

1¾"

1½"

1½"

11"

7¼"

Drill ¹⁷/₆₄" holes
so 3½" carriage
bolts will fit snugly
against edges of
2" x 8" verticals

2"

1½"

1½"

8"

spacer

END VIEW OF ARM
(drawn at half scale)

0 1 2 3

1:5 SCALE
1 square on the grid = 1"

the ground. Add a scrap of carpeting to the notched section where the canoe rests, to protect the varnish on the gunwales. Attach the carpeting with stainless-steel staples or round-headed brass upholstery tacks, positioning the fasteners so they won't scratch. Never use regular steel fasteners, as they quickly rust.

THE SAILBOARD SUPPORT ARMS

16. For the sailboard arms, simply repeat the procedure used to create the canoe supports, but use the sailboard template on p. 74 instead. This arm includes a small notch for the mast and sail.

FINISHING AND LABELLING

Sanding the entire rack is probably not a useful exercise and won't give you a coffee-table finish, as the construction-grade materials used for this rack are usually stored outside and aren't very dry. Either apply one coat of wood stain (brushed on, then rubbed off) and three coats of exterior spar varnish, or simply paint the rack with exterior enamel.

If you plan to take the rack apart for storage or transportation, use a chisel or marker to label each intersection with corresponding letters or numbers. Putting it back together after a long winter will be a lot easier.

CUSTOMIZING

Don't be afraid to tinker with the rack's design. If you want a taller rack to accommodate more canoes or sailboards, the height of the diagonal rear brace will need to be adjusted. While the lower attachment (9½" from the bottom of the vertical) should be fine, the upper horizontal brace should be raised so it's approximately 1' below the top of the vertical.

STABILITY AND SAFETY

Kids will be tempted to climb on the rack. It's quite stable, but if loaded with canoes, the rack could shift and tip, so you should deter climbers. For added support, especially on rough or uneven ground, try wedging pieces of scrap 2" x 4" vertically between the lower canoe arms and the horizontal end piece. In exposed, windy locations, you can screw several threaded eye bolts into the back of the vertical 2" x 8"s. Run strong rope or wire through these and then secure the rack to a tree or some sturdy pegs driven into the ground. (These tie-downs are easy to trip on, so be sure to keep them out of high-traffic areas.) A set of bungie cords to hold the sailboard and its mast firmly in place is another safety tip.

LOON NESTING PLATFORM

Build the loons a floating home when their natural nesting sites are scarce. By Laurie Bildfell

For many people, life on the lake wouldn't be the same without the sight and sound of loons. However, in some places traditional loon nesting sites have been lost to development, shoreline "improvements" (such as dredging and clearing), and fluctuating water levels. In such cases, an artificial nesting platform can entice the loons to stay. (Where good natural nesting sites still exist, the birds are likely to turn up their bills at artificial substitutes.) It's unlikely, though, that you'll be able to attract loons with an artificial nesting site if your lake hasn't supported a loon population in the past.

When choosing the location for a platform, think of what a loon would be looking for: a secluded, reedy, relatively shallow spot, protected from prevailing winds, wave action, and curious onlookers, and out of the way of boat traffic. The configuration of the land is important; a good-sized bay with an entrance narrow enough for the parents to patrol for predators would be ideal. Loons are territorial: Each pair needs about 250 acres of lake all to itself. And they're shy, so you won't find them taking up residence right next to your dock. They need room for take-off, weedy areas for cover, and fish in a variety of sizes.

Timing and consistency are crucial when placing the platform. It should go into the water every year as soon as the ice goes out. Loons mate for life, and are thought to return to the same nesting site each spring. If that site is gone – or if you haven't put it out in time – they may spend the summer swimming and fishing instead of nesting. Because loons copulate on the nest (and they need time to check out the site before doing so), it's not enough just to pop the platform in the water at laying time, which usually occurs around the third week of May. Moreover, if the eggs are laid too late, the chicks won't reach maturity before freeze-up.

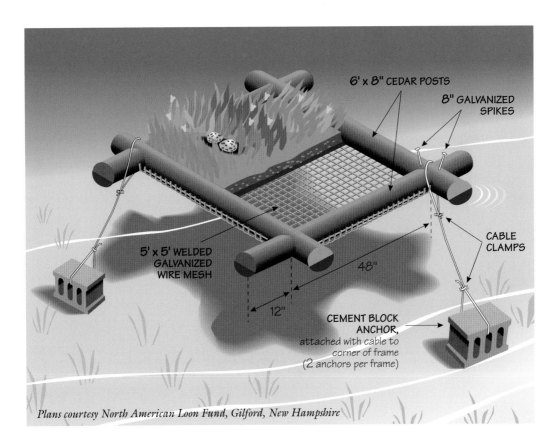

6' x 8" CEDAR POSTS

8" GALVANIZED SPIKES

5' x 5' WELDED GALVANIZED WIRE MESH

48"

12"

CABLE CLAMPS

CEMENT BLOCK ANCHOR, attached with cable to corner of frame (2 anchors per frame)

Plans courtesy North American Loon Fund, Gilford, New Hampshire

HOW TO BUILD THE PLATFORM

1. Notch the corners of four 6' x 8" untreated cedar posts with the bark removed. Fasten them together with 8" galvanized spikes. (For extra buoyancy and stability, add a fifth post to the centre.)

2. Using 1½" heavy-duty fence staples at 4" intervals, attach a 5' x 5' sheet of heavy, welded galvanized wire mesh to the underside, wrapping it halfway up the outside of the logs. Make sure there are no sharp edges sticking out that could hurt a bird.

3. With the mesh side down, build up a heavy base of sod or partly decayed organic matter on the platform, then plant about two bushels of indigenous vegetation, such as ferns, grasses, sedge, mosses, cattails, sheep laurel, and blue flag iris. Also add at least two bushels of wetland-type debris for nest building. Any additional loose material will allow the loons to replenish their nest as it gets compacted. Be careful, however, not to overload the island, causing it to float too far down in the water.

4. As soon after the ice is out as possible, anchor the nest 100–150 ft. from shore in at least 6 ft. of water, making sure you choose an area that is protected from strong prevailing winds, wave action, and boat wakes.

5. Anchor with two concrete blocks attached to opposite corners of the platform with ³⁄₁₆" cable. The lines should be on a 45° angle to the raft, with enough slack to allow for fluctuating water levels.

SPRUCE UP YOUR BOAT

Quick fix-its that give new life to your fibreglass runabout and canoe. By Chris Knowles

GOUGES, DINGS, AND SCRATCHES

Generally speaking, serious damage to a fibreglass hull is best left to the pros to repair. But if a few scratches and gouges in the gel coat and a faded hull are keeping your faithful craft from looking shipshape, you can undertake the job of fixing it yourself.

REPAIRING SCRATCHES AND CRACKS IN THE GEL COAT

Boat manufacturers often sell colour-matched kits for repairing the gel coat (the thin, outer layer of a fibreglass hull), but remember that these are mixed to match the original colour of your boat, which was no doubt significantly different from its current, faded hue. Getting the proper colour match can be the hardest part of the whole repair job. For an older boat, buy a gel coat repair kit that includes packets of pigment for do-it-yourself colour mixing.

To make things more complicated, the colour can change as the repaired gel coat cures. A light colour like yellow may darken as it dries, while darker greens, reds, and blues sometimes lighten during curing. As well, the more hardener you mix in, the lighter the gel coat will be when it dries. (Adding hardener also increases shrinkage.) But the amount of hardener you need varies with temperature and humidity. For example, on a hot, humid day the gel coat will cure faster and you'll need to add less hardener; however, on colder, less-humid days

you'll need more hardener to speed up the chemical reaction. But don't despair: To determine what colour gel coat you'll end up with, do a small test spot and let it harden. You can always remove it with a razor blade if the colour is off.

1. Always work in a well-ventilated location, and when temperatures range between 50°F and 80°F (10°C–27°C). Wear rubber gloves.

2. Start by cleaning the repair area thoroughly with acetone.

3. Closely inspect to ensure that damage is superficial and not structural. (If you're unsure, have a pro inspect the boat.)

4. If the scratch or crack is deep enough to require filling yet too narrow to accept the gel coat, enlarge it with a screwdriver, a small grinder, or the folded edge of coarse sandpaper; leave a bevelled edge so you don't get an obvious line where the old gel coat ends and the repair begins. Blow off the dust and wipe with a rag.

5. Mix the gel coat according to the manufacturer's directions.

6. Use a business card or a plastic-coated playing card as a miniature trowel to pack the mixed gel coat firmly into the crack, overfilling the repair area.

7. Gel coat usually dries in a matter of hours but, to be safe, wait a couple of days for the gel coat to cure really well before sanding. (If you sand before the gel coat has cured thoroughly, it will continue to shrink and you may end up with a depression in the surface.) Keep in mind that each gel coat application is unique, as curing time will be affected by temperature, humidity, and the amount of hardener used; using less hardener will give you more time to work with the gel coat, but you'll have to wait longer for it to cure properly.

8. After the gel coat has cured thoroughly, smooth the repair area with progressively finer grades of wet sandpaper – starting with about 220 grit and moving up to at least 600 (some people go as high as 1,500) – and then finish the job with rubbing compound and a couple of coats of wax. (See pp. 81–82.)

FIXING DEEPER CUTS

Deeper gouges that extend into the fibreglass itself may require a layer of fibreglass matting first, followed by gel coat. Fibreglass repair kits are sold by marinas, hardware stores, and boat-building supply centres. Such kits include the polyester resin, hardening agent, and sheet of fibreglass matting you'll need for this messy work.

1. Start by cleaning the area to be repaired and then grind it smooth. For good adhesion you'll have to grind right down to the first layer of fibreglass, since it's best to put fibreglass on top of fibreglass.

2. Coat the repair area with a generous helping of mixed resin and hardener, and cut a piece of matting to cover the exposed fibreglass.

3. Add more resin on top, working it into the matting until all the whiteness in the fibreglass material is gone. Allow it to cure according to the manufacturer's instructions with the kit.

4. Rough sand with 80-grit sandpaper. Clean away the dust with acetone before proceeding with the gel coat, as above.

One place gouges commonly occur is at the bow, where the boat has hit the dock during overzealous landings. Though bow nicks can look deep, the fibreglass is usually so thick in this area that structural damage is rare and a cosmetic repair is generally all that is needed. Follow the same cleaning and grinding preparation as for a hull crack, then build up the area with layers of gel coat. When the gel coat has cured, sand it with wet sandpaper and buff smooth with a finishing compound. "Micro-balloons," a powdery thickening agent available at boat-building supply centres, can be added to the first layer of gel coat to give it greater bulk and a more workable consistency.

BRINGING BACK THE SHINE TO A CHALKY HULL

If your hull has a chalky appearance, it is probably suffering from oxidation. Oxidation occurs when fibreglass is exposed to air, and it is to gel coat what rust is to metal. Usually an abrasive cleaner is required to bring back the lustre. Such cleaners contain grit that acts like sandpaper to grind off stains and oxidation. The grade of grit varies from product to product. Generally, marine products are safer for your boat than household cleaners; the abrasive in some household bathroom-cleaning products (including liquid ones) may scratch gel coat.

If an abrasive marine cleaner doesn't do the job, you may have to use a fibreglass polishing or finishing compound, which is more abrasive still – or turn to its even coarser cousin, rubbing compound, followed by a thorough waxing. However, a rubbing compound can open up a lot of pores in the gel coat, which will then oxidize even faster than before, which means you'll have to wax it more than usual.

An abrasive cleaner or rubbing compound should remove slight hairline scratches and revive the colour on lightly faded topsides. Colour restorers are another option, while some boat owners swear by a non-abrasive wood preservative called Penetrol, made by The Flood Company, for bringing back the colour to faded fibreglass.

WASHING AND WAXING TO KEEP THINGS LOOKING GOOD

Now that your hull is looking good, you'll want to keep it that way. A water-soluble cleaner – typically called "boat soap" or "marine wash" – does fairly well at chasing away loose dirt and even bird droppings from hulls and decks. Because of their mildness, these solutions are perfect for those regular midsummer washings

when you don't want to scrub away your boat's protective wax coating along with the dirt. (Repeated washings with even the mildest boat soap will eventually wear away the wax, however.) Most household cleaners, including dishwashing detergent, will strip off some or all of the wax.

For a more thorough cleaning to rid the topsides of stubborn stains and rubber streaks, as well as the old, dirty wax, you'll need a stronger product such as a fibreglass cleaner. (Some common household products can also substitute.) And since mooring lines are one of the prime culprits in getting a boat dirty, give the various ropes on your boat a regular soap-and-water wash. Simply toss them into the washing machine and air dry.

Cleaning your boat with anything but a mild boat soap will leave its surface naked, vulnerable to attack by gas spills, environmental pollution, seagulls, and oxidation. A wax provides a clear covering to protect the gel coat and help it shed water, and the smooth, reflective finish it produces gives a boat its shine. All waxes also offer some protection from ultraviolet radiation, because a glossy surface will reflect more sunlight than a dull one, but some brands contain UV absorbers as well.

Basically, a "wax" is a combination of some type of natural wax (carnauba or paraffin are two) or a synthetic substitute mixed with a polymer and perhaps other additives, and then diluted with solvent to give it a spreadable consistency. The more solvent used, the more liquid the wax. The solvent helps clean the surface as the wax goes on, but some waxes – especially the popular one-step cleaner/waxes – also contain a mild abrasive to provide greater cleaning power. If you've already cleaned your boat, the consistency of the wax you choose is a matter of personal preference.

APPLYING WAX

Different waxes require different application procedures. Read the instructions,

test in an out-of-the-way area to ensure compatibility with your boat's finish, and have a good supply of cotton or terry-cloth rags on hand for buffing. Even if you are using a cleaner/wax, it's important to make sure your boat is clean before you start waxing. Otherwise, any minor traces of dirt and grit left on the surface could be ground into the gel coat and damage the finish.

Avoid applying wax on a sun-baked surface. If you can't avoid sunlight, be sure to select a wax that allows use in direct sun; otherwise it will bake on too quickly and you may have to rub with a cleaner or a mild rubbing compound to get it off. For the same reason, work in small, easy-to-handle sections. Apply two coats of good-quality wax twice a year (once in the spring, and again halfway through the summer), especially on dark colours, which oxidize faster.

Some people like to apply (and not buff off) a coat of wax before storing their boats in the fall. This will provide extra protection against dirt accumulated over the long winter, but it probably won't save you any work; odds are you'll still have to thoroughly clean and wax the boat come spring.

QUICK REPAIRS TO SPRUCE UP THE REST OF YOUR BOAT

EXTENDING THE LIFE OF YOUR BOAT TOP

Rips in a convertible boat top should be fixed by a pro, although cloth or duct tape can fashion a temporary repair. The pros should also undertake permanent dome-snap repairs, although you can do a temporary job quite easily yourself. Dome-snap replacement kits are available from marine stores. These inexpensive kits include the special tool – called a "dome setter" – you need to replace the snaps, as well as the snaps themselves. However, many replacement kits don't have marine-grade snaps, which are made of stainless steel or nickel/brass. So buy the kit for the tool, throw out the snaps if they're not marine grade, and replace them with proper nonrusting domes from a specialty shop. In any case, DIY dome repairs are only temporary; take the top to a canvas-repair shop for permanent dome snap repairs.

Turn buttons – known in the industry as "common-sense fasteners" – are stronger than domes and won't blow undone, but they cost more and are uncomfortable if you lean on them; the experts recommend them for high-stress areas only.

A stubborn metal boat-top zipper can be helped by rubbing a wax candle along it. Nylon zippers, however, are best left alone; wax or silicone spray will just attract dirt and clog them up, and the cleaner a nylon zipper, the better it works.

Speaking of clean, a good cleaning can help old boat tops. Because they are waterproof, vinyl tops are susceptible to condensation, which leads to mildew formation. There are a host of specialty mildew removers that promise good riddance to these unsightly stains; some household products will do a good job as well. Some people use bleach to take out tough mildew stains, but none of the top experts we spoke to recommended it; household bleach can break down vinyl and make it brittle, remove waterproof coatings, and turn white tops yellow.

Once the mildew has been removed, the top can be cleaned with soap and water or an all-purpose cleaner. Scrub with a soft brush, and rinse well. Needless to say, this is a job for dry land, not for over water.

Most better-quality tops are constructed of acrylic canvas, a breathable material that – unlike vinyl – resists mildew formation and won't shrink or fade as much. It's more sensitive to harsh cleaners, though. Use mild dishwashing or laundry soap and water, then give it a light brushing.

If your top has been leaking, you can use a sealant spray such as Scotchgard on it after it's clean and dry, but you pretty well have to soak the whole top. Alternatively, "top shops" will apply a heavy-duty commercial waterproof coating. If just the seams are leaking on an acrylic or vinyl top, try waterproofing liquid (from a shoe-repair store) on the trouble spots.

HELPING VINYL WINDOWS

The clear-vinyl windows in a boat top have an infuriating habit of becoming clouded and scratched. The problem is right in the plastic, and after they've been exposed for a few summers to ultraviolet rays, your best bet may be to have them replaced.

The number of years you get out of your windows, however, is in direct proportion to the care you give them. The trick to keeping a window clear is to keep it clean. Get the dirt off with a water rinse and keep it off with a filmy coating like Armor All vinyl cleaner. Some experts advise coating the windows with non-lemon furniture polish every two or three weeks. (It's important that you use non-lemon wax, as the acid in the lemon additive eats away at the windows.) Such coatings will form a layer of film to help keep dust and dirt from digging into the soft plastic.

Never use an ammonia-based cleaner on flexible plastic windows, as the ammonia weakens the windows and makes them yellow and brittle. And don't coat yourself in bug repellent when you're near your boat top. The DEET that many bug repellents contain is one of the culprits responsible for the destruction of vinyl windows.

Once a window starts to cloud, nonabrasive cleaners and polishes designed for boat windshields may be of some help, but be prepared for a buffing work-out.

CARPET REPLACEMENT

Any good-quality polypropylene indoor-outdoor carpeting with ultraviolet inhibitors can replace your old ripped or worn boat carpet, although you may find marine carpeting comes in a more appealing range of colours for boats and, in some cases, has a little more pile to it.

1. Pull up the old carpeting and use it as a template to cut the new stuff, leaving an inch or two extra around the sides.

2. Scrape off all the adhesive residue from the fibreglass or plywood decking and allow any moisture under the floor to dry.

3. Lay the new carpet in place. Then flip up a couple of feet of carpet at one end and, using a roller or brush, coat both the rubber backing and the boat deck with exterior carpet cement. When the glue is tacky, roll the carpet back into place, being sure to smooth out all bubbles and creases.

4. Once one end is anchored, the rest of the carpet should maintain proper alignment as you glue it down.

5. Trim around the edges with a utility knife to finish the job.

While you have the carpet pulled up, it's a good idea to check the floor for signs of rot. Look for blackened plywood or floor sections that flex or spring when you walk on them. In bowriders, the walkway to the bow seats is usually the first place to rot.

Floor repairs in a fibreglass boat should be left to a professional because the floor is tied into the stringers and the sides of the hull. Consequently, a badly rotted floor can breach the structural integrity of the boat by allowing the hull to flex; this could eventually cause the boat to come apart.

One way to cut down on rot-causing moisture build-up under your carpet is to install removable carpeting. Attached to the floor with snaps, such carpeting also allows access to storage or engine-compartment hatches in the floor. It's more expensive than the glued-down type because all the edges (including the fiddly cut-outs) have to be bound. Take a template of your boat's floor to a carpet supplier, who will cut out the material, bind the edges, and sell you the snaps, which are easy to install.

LOOSE AND LEAKY HARDWARE

Loose and rusted cleats, rails, and other metalwork are unsightly, potentially hazardous, and allow water under your boat's skin. Many boat decks have a balsawood core, and water seeping through fastener holes can saturate the core, adding an incredible amount of weight. (If your boat is having a tougher time reaching plane, this could be why.) Check for leaks by dousing the boat with a hose while a friend (equipped with a flashlight) looks for drips under the deck and gunwales.

If there are leaks around the fittings, remove the hardware and dab a glob of marine sealant such as Sikaflex or 3M 5200 into all screw or bolt holes to protect against water intrusion, and coat the base of the hardware. Then reinstall the hardware by holding the bolt and tightening only the nut – not the bolt – as this will keep the sealant in place for a more waterproof bond.

If this approach fails, the hardware will have to be removed again and the stripped screw holes filled with marine epoxy and then drilled out, using a bit slightly smaller than the diameter of the screw. (Or simply drill new holes nearby, taking care to seal the old ones so they won't leak.) A strip of masking tape on the underside of the hole will keep the epoxy in place while it dries.

To really do the job right, attach cleats, rails, and other hardware using bolts that go right through the deck, with wooden or nonferrous metal backer plates on the other side. This gives a much stronger connection, and will prevent the fasteners from pulling up through the deck again. It also helps distribute the load to prevent cracking and crazing of the fibreglass.

For marine use, don't cheap out on the fasteners; always use stainless steel. They cost more, but they don't rust – and 10 years from now you'll still be able to undo them.

CLEANING DULL HARDWARE

A good rubbing with a strong fibreglass cleaner or a cleaner/wax might be all it takes to shine up tarnished stainless-steel or aluminum hardware. For more stubborn jobs, you'll probably need an abrasive specialty metal cleaner such as Flitz or Nevr-Dull (which also work well to clean and polish the chromed parts on your long-neglected boat trailer). To remove really bad corrosion, some people spray on a lightweight lubricant like WD-40, then rub the hardware with fine steel wool.

Whichever cleaner you choose, as always, read the label and test on a small, inconspicuous area first to ensure that it doesn't leave deep scratches that could invite future corrosion.

WIRE YOUR BOAT FOR LIGHT

*Making your watercraft safe for night-time travel is
simple, inexpensive – and smart. By Tom Carpenter*

If you drive at night without lights, you are not only invisible and in danger, but you are also in the wrong. Legally, the matter is quite clear. In Canada and the U.S. any boat travelling at more than 7 knots (8 mph), must carry a proper stern light and "side lights," as the red (port) and green (starboard) lights are called; slower boats must make themselves known by displaying a white light visible in all directions. Fortunately, providing lights for a small aluminum utility boat – the usual guilty party these days, as larger runabouts are factory equipped – is simple and inexpensive.

If you have neither the patience nor the urge to spend a sunny afternoon messing around with your boat, marine-supply retailers sell a variety of clip-on or clamp-on systems, glorified flashlights really, with the red and green lenses for the bow lights and something white and bright for the stern. The starting price is about $30, and you just keep them handy for those times you get caught out after dusk or want to run down to the landing as the sun is setting. With these, your only worries are a steady supply of D cells and secure storage so that nothing gets lifted at a busy public dock or spirited away by kids looking for an awesome two-tone undercover reading lamp.

If, on the other hand, the idea of drilling a few holes, squirting some caulking, and hooking up wires appeals to you, then for the same cost plus the price of some wire, a 12-volt battery, and maybe a switch or two, you can rig up something more permanent and a little less likely to run out of juice halfway across the lake.

Lighting systems for boats now come in two basic styles: fixed

MATERIALS AND TOOLS*

12-volt marine battery
Plastic battery box
Stern light (white)
Bow light (red and green)
Stainless-steel screws or bolts
16-gauge wire
Split plastic conduit
Silicone sealant
Switch(es)
5/16" and 3/8" ring connectors
Butt connectors
Heat-shrinkable tubing
In-line fuse holder (for 20-amp
   fuse)
Drill
Screwdriver

*List will vary, depending on
   your boat and the setup you
   choose*

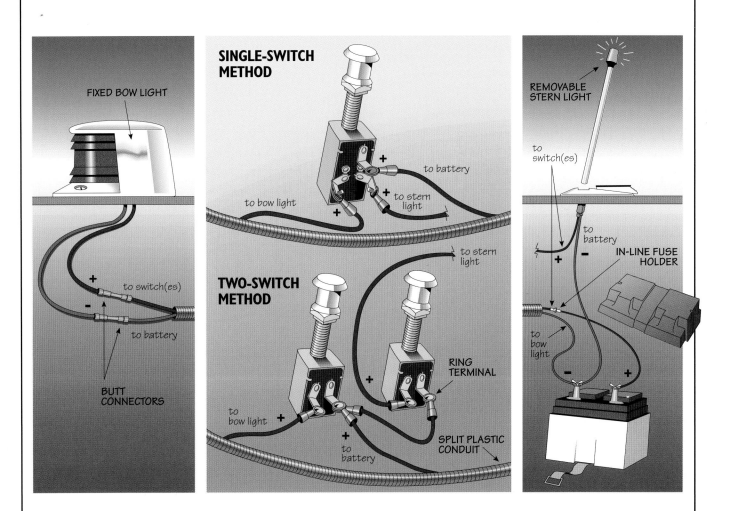

FIXED BOW LIGHT

SINGLE-SWITCH METHOD

to battery

to bow light

to stern light

to switch(es)

to battery

BUTT CONNECTORS

TWO-SWITCH METHOD

to stern light

RING TERMINAL

to bow light

to battery

SPLIT PLASTIC CONDUIT

REMOVABLE STERN LIGHT

to switch(es)

to battery

IN-LINE FUSE HOLDER

to bow light

lights that you screw down, and stowaway lights that plug into sockets mounted on the boat. Either is fine, or you can mix and match, as boat manufacturers do. (Many boats arrive from the factory with a fixed bow light and a removable stern light.)

Small bow-mounted light units, which contain both the red and green lenses, are the appropriate side lights for a small craft. Many of them cover about the same surface area as a coffee mug. That means that if you have a tiny deck – just a triangular brace at the bow of your aluminum boat, for instance – you may be able to mount a light directly to that.

Keep in mind, however, that if you already use that brace as a handle for beaching the boat you may not want a light in your way. Also consider how often you need to turn the boat over and whether or not the light will be damaged. If necessary, you can install a minimal deck of your own by screwing a board across the gunwales just behind the bow brace, and your light can then attach to that.

Wherever you plan to attach the light unit to the boat, drill a small pilot hole and use self-tapping stainless-steel sheet-metal screws. Better yet, drill larger holes and use stainless-steel bolts and, to prevent vibrations from undoing your work, also use lock-tight nuts, the kind that come with a soft plastic sleeve inside that grips the thread of the bolt. Pop rivets can also serve, but take heed: If you have never worked a pop riveter before, practise on something a little less precious than the intact hull of your boat. (You can, for example, produce a nice, harmless effect on your dog's collar with pop rivets.)

The stern light, which comes attached to a mast up to 4' high, can be similarly mounted, to either an existing corner brace or a small deck surface you install, or to a bracket of your own design. The rear seat can also serve, as long as it has a good, solid top surface to take the screws, bolts, or pop rivets, and as long as you can get underneath the seat to do the wiring. Wherever you put it, ensure that the mast stands high enough to be visible through 360° and that the driver of the boat will not block the light. Do not make it any taller than necessary, however; a long mast on a boat bouncing across a choppy bay can tear itself loose.

At either the bow or the stern, receptacles for stowaway lights cover even less area than the base of fixed units and need not interfere with any other use of the boat, since you remove the lights when they are not in service.

Hooking up the wires seems scarier to the weekend handyperson than actually installing the lights. Yet, despite the fact that you should treat the 12-volt marine battery you need for this job with due respect, the actual wiring could not be simpler. Each bow and stern light comes with two wires emerging from it. You provide a connection from either one of those wires to either one of the battery posts, then connect the other wire to the other battery post. That's the basic principle.

Switches anywhere along the positive lines turn things on and off. (More detail on this in just a minute.)

THE GENERAL PRINCIPLES

You can use a 12-volt dry cell to supply your lights, but it will eventually run down, leaving you with one of those guilt-inducing toxic garbage problems. You can also use smaller 6-volt dry cells, which not only raise the disposal issue but also require you to switch over the bulbs in the lights you buy to 6-volt replacements. Your best bet is a 12-volt wet battery. Used only now and then for lights, it should last all summer and can then be recharged for next year.

Place your battery inside a plastic battery box. The box should be covered with a proper top that straps in place and should be fastened to the transom or to the side of a seat so that it cannot tip over. This is useful advice: If both posts of a 12-volt battery come in contact with the metal hull, the battery can explode.

Locate your switches where they will not be bumped and broken or accidentally turned on. You may be able to attach them to a seat, or perhaps they will need to be mounted on a small, aluminum bracket which has been pop riveted to the hull.

Run all wires (use 16-gauge) from the battery to the bow and stern either by tucking them up under the gunwales of the boat or, if the design of the boat does not allow that, by stringing them along the tops of the seats. In either case, slip the wires inside some split plastic conduit for protection against wear and tear and

UV damage, and fix the conduit in place with blobs of silicone sealant. Where the conduit crosses a seat, run a full bead of silicone across the width of the seat for further protection. Whatever you do, avoid running wires anywhere down in the bottom of the boat where people walk and gas tanks get banged about.

THE SPECIFIC CHORE

To provide your boat with a bow light and a stern light, each switched so that you can operate it independently of the other, first mount your lights and battery box and two switches, then follow the instructions below.

Deep-cycle marine batteries – so-called because they withstand the rigours of repeated discharges and recharges – come with the threaded post to which you connect the wires already in place. If, however, you are using an older marine battery or a car battery, begin by installing a pair of terminals. These clamp around the large positive and negative posts of a standard 12-volt battery to provide smaller threaded posts with wing nuts so that wires attach easily. The positive and negative posts are different sizes and so are the corresponding terminals. The ring connectors you will need for the job are also available in the different appropriate sizes.

Ring connectors are just what their name suggests: rings that crimp onto the ends of wires and make it easy to hook those wires to terminals. They keep things tidy and prevent the wire from wearing out with repeated connections and disconnections. Buy ⅜" rings for the line that will connect to the positive terminal of the battery, and ⁵⁄₁₆" rings for the negative connection. Make a habit of using the correct sizes; the whole system is designed to help forestall confusion about which wire goes where.

Attach ⁵⁄₁₆" ring connectors to two separate pieces of wire, one long enough to reach from the battery to the bow light, through whatever circuitous route you have planned, and a shorter length that reaches from the battery to the location of the stern light. Slip both these ring connectors over the negative post of the battery and tighten them in place with the wing nut.

Connect each of these wires to one of the loose wires emerging from the appropriate light unit, using butt connectors, plastic-coated sleeves that crimp onto the wires, to join them firmly. These provide a better connection than the old twisting and taping method.

As well, protect every splice you make with heat-shrinkable tubing. This material comes in rolls or in short lengths, and slips onto the wire so that once the connection is made, the tube can be positioned over the splice and then heated with a flame. It contracts to provide form-fitting protection.

With each light hooked up to the negative post of the battery, one half of the circuit is complete.

Next, measure out enough wire to reach from the positive post of the battery to the location of your switches, again allowing some slack so that you can tuck everything out of sight. Attach a ⅜" ring connector to the battery end of the wire, but *do not attach it to the battery until after you have hooked up the switches.*

MAKING THE SWITCH

Separate switches, of course, provide flexibility. When you're at anchor, jigging for some midnight walleye, you can turn off the bow light and show only the white stern light. But two switches also complicate the wiring a bit, and if you don't care for complexity, remember that you can choose to run both lights with a single switch. And once you understand the principles involved, you also have the option of installing a three-position switch. (More on that in a moment.)

The switches you buy will either have two wires emerging from the housing, just like the lights themselves, or will have small screws to which the wires attach. If yours have the wires, attach one wire from each switch to the single positive line that you have stretched from the battery. Again, use a butt connector and crimp the wire from the positive post of the battery into one end of the tube, and the two wires (one from each switch) into the other end of the tube.

If your switches have screw posts, attach the wire from the positive post of the battery to one side of one switch, then run another short length of wire from that same post over to the corresponding post on the other switch. (See diagram, p. 87.)

Now run a wire from the remaining side of one switch up to the bow and use a butt connector to attach it to the free wire emerging from the light there. Do the same from the other switch to the remaining loose wire on the stern light.

If you prefer to have only a single switch, but still want slightly more flexibility in controlling your lights, you can install a three-position switch. Such a switch allows you to have either all the lights on or just the stern light showing, and once you understand the principles behind the two-switch system, installing the single, three-position alternative comes easily.

To hook up a three-position switch, make the same connection between the lights and the negative post of the battery, then run the positive line from the battery to the clearly marked "in" wire on the switch. That leaves two remaining "out" wires; connect one to the bow unit, and the other to the stern unit. The "Stern On" or "Both On" settings are simply different positions on the switch. (The third position, of course, is "off.")

Whichever switching system you choose, in order to prevent your lighting system from melting down in the event of a short circuit, include a fuse in the setup.

STOWAWAY LIGHTS INSTEAD OF SWITCHES

If you don't like the idea of installing switches, stowaway lights can relieve you of the problem. You plug them in when you want light, and unplug them and put them away when you do not. In fact, you can control the bow and stern lights independently of one another, just as you can with the switching arrangements described above. You can purchase clips that mount on the sides of the seats to hold the lights during the daylight hours.

If you choose stowaway lights for both the bow and the stern, connect the negative lines to the negative post of the battery, as described above, and run a single line away from the positive battery terminal. Install the fuse holder, and beyond that point use a butt connector to branch the positive line into two lines, one to each of the lights.

Install an in-line fuse holder containing a 20-amp fuse on the positive line that runs from the battery to the switches. You just cut the wire and crimp the fuse holder in place.

Everything should now be ready to go. Hook up the line to the positive post of the battery and flip the switches.

With every connector crimped and wing nut tightened, and the whole thing tested, you have accomplished several things. You have made your little boat safer. You have made it legal for travelling at night. You have made it reasonable to run to the marina or landing at dusk, and you have removed the need to abandon a good fishing spot when darkness falls.

HAND-CARVED CANOE PADDLE

This traditional ottertail paddle is lovely to look at – and a pleasure to use. By Ron Frenette and Greg Gorgerat

Our traditional ottertail paddle is simple to make and can be completed in about 12 hours of work by anyone over the age of 14. Essentially it requires only one hand tool, the venerable spokeshave.

We've chosen black cherry for our paddle because it's light, strong, and can be worked comfortably with the spokeshave. It also sands well and displays a wonderful variety in colour and grain pattern.

You need to start with a board that's 1¼" x 6" and about 5' long. Do *not* settle for 1" stock, or the paddle shaft will be too thin when it's completed. The board should be planed smooth on at least one face; some suppliers will do this for you. Make sure there aren't any knots in the area from which your paddle will be cut, as they will weaken it critically. If there are knots, no matter how small, you should get a new piece and start again.

The board should be a bit longer than the intended length of your paddle. To decide on the overall length, have its intended owner hold a broomstick over his or her head with arms parallel. Use the rough distance from hand to hand, and then add 25" for the blade. Another method is the "toes to chin" rule: Take this measurement and subtract 25" for the shaft length.

Alternatively, you can start with a presawn paddle blank, available from some traditional canoe builders; if you choose to do so, begin working at step #5.

TOOLS AND MATERIALS

1¼" x 6" x 5' planed black cherry board, or presawn paddle blank

Jigsaw or band saw (unless you start with a paddle blank)

Spokeshave (Expect to spend at least $20 for a good one; don't bother with bargain models, as they're poorly cast and the blades don't hold an edge. Look for two adjusting screws for the blade, not just a single butterfly screw.)

Hard, black Arkansas sharpening stone and honing oil or 3-in-1 oil

1–2 C-clamps or Jorgensen wood clamps (with opposing handscrews)

Long ruler or straightedge

3–4 sheets each of 80, 120, and 220-grit sandpaper, as well as 320 or 360-grit wet-dry emery paper

Good-quality marine spar varnish

Tack cloth

Good-quality bristle brush

Mineral spirits or turpentine

1. Make a full-size drawing of the paddle blade and grip from the reduced-scale drawings on the next page.

2. Lay out the pattern on the cherry board. Try different positions, in order to get the straightest grain lines along the paddle shaft. Trace the outline on the board.

3. Draw a centre line lengthwise down both sides of the board, ensuring that the paddle's blade and grip are symmetrical, with equal portions on both sides of the line. (At this point the shaft is 1½" wide, so there should be ¾" on either side of the centre line.) See Diagram A.

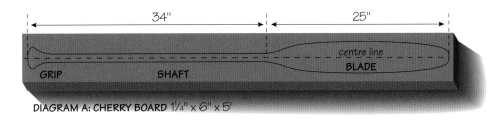

DIAGRAM A: CHERRY BOARD 1¼" x 6" x 5'

4. Cut out the paddle blank using a band saw or an electric jigsaw, or you can purchase a presawn paddle blank instead.

5. Draw a centre line along the new *edges* that you just revealed by cutting out the paddle blank. Now, you should have centre lines on both flat faces and all around the edges. These guidelines help you carve evenly from the board for a symmetrical paddle.

6. Around the paddle's blade area only, draw two more guidelines ⅛" to either side of the edge line you just created. These new lines, ¼" apart from each other, represent the unfinished edges of the blade, and will help you keep a consistent blade thickness. See Diagram B.

Steps 4 & 5

DIAGRAM B: Draw lines ⅛" either side of centre line

7. Now you're ready to begin shaping the paddle blade. Clamp the paddle blank to a flat place like a sturdy table or a balcony railing, where it's easy to get at the work surface. Make sure the blade in your spokeshave is razor sharp. (See box, p. 95.) Adjust the spokeshave so only a very small amount of blade is exposed. Holding the spokeshave in two hands, you can either pull or push it to make cuts. Remove equal amounts of wood from each of the four quarters of the paddle blade, *without* removing any of the lines you drew earlier. See Diagram C, p. 95. Your cutting strokes should be long and even. You don't need brute force to remove clean curls of wood; strokes with moderate, even force are the most effective and yield the best finish. (If the spokeshave chatters or hops, either you have too much blade out or the blade needs sharpening.)

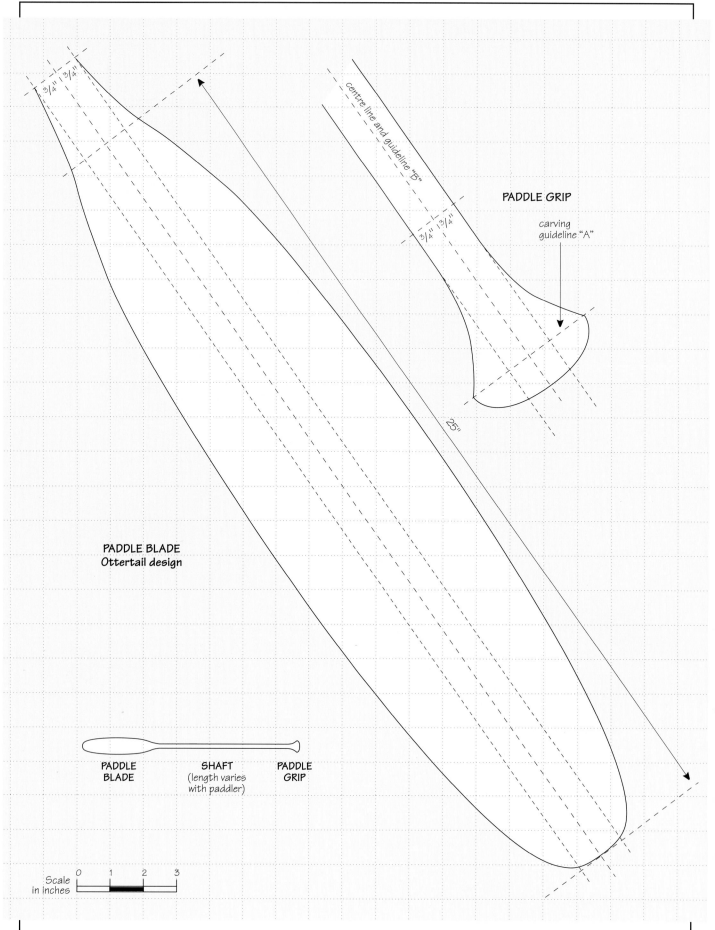

3/4" 3/4"

centre line and guideline "B"

PADDLE GRIP

carving
guideline "A"

3/4" 3/4"

25"

PADDLE BLADE
Ottertail design

PADDLE
BLADE

SHAFT
(length varies
with paddler)

PADDLE
GRIP

Scale
in inches

0   1   2   3

HOW TO MAKE SURE YOU STAY ON THE CUTTING EDGE

The key to clean, smooth cuts is a sharp blade. A dull blade tears or gouges the wood fibres, actually making you work harder for a poor-quality job.

For best results, spokeshave for 12–15 minutes, then sharpen for 2–3 minutes on a hard, black Arkansas stone. If you own a spokeshave in poor condition, regrind the blade to its original angle. Most places that sharpen saw blades can do this for $2–$3.

To begin, firmly clamp the sharpening stone to your table or hold it in a vise. Generously apply honing oil or light 3-in-1 oil to the stone. Hold the spokeshave blade evenly, with the thumb and forefinger of both hands, and lay the bevelled edge absolutely flat on the stone. Move it back and forth across the stone. To ensure perfect contact between stone and steel, rock your body and keep your arms rigid. Check the edge after about 15 passes. If there are uneven, shiny spots on it, the bevelled edge wasn't perfectly flat on the stone.

After 2–3 minutes of sharpening, turn the

Use long, even cutting strokes: If the tool chatters or hops, it needs sharpening.

whole blade over and lay it flat on the stone (bevelled side up). A few circular passes to remove the burr or "wire" from the back of the leading edge and you're done. Now get back to spokeshaving.

8. After the paddle blade has achieved a shape similar to that in Diagram C, you can next remove the bulk of the wood from the central "spine" on both flat faces. You should remove wood until the central area of the blade is about ⅜" thick and now has a more oval cross section. At this point, you will be removing the guidelines.

Do a bit more gentle spokeshaving towards the edges to reduce the edge thickness to ³⁄₁₆"; sanding will bring that to the final ⅛" thickness.

9. Begin shaping the grip next. An uneven grip causes cramping, and a rough one will create blisters, so pay special attention to detail here. Clamp the blank in an upright position, with the paddle grip at eye level, and draw the grip guidelines on the paddle blank. See Diagram D, next page. Starting at guideline "A," work *downward* (towards the blade), covering a distance of about 3½", all around the evolving grip. Make sure the transition zone between grip and shaft doesn't get thinned out – it should remain about 1" thick. Again, do not cut away guidelines "A" or "B."

Steps 7 & 8

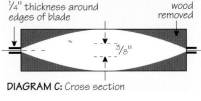

¼" thickness around edges of blade

wood removed

⅜"

DIAGRAM C: *Cross section*

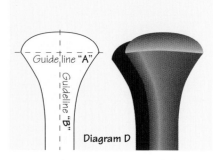

10. Now, cut upward from guideline "A," by pushing the tool and working constantly around the grip. You want a full radius curve that feels comfortable in your hand. At this point, you can remove the guidelines and touch up the handle so the grip is symmetrical and the dimensions are close to those in Diagram E.

11. Next, tackle the shaft. Clamp the blade to your work surface, protecting it with pieces of scrap wood. Remove wood evenly from all four edges of the shaft so that a cylindrical shape emerges. It should be about 1″ in cross section. To keep the paddle shaft straight, use only a small amount of blade and long cutting strokes. Be sure to blend the shaft into the blade and grip; you don't want abrupt lines.

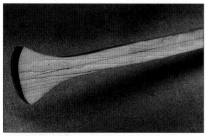

Steps 9 & 10

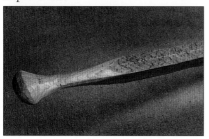

12. Sand the paddle by hand, or with an orbital sander. First, do the entire paddle with 80-grit paper, ensuring all edges are removed and all surfaces flow together. Next, do final sandings with 120 and 220-grit sandpaper. Clean the entire paddle with a tack cloth, then wipe it with a damp (not wet) cloth, which causes loose fibres to stand up. When it's dry, remove the fibres by sanding with 320 or 360-grit emery paper.

13. Clean the paddle again with your tack cloth. Then apply four coats of marine spar varnish (thin the first coat 15% with turpentine or mineral spirits), sanding with 320 or 360-grit emery paper between the second and third coats. (Remember to wipe the paddle clean with your tack cloth before applying further varnish.)

Use a good-quality bristle brush for varnishing, always working from the blade to the grip. Either suspend the paddle from a tiny cup hook screwed into the butt of the grip (once removed, a small dab of varnish

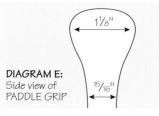

DIAGRAM E:
Side view of
PADDLE GRIP

will erase the hole), or lean it against a wall, putting waxed paper where it meets floor and wall.

14. If you want to add some artwork to your paddle, sand and clean it as above. Apply a single coat of sanding sealer (available in paint stores) and then apply your art with an enamel, such as One Shot Lettering Enamel (available at graphic arts stores); varnish as above. Allow to dry in a dust-free area to avoid marring the finish with unsightly bumps. (The varnish will cause the colours to darken a few shades.)

PADDLE SHAFT WRAP: GET A GOOD GRIP – AND PROTECT YOUR PADDLE

Do your hands and your favourite paddle a favour: Make a sturdy shaft wrap that provides a firm grip, saves wear on the shaft (and your canoe's gunwales), and looks good for years. A popular craft project at the Taylor Statten Camps in Ontario's Algonquin Park, the wrap takes just a relaxing hour or so to do (not counting varnishing). To determine where to wrap, check where you grasp your paddle, and where it tends to rub against the gunwales during various strokes – when you pry, for instance. Most paddlers will find that a wrap about 8" long, with the lower edge at or just below the paddle shoulder, works best.

Since the paddle should be freshly varnished to seal the wood under the wrap, we suggest you do your wrap when you're refurbishing – sanding down your paddle to resharpen the blade edges and smooth out the rough spots. Before starting, apply two coats of marine spar varnish as usual, allowing both coats to dry.

HOW TO DO THE WRAP

With the paddle across your lap, lay an end of cord lengthwise along the base of the shaft, leaving a "tail" of several inches hanging down the blade. Tape it down securely about 2" below the paddle shoulder. Run the cord along the shaft to a point an inch or two past the intended upper edge of your wrap, form a loop and tape it flat, then run the cord back down the shaft to the shoulder. At the intended lower edge of your wrap, place a small, neat piece of tape over this strand only. (Don't tape over the first strand.) Just below this last piece of tape, begin to wrap the shaft, moving upward towards the loop. Your small piece of tape will be neatly covered by the first few strands. Turn the paddle over and over (instead of winding the cord) as you wrap. Lay the strands as close together as you can. Wrap snugly, keeping some tension on the cord, but don't pull it too tight or finishing will be difficult.

At the top edge, cut the cord (leaving several inches of tail) and, removing the upper piece of tape, thread this tail through the upper loop. At the bottom edge, remove the lower piece of tape, grasp the lower tail, and pull just until the top loop disappears under the upper edge of the wrap. Cut off both tails flush with the wrap edges.

To finish your paddle, apply two more coats of varnish, covering both paddle and wrap. Sand and wipe wood (not wrap) between coats as usual. —*Jo Currie*

With thanks to Laura Felstiner of Taylor Statten Camps for instructions.

> **MATERIALS**
> Fine or medium butcher cord (or use 40-lb.-test nylon fishing line)
> Marine spar varnish
> 80–220-grit sandpaper
> Masking tape
> Brushes
> Tack cloth

TOW-BEHIND-THE-BOAT DISK

Make this old-fashioned water toy and help revive a silly sport. By Judy Ross

What's wooden, round, and flat, and skims across the lake with a person sitting on a chair waving wildly with one hand and holding onto a ski rope with the other? It's a water toy called a disk, and if you've never heard of it you're probably under 30. Disks were popular in the 1960s, long before the word was prefaced with floppy, hard, or compact.

Make your disk 3' to 4' in diameter. The more experienced a disker you are, the smaller the disk can be

Towed behind a motorboat, the disk was a platform for feats of agility and derring-do. Experts would try to outperform each other, doing fancy turns and balancing on chairs, stepladders, and stools. It wasn't until the 1980s, when water-skiing became a world-class sport, that interest in disking faded.

However, we think it deserves a revival. It's fun, inexpensive, and safe, and it doesn't require a powerful boat. Here's what you need to get started.

MAKING YOUR OWN DISK

1. Get a 4' x 8' sheet of ¾" plywood and cut a circle, 3' to 4' in diameter. The more experienced you get, the smaller the disk can be.

2. Use a sander to round the edges and smooth the entire surface.

3. Finish the disk with a few coats of varnish, or paint it with a good-quality exterior paint. For maximum durability, high-gloss marine enamel is the best choice. One advantage of brightly coloured paint is its greater visibility in the water. Put additional coats of paint on the edges. Since the disks are awkward to lift and tend to be rolled like tires along the ground and onto the dock, it's important to protect the edges. If they chip and water is able to seep into the wood, the disk will get very heavy and warp.

4. Creating traction is optional, but a non-skid surface is helpful for maintaining your footing on a wet, slippery board. Sprinkle fine sand over the disk while the paint or varnish is still wet, or buy adhesive strips of non-skid material (available at water-ski and hardware stores) and apply these to the top of your disk. Alternatively, hardware stores sell a paint product that has a gritty surface.

5. Decorate the disk with your favourite decals.

WHAT ELSE IS REQUIRED?

1. A 10-hp motor on an aluminum boat. As speed is not necessary, this combination will easily pull a child on a disk. Even adults can be towed with a 15 to 20-hp outboard.

2. A driver and a spotter, just as in water-skiing. And use the same hand signals as in water-skiing: thumb up for faster, thumb down for slower, and an A-okay sign for everything's fine.

3. A water-ski rope with a standard single handle. A shorter rope gives a better ride, so loop the rope to shorten it to about half the regular 75' length.

4. An approved life jacket or PFD.

HOW TO GET GOING ON YOUR DISK

1. Lie flat on the disk with your weight positioned aft and your fingers holding the tow handle over the front of the disk.

2. Give the boat driver the go-ahead. (Yelling "Hit it!" is a good signal.) Once the disk is up on a plane, the driver should continue at a steady speed. He or she should try to keep you planing at the slowest possible speed.

3. Next, pull your knees up, still keeping your weight to the back of the disk. The basic rule of disking is to keep the front edge up at all times. If you're too far forward, the front edge of the disk will catch and it will slide out from under you. If your knees are too far back, the disk will bounce.

4. Once on your knees, you can swing the disk outside the wake or ...

5. ... try to stand up. Go from kneeling to standing one foot at a time. Relax and get your balance.

6. Then try turning, slowly and carefully, in a complete circle, reaching around behind you to pass the tow handle from one hand to the other. (Keep the handle close to your body or you'll be pulled over backwards.)

The ultimate disking skill is "balancing." Expert diskers can put a wooden chair, stepladder, stool, or other floatable object on top of the disk and then get up on it. How do they do it? First, they hold the chair or stool alongside the disk as they get stabilized. Then they stand up, while still holding the chair in one hand and the tow handle in the other. Once standing, they bring the chair around behind them, pass it between their legs, and set it on the disk. They sit down – very carefully – relax, and enjoy the ride.

SWIMMER'S SUPPLY RAFT

Get in the swim of things with this handy towable float.
By Paul Howard

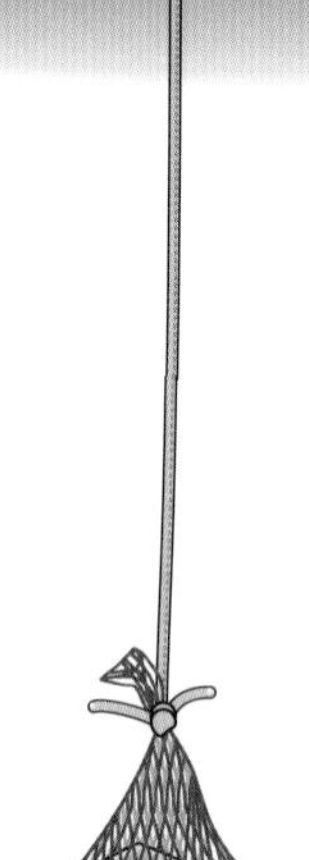

MATERIALS

1 inner tube or inflatable float ring
⅜" exterior-grade plywood
Piece of ½" plastic hose (such as garden hose)
¼" nylon or Dacron rope
¼" polypropylene rope
Mesh bag

TOOLS

Jigsaw
Drill
Shears
Sandpaper

I t's handy to have something to hold your sunscreen, towel, book, soft drink, and snack when you swim out to an island, rock, or raft. A towable float consisting of an inner tube or float ring with a plywood floor makes the perfect carrier.

Inflate your tube or ring until firm. (We used the king of inner tubes – a 48" tractor tube given to us by friends – but unless you've *really* got a lot to carry, a smaller tube should suffice.) Using a jigsaw, cut a circle of ⅜" exterior-grade plywood about 10% larger than the diameter of the hole at its narrowest point, and sand the rough edge. This disk will form the floor of your float.

With strong shears, cut a piece of ½" plastic hose (garden hose works well) equal to the disk's circumference. Next, cut a slit along the length of the hose and force it around the edge of the plywood. (Be sure the cut is straight or the hose will not lie evenly.)

Drill four ⅜" holes spaced evenly around the disk and about 2" in from the edge. With the inner tube lying on the floor, inflation stem down, place the disk in its centre, and tie it in place with four pieces of ¼" nylon or Dacron rope. (Before tying, burn the ends of the rope to prevent unravelling.) Make a loop in one end of each rope (practise your bowline) and force the other end through one of the ⅜" holes. Cinch the rope tight enough around the tube to squish it slightly, and tie off with a couple of half-hitches, leaving a tag end to hang onto.

A rock in a mesh bag makes a disposable anchor. Tie your anchor line to the underwater portion of one of the cinch lines. It can double as a tow rope, or you can attach a separate shorter line for towing; use ¼" polypropylene for your tow rope so it will float.

Since the floor is lower than the top of the tube, your things won't slide off into the water; however, you may want to put them in a plastic bag or container to keep them dry.

This device is designed to follow you during a leisurely swim, and is not recommended for any high-speed towing.

SAILBOAT STORAGE PORT

An inspection port gives you access to the inside of the hull –
and a dry place to store your stuff. By Paul Howard

You're heading out in the dinghy for a rollicking good sail. You'd love to be able to stop and relax along the way – but there's no place on board to carry a soft drink, sandwich, paperback, reading glasses, sunscreen, or other small articles where they are safe from an accidental dunking.

No problem. Install an inspection port (also known as a deck plate) with a removable bag in the dinghy's buoyancy tanks. Inspection ports (generally 4", 5", or 6" in diameter) consist of a flange with a screw-on cover, and an optional nylon bag.

The ports and bags are available from sailboat dealers and at marine stores that

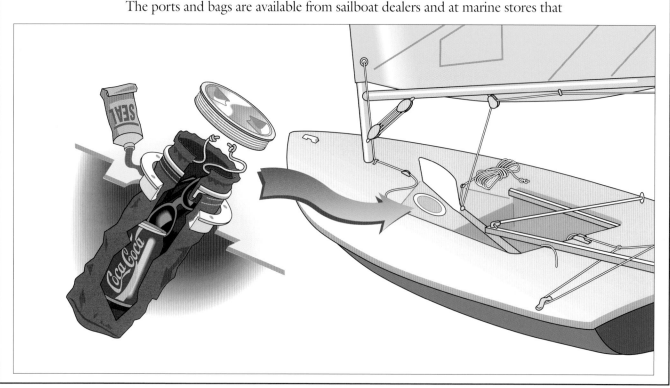

STORAGE PORT / 103

sell sailing supplies. The popular 5"-diameter port often used on Lasers can be had with a 12"-long tube-shaped "Cat Bag" or with a "Fat Bag," also 12" long but wider (12") at the bottom. Not all makes of inspection port are designed to accommodate a bag – those that are have a ¼" lip inside the flange – and one manufacturer's bags do not necessarily fit another manufacturer's ports. Keep this in mind if you want to retrofit a bag to an existing port.

An inspection port can be installed in any dinghy that has a sealed cavity with a flat – horizontal, vertical, or in-between – surface. (Of course, besides opening up a storage space, an inspection port allows repairs to be made in, and water to be sponged out of, previously inaccessible areas.) To install, unscrew its cover and position it upside down where desired (on the foredeck or afterdeck, or on either side of the daggerboard trunk), allowing space for the outer flange and clearance for a jigsaw or compass saw to cut the hole. Using a pencil, draw a circle around the outer lip of the cover, which will give you the correct size hole for the flange to sit in. Drill a ⅜" starter hole for the saw anywhere inside this mark. *Carefully* cut the hole.

Lay a bead of marine sealant under the rim of the flange where it makes contact with the surrounding laminate of the dinghy and press the flange in place. Wipe off excess sealant. Fasten with all-aluminum pop rivets or stainless-steel self-tapping screws. ◂━

MATERIALS
Inspection port and bag
Marine sealant
Aluminum pop rivets or stainless-steel self-tapping screws

TOOLS
Jigsaw or compass saw
Drill
Pop rivet tool or screwdriver

SET-IN STEPS ON A SLOPE

A simple solution when the terrain is steep – but not steep enough to require a staircase. By Charles Long

The cottage adds a third certainty to death and taxes: It is always uphill. The wider the view and the sweeter the breeze, the greater the climb from the water to the veranda. If you've got a steep and rocky climb, you'll most likely find yourself building a flight or two of wooden stairs. (See next chapter.) However, if you have a somewhat gentler, soil-covered slope, setting in some steps is a simple, attractive solution.

Coping with the slope requires a little understanding of *rise* and *run* – that bit of math that makes the difference between an easy climb and a toe-stubbing drink spiller. The numbers can tell you whether you need steps, where to put them, how many, and what size.

To measure the slope between any two points, divide the vertical rise by the horizontal run. (For an easy way to calculate rise and run, see box on facing page.) Thus, if the path from the dock to the door rises 8' in a straight, horizontal distance of 67', then the slope is 0.12, or 12%. That's too steep for wheelbarrows or even for comfortable walking. An 8% slope is the usual maximum for paths or ramps.

The simplest way to take the misery out of steeper slopes is to make the path longer, zig-zagging back and forth across the slope instead of straight up. When there isn't time or room to meander, you might have to add some steps. Where to add the steps is usually obvious – they go in the steepest part of the path.

How many steps is a little trickier. A single step in the path is a hazard – it's too easy to overlook. On the other hand, a long flight of steps requires railings. The best compromise, for safety and the landscape, is to group steps in sets of three or four each, with paths, landings, or turns between them.

You can calculate the size of the step by starting with the rise, and with the knowledge that a comfortable step is 5"–7" high. If the steep portion of the path has a vertical rise of 24", for example, you might consider reaching that height with four 6" steps, five 5" steps, or three-and-a-half 7" steps. Three-and-a-half steps? Absolutely not! The one unbendable rule of steps is they must all be the same height. Pick any height within the range of comfort, but keep the dimension uniform from the top of the flight to the bottom. No half steps. When it doesn't come out even, add a whole extra step, then raise the path to match the top step.

With simple, timber steps, it's often easier to start with the material. If you want to use 6" x 6" timbers, for example, consider that they are actually 5½" high, and accept that dimension as one step. Five steps, each 5½" high, will reach an overall height of 27½". That's 3½" more than needed, so raise the path at the top to match.

The height of a step will determine its depth or tread. Again, it's a matter of rise and run. Here, however, it is the product of rise times run that counts: The product should be not less than 70" and not more than 75". Check your local building code, but each of these combinations probably meets the code:

Rise:	5"	5½"	6"	6½"	7"
Run:	14"	13"	12"	11"	10"

HOW TO COPE WITH MEASURING SLOPE

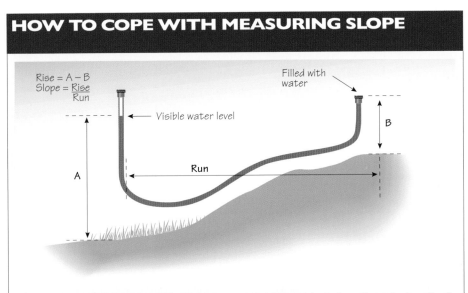

One method of measuring slope, based on the principle that water seeks its own level, requires only a helper and a length of transparent garden hose. Fill the hose completely and ask your helper to hold one end at the top of the slope. Take the other end down the hill and raise it until it's higher than the helper's end. Remove any nozzles – both ends of the hose should be open. Shake out any loops or air pockets along the length of the hose. Now the water should be at the same level at either end of the hose. Measure the vertical distance from the water level to the ground. Ask your helper to do the same. The difference between those two heights is the rise. The distance between you and the helper is the run. The rise divided by the run defines the slope.

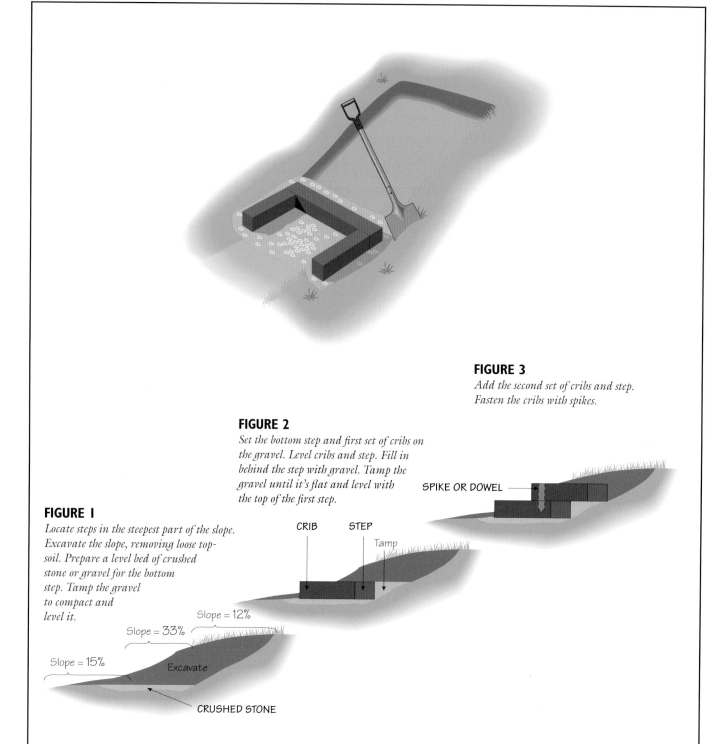

FIGURE 3

*Add the second set of cribs and step.
Fasten the cribs with spikes.*

SPIKE OR DOWEL

FIGURE 2

*Set the bottom step and first set of cribs on
the gravel. Level cribs and step. Fill in
behind the step with gravel. Tamp the
gravel until it's flat and level with
the top of the first step.*

CRIB   STEP

Tamp

FIGURE 1

*Locate steps in the steepest part of the slope.
Excavate the slope, removing loose top-
soil. Prepare a level bed of crushed
stone or gravel for the bottom
step. Tamp the gravel
to compact and
level it.*

Slope = 12%

Slope = 33%

Slope = 15%

Excavate

CRUSHED STONE

If the natural terrain allows, lower steps with a longer run (12"–13") are more comfortable – plus they allow you to use readily available materials. The width of a step,
from side to side, is partly a social question. A 3' width is sufficient for one, but we'll
need 4½' to 5' in order to walk two abreast. That seems extravagant when compared
to indoor stairs, but wider steps are friendlier, and easier to fit into outdoor spaces.

To build these steps, you'll need 6" x 6" pressure-treated timbers, a shovel, saw,
hammer, carpenter's level, and galvanized spikes (or a drill and hardwood dowels

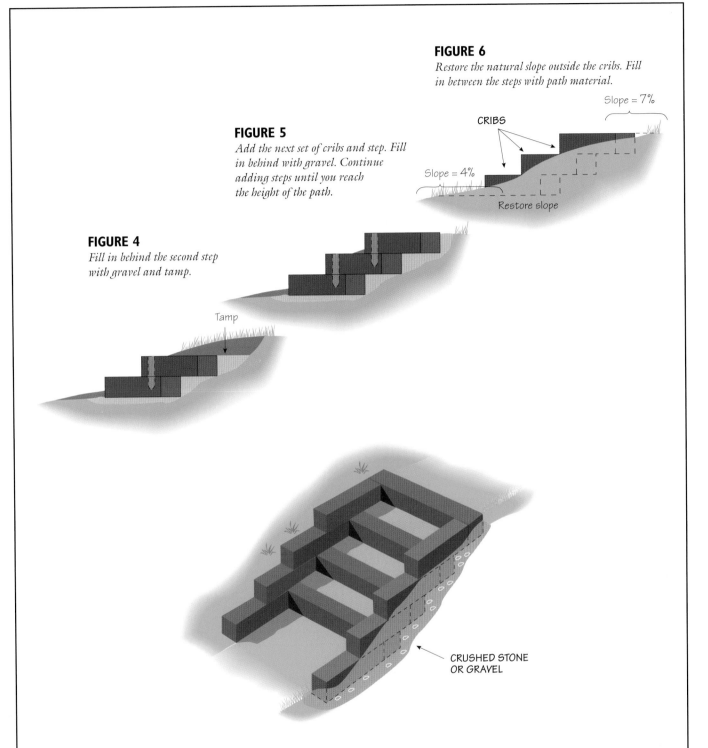

FIGURE 6

Restore the natural slope outside the cribs. Fill in between the steps with path material.

Slope = 7%

CRIBS

FIGURE 5

Add the next set of cribs and step. Fill in behind with gravel. Continue adding steps until you reach the height of the path.

Slope = 4%

Restore slope

FIGURE 4

Fill in behind the second step with gravel and tamp.

Tamp

CRUSHED STONE OR GRAVEL

for a nicer finish). You'll also need some crushed stone or gravel for the base and back fill. Round gravel from the shore may be free, but it's best left where it is and, in any case, ¾" crushed stone is more stable when tamped.

The top fill, behind the steps and atop the path, is a matter of taste. It can range from fancy bricks to free wood chips, or flat stones. Whatever you dress the top with, be sure it's porous enough to let the water drain through, and not too rough for bare feet.

A FLIGHT OF WOODEN STEPS

Build a sturdy outdoor staircase that won't sag, rot, or trip you up. By Tom Carpenter and Jeff Taylor

A stairway is perhaps the most complicated individual bit of work in the entire science of carpentry. If you would like to create stairs of your own, first examine your skills honestly. Keep in mind that there are lots of ways to build stairs badly; maybe you know a technique or two, such as nailing little cleats to some stringers and then balancing treads on the cleats. Unfortunately, such stairs sag and rot and twist far sooner than the real item, and in the long run it's easier – and safer – to build your stairs properly in the first place. If you do not panic when you pick up a framing square (see box, p. 111), and work through each stage of construction methodically, you can build a first-rate flight of stairs.

BEFORE YOU START

There is good reason for taking care. People get injured falling down badly built stairs, rising from their bed of pain just long enough to get X-rays and hire legal talent, so you probably do not want one step to be a negligent ½" higher or lower than the others.

Most building codes require that the dimensions of each individual tread and riser be equal to within ¼" of every other, because walking is an almost unconscious activity, and the human foot tends to assume that stairs will be identical. If the top tread is 10½" wide, all the treads should be that width. If the first riser is 7" high, so should every other riser, and so forth. If you are a weekend carpenter who tends to dismiss differences of ¼" or less, keep in mind that if you make just a ⅛" mistake in your calculations and then multiply that by nine stairs, the finished flight will be out by more than 1".

Working outdoors simplifies the stair-building task. You do not, for instance, have

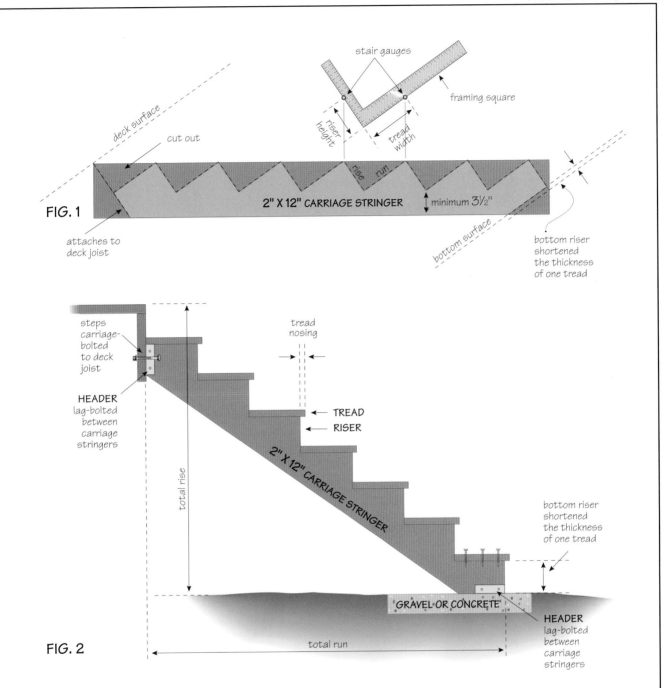

stair gauges

framing square

riser height

tread width

deck surface

cut out

rise

run

2" X 12" CARRIAGE STRINGER

minimum 3½"

FIG. 1

attaches to deck joist

bottom surface

bottom riser shortened the thickness of one tread

steps carriage-bolted to deck joist

tread nosing

HEADER lag-bolted between carriage stringers

2" X 12" CARRIAGE STRINGER

TREAD

RISER

total rise

bottom riser shortened the thickness of one tread

GRAVEL OR CONCRETE

HEADER lag-bolted between carriage stringers

FIG. 2

total run

to worry about headroom considerations; you need not make careful allowances for the thickness of the finish flooring at the bottom of your flight of stairs. You may want to include a landing, but a landing is little more than a frame of 2" x 6"s or 2" x 8"s with decking nailed in place and does not complicate things. In fact, landings should be used to break stairways longer than 12' in total rise. They provide a place for the stair climber to rest, and prevent long Hitchcockian tumbles that may result in a broken neck. Landings should be at least as wide as the stairway but no more than 4' long, unless the stairway changes direction.

Before you start to build your stairs, measure your site well, noting the precise vertical distance you have to rise, and the amount of horizontal space you have avail-

12 STEPS TO BETTER STAIRS

1. Many building codes require *treads* to be no less than 9¼" wide. *Risers* should be no more than 8" high.

2. The number of treads will usually be one less than the number of risers.

3. The topmost riser is formed by the step down from the deck to the first tread.

4. The sum of two risers and one tread should equal 25".

5. One riser height plus one tread width should total between 17" and 18".

6. To begin all stair-carriage calculations, divide the total rise by the magic number 7.

7. After all the cuts have been made, the stringers forming the carriage of your stairs must be no less than 3½" thick at their narrowest points.

8. Check your calculations by multiplying the number of treads by the width of the tread to make sure that you have enough room for the horizontal distance your stairs will cover.

9. The bottommost riser is shorter than the others in the carriage stringer by the thickness of the tread material you are using; otherwise, the bottom step will be higher than all the rest and the top step will be shorter by the same amount.

10. Attach the finished stairs to the edge of your deck using at least three lag bolts or carriage bolts spaced no more than 12" apart.

11. Landings should be used to break stairways with more than 12' of rise.

12. Landings should be at least as wide as the stairway but no more than 4' long, unless the stairs change direction.

able in which to do so. Be sure that if the stairs lead down to the ground, you have a flat area of rock or patio stones or gravel to support the lower end.

THE BASIC RULES OF STAIR BUILDING

Stairs have two parts: the *treads* you walk on and the *carriage* (or the *horse,* as some carpenters name it) underneath that holds them in place. Plank treads are easy to cut, the only requirement being that all are the same length, width, and thickness. But the two stringers (sometimes three if the space between them is greater than 3') that form the carriage require some head-scratching and worry.

In order to understand how it all works, you need to keep in mind the following basic nomenclature: *treads* are the part under your feet, *risers* are the vertical parts your toes point at when you are on your way up the stairs. Remember, treads are horizontal, risers are vertical.

And you need to remember three basic rules: 1. The number of treads will (usually) be one less than the number of risers. 2. The sum of two risers and one tread should equal 25". 3. The height of one riser plus the width of one tread should yield a figure between 17" and 18" and, since many building codes limit the maximum height of the riser to 8", you can assume the width of the tread should not be less than 10". Rules 2 and 3 together force you to create an angle of inclination within the range of 33°–37°, neither too steep nor too shallow.

Hypothetical outdoor stairs for the purposes of this explanation can be perfectly straightforward. Let's say the total rise (vertical height from one landing to the next) is 4½', and the total run (the total horizontal distance covered by the stairs) is about 6½'. The total rise is almost always a fixed dimension, something you can't change, but you can usually play with the total run to make your stairs come out right. More on that later.

For outdoor stairs, use treated wood, which you can stain; painting stairs is not a great idea because paint can hide structural cracks. Pressure-treated wood provides greater strength than cedar, and resists the rot that afflicts sturdier woods such as fir. Be sure that wherever you cut into pressure-treated lumber, you treat the exposed surface with additional preservative. Use 3½" wood screws or galvanized 3½" ardox spikes to fasten everything together.

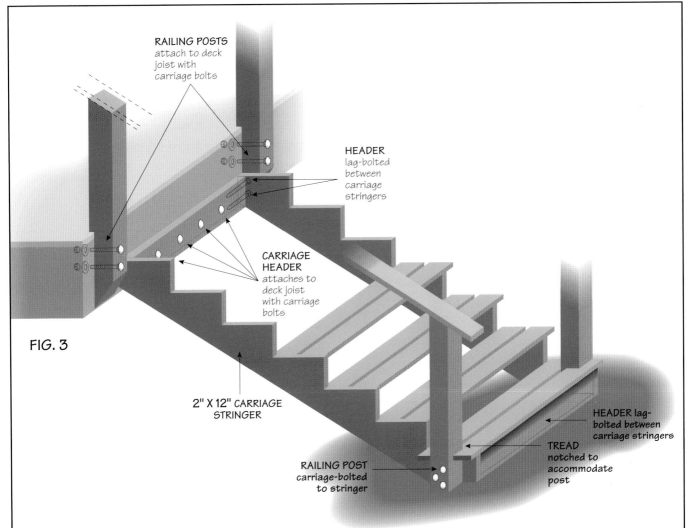

RAILING POSTS
attach to deck
joist with
carriage bolts

HEADER
lag-bolted
between
carriage
stringers

CARRIAGE
HEADER
attaches to
deck joist
with carriage
bolts

FIG. 3

2" X 12" CARRIAGE
STRINGER

HEADER lag-
bolted between
carriage stringers

TREAD
notched to
accommodate
post

RAILING POST
carriage-bolted
to stringer

CALCULATING HOW MANY STAIRS YOU NEED

There's no getting around it – into the beautiful summer day on which you build your stairs, a little mathematics must fall. To find the number and size of risers and treads requires some work with a calculator. Begin by dividing the total rise by 7, a magic number that can be used for stairs of any length. We have a 4½' rise, so 54" divided by 7 = 7.71, which we round off to 8, because we need a whole number of risers, right? And there will be one less tread than the number of risers, which means we need 7 treads.

To find out *approximately* how high each riser should be, divide the number of risers (8 in this case) back into the total rise of 54".

To find out *exactly* how high each individual riser will be, mark the overall rise

THE ESSENTIAL TOOL FOR FIRST-RATE STAIRS

You can design the roof of a cathedral using a framing square, and you cannot construct a perfect wooden stair carriage system without one.

The long blade of a framing square extends 24" and is used to measure off tread width. The shorter tongue extends 16" and is used to measure riser height.

A new square costs $11–$50, but used ones can be found for less.

Stair gauges are little hexagonal brass clamps that attach to the outside of the framing square, to lock in the tread/riser measurements on the tongue and blade. They are invaluable for building stairs, and cost $5–$10. There are also specialty squares available, incorporating a fence that does the same job as the stair gauges.

of 54" on a board (any scrap board will do). Divide 54" by the number of risers, which gives you 6.75, or 6¾". Set a pair of wing dividers at 6¾" and step off the board eight times; you want the last step of the dividers to hit exactly on 54". If it goes beyond, reduce the divider step a mite and try again; if under, then increase the divider step the teeniest bit. Keep trying until eight steps of the dividers arrive exactly at 54". This technique will catch any minor arithmetic mistakes, and is especially useful if, instead of a nice round number such as 6.75", your site calls for a riser dimension of 6.86".

Transfer the dimension on the wing dividers to the shorter "tongue" of the framing square by placing one of the points of the dividers at the outside corner of the square and marking where the other divider point falls with a pencil or stair gauge. (See Fig. 1.) Subtract the riser height from 17½" – remember, one riser plus one tread should equal 17"–18"– and the resulting number is the width of your tread for each step. (You can round it off.) Mark the tread width on the longer "blade" of your framing square, again using a pencil or the second stair gauge. It will be about 10¾". Now before you lay out the carriage, multiply the number of treads by the width of each tread and make sure that you have enough room for the horizontal distance your stairs will cover. In this hypothetical example it will all work out: 7 treads @ 10¾" = 75¼", which just fits in the 6½' we allowed. (See Fig. 1.) If your stairs turned out too long, then you would reduce the width of each tread until the total fit into the available space. Keep in mind, however, that you would be defying rules 2 and 3, steepening your stairs and making them less comfortable. You might also find yourself defying the building code.

MARKING OFF THE CARRIAGE STRINGERS

Now you can mark off 7 treads and 7 risers; the "riser" formed by the edge of the deck accounts for the fact that while you calculated 8 risers, you only mark 7 onto

LEAN ON ME: HOW TO BUILD A RAILING

Install posts for the railing in the manner illustrated in Fig. 3. Note that the top post connects to the deck and not to the stairs themselves. The railing should be precisely parallel to the bottom of the carriage, and you can use a sliding T-bevel to transfer that angle to the tops of the posts in order to ensure that you get them just so. Building codes usually require railings between 31" and 36" high.

Having the wooden treads of the stairs line up flush with the sides of the carriage stringers makes for the easiest method of railing attachment. But the stair treads *can* be cut wider than the carriage, and overhang by up to a foot at either end. If you decide to make this adjustment, you will have to examine the site for your stairs and decide on an alternative means of anchoring the railing posts since the overhanging tread ends will interfere. For example, the treads shown in Fig. 3 have been notched out to accommodate the posts.

Once you understand the instructions for laying out these stairs, there is another simple modification you can make. The stair's wooden treads can be wider front to back than the cutouts you made in the carriage stringers, so that they overhang up to a couple of finger widths. This small overhang is called the nosing and provides a wider surface for feet. (See Fig. 2.)

your carriage stringers. (See Figs. 1 and 2.) However, in cases where you need the top tread to rest flush with the surface of the deck, do not subtract that last riser. Such an installation may be necessary if the header joist of the deck is not as wide as a full riser, but otherwise avoid it since it will complicate the placement of the top handrail post, and it is inelegant besides. Notice, as well, that it will extend the total horizontal distance covered by your stairs.

In order to actually mark the carriage stringers, start by placing the framing square against the wood near one end of the material from which you plan to cut one of the stringers. Trace lines along the tongue (the riser) and along the blade (the tread) with a sharp pencil. Then, keeping the square oriented in exactly the same manner, slide it along the stringer until it is positioned so that the line for the next riser will meet the line you just drew for the previous tread. Repeat until you have all the risers and treads marked, then extend the lines at each end so that you know where to cut away the extra material.

MAKING THE CUTS AND ATTACHING THE TREADS

Use a power saw to rough-cut the notches in the stringers and a hand saw to finish each cut. Here again, take care. A power saw has a blade ⅛" thick, and minor inaccuracies in your cuts will add up quickly. A good rule is that you should always try to leave the lines marking your cuts. This will ensure your saw cuts are bang on.

Now shorten the bottommost riser by exactly the *thickness* of one stair tread; otherwise, when you attach the treads, the bottom step will be just that much taller than all the rest, and the top step down from the deck will be too short by the same amount. To avoid having to measure each stringer individually, once you have cut the first to size, carefully transfer the cutting lines onto the next stringer to be cut. Keep in mind that any minor errors you made when cutting the first stringer will be *magnified* when you transfer the cutting lines.

Put the carriage stringers up on a pair of sawhorses and nail or screw the treads in place with a couple of fasteners driven into each stringer. You can attach riser boards, patterned or plain, to fill the vertical spaces between the treads, or you can leave the risers open. Measure the exact distance between the carriage stringers and install a header (2" x 6" or larger) between them at the very top, then use that header to attach the stairs to the edge of the deck, using at least three hefty (⅜" x 3") lag bolts or even carriage bolts (⅜" x 3½") spaced every 12" or less. Position the stairs as shown in Fig. 2, locating the top of the first tread exactly one riser height down from the *top* of the deck. You can also install a crosspiece at the bottom of the stairs and use it to anchor the bottom of the carriage to a lower deck. ⬥

PUT IN A FLAGSTONE PATH

This rugged alternative to a paved walk suits the spirit of rustic living. By Charles Long

It doesn't take long for the pitter-patter of feet to wear a path to the door. And on rainy days the path becomes a runnel of mud. Concrete slabs or patterned pavers would solve the problem, but they hardly seem fitting in a rustic setting. Here, flagstone paths look more at home. They can be as formal or casual as you like. We built one in a day with straight edges and a proper base. That's about as complicated as it gets. Less fuss with the fit, and irregular edges, would finish the job faster with a less formal appearance.

Indeed, a flagstone path can be as simple as setting a series of flat stones in sod. On dirt without a proper base, the stones would shift more and heave with the frost, but those little faults are hard to see and easy to fix. Unlike cracks in concrete or interruptions in the tight geometry of interlocking bricks, a little irregularity in a flagstone surface looks like it belongs there.

The essential ma-

Mark the boundaries of the path with stakes; a garden hose will help you draw a sweeping curve. Then excavate between the stakes, removing enough soil to leave sufficient depth for the base material and stones.

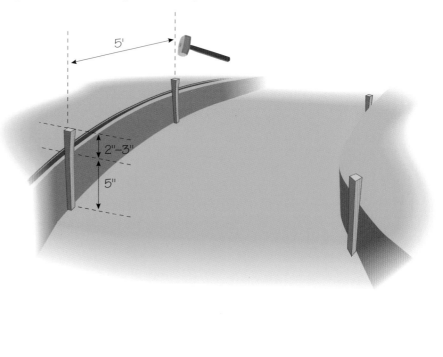

terial is stone – lots of large, flat stones. All that really matters is that they be flat on top. You can accommodate a lumpy bottom by digging out the base material until the stone settles level with its neighbours. The bigger the stone, the better. Large ones cover a wider area with fewer edges to fit. More importantly, the bigger slabs are more stable. They distribute weight like a snowshoe, and don't sink into the ground the way smaller pieces do. In practice, however, any question about the ideal size and shape for a flagstone is dwarfed by the more relevant matter of what is available.

In my area, we can find them in our fence rows and woodlots. (But don't pull them off the shoreline or out of the lake – not only is it illegal without a permit in many jurisdictions, but you'll also be destroying valuable fish habitat.) If flagstones are scarce, you'll have to buy them from a quarry or a landscaping centre. Look in the *Yellow Pages* under "Stone" and pick the nearest supplier; haulage is the most expensive part of the job.

Like flagstones, the base materials – crushed stone and stone dust or sand – are more expensive to haul than buy. If you have access to a small truck or trailer, you can fill up at most quarries for a few dollars. If you have to order the material delivered, a full load is not much more expensive than a part load – so consider a co-operative stone-building venture with the neighbours.

Obviously, how much stone you need varies with how long your path will be: a 4' x 10' path, for instance, will require about 1 ton of 3" flags, 1 ton of crushed stone, and ¼ ton of stone dust.

Let the path follow the lay of the land. If it sinks below the natural surface, it will become a creek on wet days. Better to plan the paved surface an inch or two higher than the natural surface. You can use what you excavate to fill and slope at the sides.

PAVING THE WAY

Furrow the sand on top of the crushed-stone base before the flags are put in place; the stone's impression will indicate where to add or remove sand.

1. Mark the boundaries of the path with stakes. A stretched string will define a straight edge; a garden hose will help you draw a sweeping curve. Drive a stake about every 5' along these lines. Hammer them in until the tops are at the desired height for the finished surface. You can leave

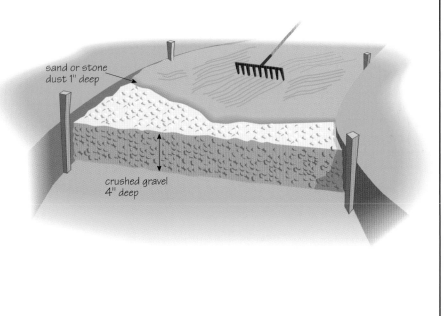

sand or stone dust 1" deep

crushed gravel 4" deep

the tops an inch or two above the ground, following the contour of the land, or get a more uniform surface by setting the tops of the stakes level with one another.

2. Excavate between the stakes. The object is to remove the sod or soil and to leave enough depth for the base material and stones. Start with the average thickness of the pavers. We measured our stones at 2"–3", then added 1" for the fine bedding material and another 4" for the coarse base, and calculated a total depth required of at least 7". Remember, that's 7" from the tops of the stakes. In effect, it meant moving about 5" of dirt – so have your wheelbarrow ready for intensive action.

3. Lay a 4" base of crushed stone. You can skimp on the base if the soil is porous enough to drain quickly, or if you're prepared to re-set a few pavers in the spring. Rake the base level, then compact it by tamping or rolling.

4. Spread a thin layer of stone dust or sand atop the base. This bed accommodates the varying thickness and rough undersides of the stones. It's a gap filler. Rake it level.

You can always knock off a piece to make a stone fit. Mark the line to be cut, then chisel back and forth along it. Go gently at first.

5. Set the largest stone in the busiest spot – where a gate or steps might concentrate the traffic. And set the heavier stones along the edges where lighter pieces might be dislodged by mowing or weeding.

6. Level each stone as it's set. This is where the stakes are most useful. A long, straight board set atop two stakes defines the desired surface level. Raise or lower the stone until it just meets the underside of the board. You can set the board across the path, along an edge, or on diagonals, levelling in all directions. To lower a stone, simply tip it out of the way and rake away some sand. To raise the stone, add more sand. If the bed is furrowed with a rake, or slightly damp, the stone's impression will tell you where to add or remove sand.

A long, straight board set atop two stakes defines the desired surface level. Raise or lower the stone until it just meets the underside of the board.

7. Fit the stones edge-to-edge. If you can do jigsaw puzzles, you can do this. Even the rules are

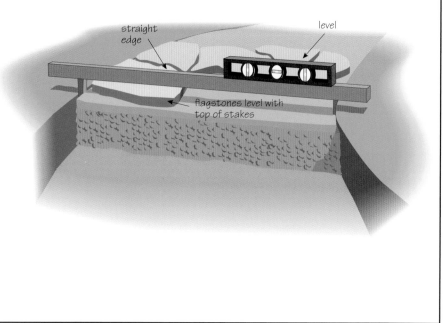

straight edge

level

flagstones level with top of stakes

the same: Do the straight edges and big pieces first, then fill in the fiddly bits. If you're not fussy about straight edges, you can lay the middle of the path first and then add on at the edges.

In one critical way, flagstones are even easier than jigsaw puzzles – if the piece *almost* fits, you can knock off a bit to *make* it fit. You'll need a hammer, a cold chisel, and good eye protection. Mark the line to be cut, then chisel back and forth along the line. Go gently at first; too heavy a hand on the hammer will break the stone in the wrong place. Weaken it first in the right place, then bang away harder.

8. When the mosaic is complete, sweep more stone dust or sand into the cracks. Now get the garden hose and squirt a hard stream of water into the cracks, washing the sand under the edges of the stones and into any remaining gaps. If any stone sinks a little, raise it back into a level position with a crowbar and hold it there while you wash more sand in. It will take several days of walking on the surface to find all the wobbly rocks, and several days of sweeping and squirting to stabilize them.

Finally, the bad news: You decided to pave the path when the grass wore away to a barren rut. Now you have to face the irony that the paved path will sprout weeds in profusion. You can pull them, or fight back by seeding even tougher plants. Crocus, portulaca, and creeping phlox will bloom in the cracks (and turn a poor fit into a virtue). Mother-of-thyme will spread in a rough mat that releases a delicate scent when walked on. No summer is long enough to wear a rut in mother-of-thyme and flagstone.

To stabilize the pavers, sweep stone dust or sand into the cracks, washing the filler in with a stream of water. If any stone sinks a little, raise it back into a level position with a crowbar and hold it there while you wash in more sand.

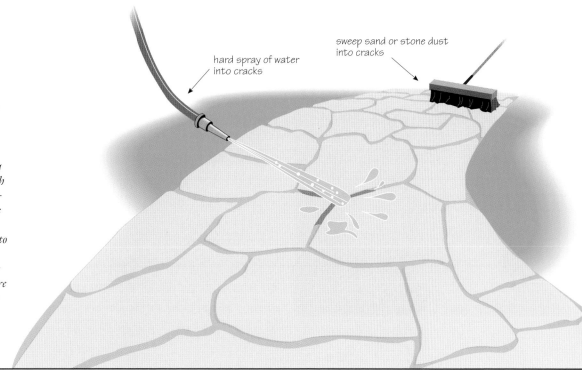

sweep sand or stone dust into cracks

hard spray of water into cracks

SHOWER WITH A VIEW

This open-air shower stall lets you come clean while soaking up the great outdoors. By Ken Campbell

In the old days, waterfront dwellers often took their soap into the lake with them. But bathing in the lake doesn't wash in these more environmentally aware times. An outdoor shower allows you to enjoy the lake without actually being in it – and offers the added advantage of hot water, whatever the weather.

Depending on local laws, the following plans and suggestions may not be legal in your area, so check with the appropriate authorities before beginning construction.

1. Choose the location for your shower. Pick a site where water hook-ups are easily accessible and where drainage will not create a problem. Environmental considerations may also dictate location. Because washing anything produces grey water (the soiled and soapy water), outdoor showers must meet minimum setbacks for grey-water leaching pits. Allow at least 100 ft. between your shower and open water or a well, and 50 ft. between shower and any wetlands.

2. Determine the size of the shower by hammering some stakes in the ground, standing

STRUCTURE

WATER SYSTEM

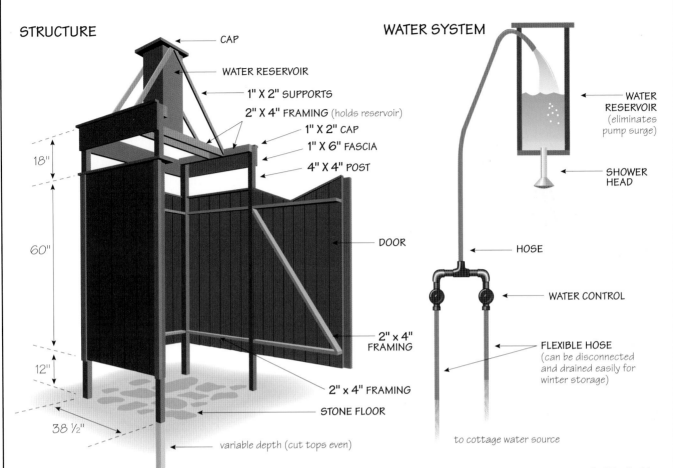

CAP

WATER RESERVOIR

1" X 2" SUPPORTS

2" X 4" FRAMING (holds reservoir)

1" X 2" CAP

1" X 6" FASCIA

4" X 4" POST

18"

60"

12"

38 ½"

DOOR

2" x 4" FRAMING

2" x 4" FRAMING

STONE FLOOR

variable depth (cut tops even)

WATER
RESERVOIR
(eliminates
pump surge)

SHOWER
HEAD

HOSE

WATER CONTROL

FLEXIBLE HOSE
(can be disconnected
and drained easily for
winter storage)

to cottage water source

* materials and dimensions can be varied to suit builders' whims

in the middle and pretending to take a shower, making sure you have enough room. Unless you enjoy bruising bits of your body, no shower should be less than 2'8" square. Ours is just over 3' square; the exact size of 38½" resulted from the cedar siding planks, seven 1" x 6"s (7 x 5½" = 38½").

3. Dig postholes and set four 4" x 4" posts standing up straight in a square; pour concrete around their bases to hold them in firmly. For those not keen on digging, metal post-holder "spikes," which have a built-in post base attached to a 2'–3' long spike, can be driven into the ground. Because the post holder keeps the wood above ground, the legs of the shower are therefore less likely to rot.

If you're on solid rock, the best solution is to build a form and pour a concrete pad, embedding a prefabricated metal post base (designed for such applications) into the concrete. This makes a strong connection to earth and also keeps the wood above ground. Prefabricated concrete post-holders (which just

MATERIALS*
LUMBER

4 4" x 4" x 10' pressure-treated posts

16 pcs. 1" x 6" x 10' cedar (for sides 5' high)

8 pcs. 2" x 4" x 8' pressure-treated lumber

7 pcs. 1" x 2" x 10' cedar (trim and supports)

1 pc. 1" x 10" x 8' cedar (for water reservoir)

OTHER

2½" and 3½" galvanized nails
Concrete mix and mortar mix
Hinges
Waterproof caulking
(Supplies for plumbing hook-up will vary, depending on your water system.)

sit on the surface of the ground) will work on rock or soil, but don't provide any bond to earth other than what's available from gravity.

4. The design of the floor will be dictated largely by local regulations and the type of water system connected to the shower. Showers fed by high-pressure systems will need a dedicated drain leading to a leaching pit or the cottage's plumbing system. This can be done with a central drain, as seen in typical indoor showers, or an open perimeter drainage "ditch" which runs around the outside edge of the shower stall. This ditch is similar in concept to the eavestrough around the roof of a house, collecting the runoff and directing it to a central drain (which in this case would lead to a leaching pit or plumbing system). The advantage of the ditch system is that it allows you to get creative with the shower floor, using brick, wood, or rock.

The shower illustrated here gets away with a rock floor without drainage because it is connected only to a minimal pressurized system. This would also be suitable for showers fed by rain barrels and such. (Check with local authorities for regulations in your area.)

If you go with a rock floor, placing the rocks on a bed of ⅜"–½" gravel, covered in sand, will allow for sub-surface drainage, thereby lessening the chances of frost heave destroying your handiwork. After the rocks are arranged, pour mortar mix between them and trowel evenly.

5. Frame and side the shower next; 2" x 4"s cut and toe-nailed into the 4" x 4"s support the cedar siding, and make great shampoo and soap shelves on the inside. The 1" x 2" trim on the top and corners gives a decorative finished look. The V cut in the door is decorative, but also allows the bather a grand view of trees and lake – an important factor.

6. If your water pressure is minimal (or fickle), a water reservoir for the shower is a necessity. The reservoir not only gives a constant flow from the shower head, but also guarantees a constant temperature – none of those extremes when someone "accidentally" flushes the toilet when you are in the shower. We made the reservoir approximately 24" high out of 1" x 10" cedar and just caulked the seams, but you may want to line the reservoir with plastic just in case. A large, plastic 3.5-L juice container would work well. If you're using rainwater to fill the reservoir (perhaps from the roof of the cottage), a larger dark-coloured (to absorb the sun's heat) food-grade plastic pail (usually available at bulk-food stores) would be dandy.

7. Our shower head is made of PVC tubing and a slew of 90° elbows, although a "sunflower" head would work just as well if the holes are large enough so they don't clog. Naturally, the larger and more numerous the holes, the more water used. Holes could also be drilled directly into the bottom of the tank. Some experimentation probably will be in order to regulate a proper flow for each individual system.

8. Place the reservoir 7½' off the floor on 2" x 4" crosspieces; 1" x 2" supports keep it from blowing over. Cut the 4" x 4" post tops off evenly, then add 1" x 6" fascia and 1" x 2" trim.

9. Install taps at the cold and hot-water sources to act as hook-ups and cutoff valves. The shower controls are faucets soldered to a copper T using two 90° elbows and short pieces of pipe. Lengths of flexible hose with double female ends are the water sources – very easily disconnected and drained for winter storage. For showers not hooked up to a pressurized water system, a simple tap at the reservoir spout will suffice. In any case, be sure to seal off the top of the reservoir at season's end, leaving any tap at the bottom open. Otherwise, water could collect in the reservoir and freeze, which could in turn crack the reservoir.

FLY THE FLAG PROUDLY

Put in a pole, hoist your country's colours – and follow the protocol. By Charles Long

A flag is like a kite on a very short string. It measures the wind and brings a tranquil landscape to life. It portends the weather and guides the sailor home. That it also proclaims our loyalties gives the flag a language as well as a life.

For getting a flag aloft, rustic tradition calls for a slim cedar pole. It's not quite as simple as it sounds, however. First, few trees grow perfectly straight. Secondly, the simplest mounting, the sleeve base (see pp. 123–124) doesn't work with a solid wooden pole. You have to build a tilting base or plant the pole permanently upright – which makes rigging and rerigging tough. Finally, a natural pole has to be debarked and smoothed to eliminate the snags that would shred a wind-whipped flag. And it may need lots of paint to keep it smooth.

The commercial alternatives include steel, aluminum, or fibreglass poles; fixed or tilting bases; standard or nautical poles (with yardarm and/or gaff); and a variety of finials (the decorative elements that go at the top of the pole) and hardware. Flagpoles, like flags, are in the *Yellow Pages.*

Aluminum poles 20' and 24' long are popular for residential use; such poles are small enough for do-it-yourself installation, come with a sleeve base (others come with a socket base, installed in much the same way), and are maintenance-free. Steel poles are cheaper, but they must be painted to keep ahead of the rust.

Ideal flagpole height is between you, your budget, and your sense of proportion. Do remember two things, however; the taller the pole and the bigger the flag, the more substantial the base required to hold it upright in the wind. Secondly, sooner or later, you'll have to take the pole down, if only to unsnarl the rigging.

The size of the flag should be in proportion to the height of the pole. A standard 3' x 6' flag is recommended for the popular 20' and 24' poles. Stitched or sewn

SLEEVE BASE

TILTING BASE

flags last longer than ones where the design is silk-screened on; ones made of sewn nylon appear more brilliantly coloured than ones made of polyester. Etiquette says if you're flying more than one national flag, they should all be the same size and should be flown at the same height on separate poles – with your own national flag given the place of honour, of course.

Where? Not too close to trees, of course. Easily seen from lake or cabin, but a lightning-safe distance away from the latter. Last but not least, look for a pocket of soil in which to plant the base. You can buy a "rock and dock" base that bolts into place for use with smaller flagpoles. But drilling holes into Precambrian granite is usually as tough as finding a pocket of soil. (You'll need to rent a rock drill for the task.) On a bare-rock site, consider a smaller flagstaff and a dock mounting or a bracket that screws into the wall.

THE SLEEVE BASE

It's dangerous to lean a ladder against a flagpole. And a shinny up loses its appeal at puberty. When the rope tangles – and it will – you'll have to lower the pole. A sleeve lets you remove the pole without uprooting the base.

You'll need a hollow flagpole and a slightly smaller base, about 5'–6' long. The pole slides over the fixed base: not too tightly or you'll never get the flagpole off, and not too loosely or the pole will wobble and lean.

Dig a hole about 1' across and 4' deep. If you hit bedrock before that, don't worry. The depth is meant to get below the frost line, and frost won't heave the bedrock. But if the hole is shallower, make it a little wider and brush the dirt off the rock. Taper the sides so the hole is wider at the bottom than at the top.

It will take five or six bags of concrete mix to fill the hole. Mix as directed and shovel it in. When the hole is about half full, set the base piece in the centre and sink it into the soft concrete just enough to hold the bottom end in place. That leaves about 2'–3' sticking out of the hole. Plumb it and secure the top with guy wires or braces. Finish filling the hole with concrete, tamping it to settle.

Do a final check with a plumb bob or level to ensure the base is perfectly vertical, and leave the concrete to harden for at least three days. Then you can assemble the pole and slip it over the base like a sleeve.

THE TILTING BASE

A tilting base is a little harder to install than a sleeve base, but is well suited to wooden poles, and it makes raising and lowering even easier.

You'll need two 8' posts for the base. Use natural cedar posts, treated 4" x 4"s, or steel. You'll also need two long threaded rods, four nuts, and a dozen washers.

Assemble the flagpole and posts on the ground. Lay out the pieces with each post overlapping the bottom of the pole by 4', and drill two holes. If you don't have a long bit, drill the flagpole first and then use that hole as a guide to start drilling the post on either side. Push the rods through and insert two washers at each point between post and pole. These inside washers let the pole pivot without binding. Add one more washer at the outer end of each rod, then add the nuts – snug but not tight.

Dig a hole 4' deep, or to bedrock if that comes first. Taper the hole so it's wider at the bottom. The butt of the flagpole has to clear the ground by a few inches, so adjust the posts or the depth of the hole to meet that goal.

Recruit some help to raise the post-and-pole assembly. Set it in the hole, check the pole for clearance, then rig guy wires, props, or whatever it takes to secure the pole in the vertical postion. Fill the hole with concrete and then check the vertical again. Leave the concrete to harden for at least three days before removing the props. You can use either rod as the pivot, but the upper pivot gives you more leverage.

"Nailing your colours to the mast" is a no-no, brave clichés notwithstanding. The only proper way to fly a flag from a pole is on a rope, or halyard. You'll need a piece twice as long as the pole is tall. You'll also need two flag clips, a cleat, a pulley, and a bolt. (All are available where flags and flagpoles are sold.)

When the pole is still safely on the ground, bolt the pulley near the top and thread the rope through. Pass each end of the rope through a clip, then tie the two ends together so the clips are as far apart as the two grommets in the flag. Now raise the pole and fit it over the sleeve base, or anchor a tilting base in the upright position. When the pole is secure, attach the flag with the clips and adjust them so that the flag is taut on the halyard. Fasten the cleat to the pole. Finally run the flag up to the top of the pole and tie off the halyard at the cleat.

FLAG-FLYING ETIQUETTE

Now, look over your shoulder to see who's saluting...or sputtering. Etiquette says: Raise the flag quickly and lower it slowly. Hats off, please.

Precedence always goes to one's national flag (unless, in Canada, a member of the Royal Family, the Governor General, or the Lieutenant Governor should happen to be visiting, in which case their personal flags take precedence). With two flagpoles, the national flag flies at the observer's left. If you've got just a single pole, no other flag should fly above the national flag. (It is never appropriate to fly a foreign flag without a national flag in the honoured position.)

Officially, the second spot is for flags of other nations. After the flags of other nations come provincial or state flags, city flags, family crests, and any other kind of silliness that flag makers are willing to sew on cloth. The Maple Leaf or the Stars and Stripes (depending on your locale) should be raised first and lowered last.

Many people leave the flag up for the season, but suffer a twinge of guilt when sticklers suggest it should be lowered at night. Canadian government protocol experts say you can leave it up all night if you like (the Peace Tower does); American protocol specifies that it should be "properly illuminated during the hours of darkness." Suit yourself – but remember the flag will last longer if you take it down in bad weather and when you're away for an extended period.

The simplest elements of flag language are half-mast for mourning and upside down for distress. Since the advent of the telephone, few of us have needed to reverse the flag to call for help. Today, the distress signal is more often a result of inattention when clipping the flag to the halyard, or running it up the back side of the pulley. Chances are no one will come to the rescue anyway, but you may attact a few deserved tut-tuts from passersby.

MORTARED STONE WALL

When you want to hold a slope or terrace a garden, local stone is the logical choice. By Charles Long

Stone is the primal spine of rustic landscapes, the natural companion of water and pine. No wonder then that when you need a little wall somewhere – to hold a slope, terrace a garden, or simply keep the neighbour's ATV at bay – local stone is a logical choice.

The problem is that a wall with footings above the frost line can suffer from heaves. Freezing soil expands, lifting the earth unevenly; one part of the wall heaves, while other parts settle. If the wall is built "dry" (without mortar), the individual stones might settle back near their original positions. But any attempt to strengthen such a wall by mortaring together is usually self-defeating. Frost movement will break these rigid joints instead of flexing them, and the wall is doomed.

A mortared wall requires a frost-proof base. And where that means excavating a grave-deep trench to pour a footing, a stone wall may not be feasible. However, if you can dig that far without hitting bedrock, you probably don't have enough rocks lying around to build a stone wall anyway.

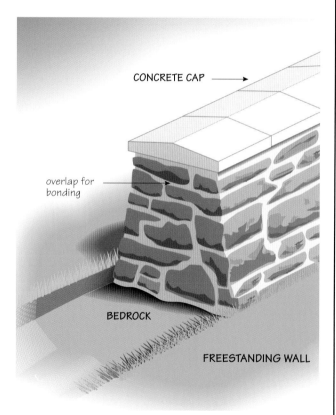

CONCRETE CAP

overlap for bonding

BEDROCK

FREESTANDING WALL

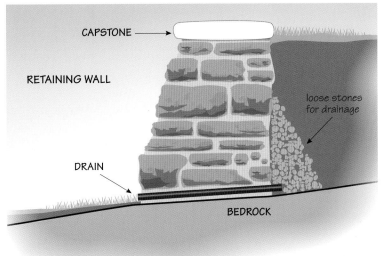

A rocky landscape, on the other hand, usually means that bedrock isn't far below. Scrape off the dirt down to a solid bottom that can't be moved with crowbars. That's nature's footing.

Unlike strait-laced brick and block, stone walls look best undulating across the landscape, disdaining straight lines. Forget the stretched string and lay out this wall by eye, or with a sinuous garden hose. Do, however, plan to keep the face of the wall plumb or, better still, raked back – with a wider base than top.

Now consider storm water and seepage. A solid wall across a slope becomes a dam. Even if you can't see any water, the soil behind the "dam" may stay damp. Frost will expand the damp soil, pushing at the side of the wall. Set drains across the base (old pump pipe is fine), covering the uphill ends with loose rock to keep the pipe from clogging.

CHOOSE YOUR STONES

Some rocks are undoubtedly more user-friendly than others. Flat rocks are simpler to fit than round ones. If they're too big, your back will be sorry; if they're too light, you'll end up with a fussy little pebble wall. In truth, however, the best rock is still the one nearest the site. The shorter the haul the better, and the better the odds that your wall will match the natural stone in the landscape.

You'll want a crowbar to pry rocks loose and a heavy-duty wheelbarrow to move them around. Don't try to lift the big ones. Tip the barrow onto its side and roll the stone into it. Then tip the loaded barrow upright again. If you're using a truck or trailer, take along a stout plank to roll the stones from the ground to the bed.

GET THE OTHER INGREDIENTS

For a mortared wall, you'll need sand, cement, and water as well as the rocks. Masonry sand, available from quarries or building-supply dealers, is better than beach sand. It's cheap if you haul it yourself and saves you the trouble of screening. Cover the sand pile to protect it from falling leaves, Tonka toys, and incontinent cats.

Cement terms can trip up a novice, and stumbling over the jargon is almost as bad as walking into the local building supply with unscuffed work boots. Just remember this: *Cement* is the fine powder sold in a bag. You mix cement with water and sand to make *mortar*. Mix cement with water, sand, and coarser aggregates – like crushed rock or gravel – and the result becomes *concrete*. So, it's a bag of cement, mortar between the stones, and a concrete sidewalk.

The common choice at the store is between Portland cement and masonry cement. Builders use Portland cement to make concrete, and masonry cement to make mortar. Portland is manufactured by burning and grinding a mix of limestone, clay, gypsum, and other minerals. Masonry cement is Portland plus other compounds to make it more workable with the trowel and softer in its finished state – deliberately softer so the mortar "gives" before the stones break.

Here, we want masonry cement. How much we want, though, is a guess because the amount of mortar varies widely with the shape of the stones and the spaces between them. In any case, it's better to pick up a few bags at a time and avoid storage problems.

Pre-mix is a convenient alternative for small jobs. Mortar mix, for example, is a bag of sand and masonry cement. The pre-mixes are expensive ways to buy sand, but they are easy to transport and resolve any uncertainty about the proper ratio of sand to cement (3 to 1 by volume). Buying pre-mix, by the way, is akin to wearing unscuffed work boots in some high-testosterone stores.

MIX YOUR MORTAR

Whether you mix the dry ingredients yourself or buy pre-mix, the tricky part is adding the right amount of water. First, throw out the measuring cup. This part is art, not science. The sand has already absorbed some moisture from the air. Your job is to top up the water level until the wet mix is the right consistency, and that, I'm afraid, means trial and error and a load of self-discipline at the end.

A heavy-duty wheelbarrow makes a convenient and portable mixing pan. Measure in the sand and the cement, and mix it up dry with a hoe or shovel. When it's all a uniform colour, make a hollow crater in the pile and pour in clean water. Pull the dry sides into the crater and hoe it around until all the water disappears. Make another crater and add more water – less this time than before. Keep turning the driest parts of the pile into the crater until the whole mess is uniformly damp and crumbly. Now consider the texture. Mortar has to be past crumbly, yet stiff enough to stand up on the trowel and in the joints. Aim for the consistency of mashed potatoes.

Now – here's where the self-discipline comes in – there is only the tiniest difference between too dry and too wet.

MAINTAINING A WEATHER EYE

Rain washes new mortar out of joints. Extreme heat can dry mortar too quickly, either by direct evaporation or by heating the materials, which then draw moisture from the mortar. Cold can freeze the water inside masonry, expanding and breaking it, or scaling off the surface.

In all seasons, keep plastic sheets or tarpaulins handy to ward off showers and – at the end of the day – to hold the curing moisture in.

In summer, work in the shade if possible. Certainly shade the mortar pan and don't leave the water hose exposed to the sun. Pile stones in the shade, or spray them with water the night before. And, once again, cover the finished work with plastic to slow evaporation.

If you must work in cold weather, heat the water and the materials, and cover the work to keep the heat in.

The mix seems stiff, crumbly, and hard to move with the hoe, but add one more slop of water and it turns to instant soup. Dump the soup and try again. This time, add the last of the water a tiny bit at a time and keep mixing. There's a fine touch at the end, like letting out a clutch. Test the mix by slicing a fresh pile in half. It should be wet enough to leave a smooth, damp slick on the vertical face, and dry enough to stand hand-high without slumping.

The best-made mix has a useful life of about an hour – less on a hot, windy day and longer on a cool, damp one. If the mortar stiffens in the pan before being used, do not add more than a few drops of water. Instead, remix it with shovel or trowel. If that doesn't make it more pliable, throw it out and start afresh.

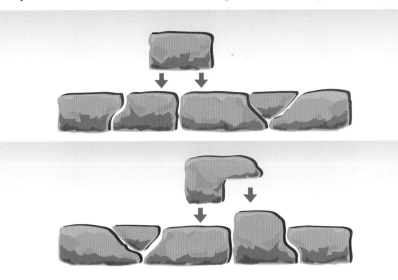

LAY OUT THE COURSES

Spread a thick bed of mortar on the footing – bedrock, in this case – and wriggle in a course, or layer, of stones. If possible, match them by height. Place the stones "flat" rather than upright, and lay the straightest edge of each stone along the face of the wall. In most cases, the wall will be wider than a single row of stones, so each course will have two faces – one at the front and one at the back, with odd gaps left in the middle. Lay out the two faces carefully, then stuff the gaps with fillers – the odd and ugly stones plus lashings of mortar.

In the second course the stones have to overlap, or bridge, the joints in the course below. (See illustration above.) Overlapping is easier if the course below is more or less even on top. If it's a jagged roller coaster of uneven heights, fitting the course above is tougher. The rounder the stones, the more awkward the fit. The principle is the same, however. A round stone bridges a joint by resting in the "V" of two round stones beneath.

At each course, spread the mortar, lay out the two faces, and stuff the gaps in the middle. Careful overlapping of joints will bond the wall end to end, but we also have to bond the front face to the back face. The easiest way to do this is to place the occasional stone that spans the whole width of the wall. Second best is to overlap face stones from opposite sides of the wall. One solid overlap every couple of yards will do the job.

SMOOTH THE MORTAR EDGES

Setting a stone at the face may squish out a little excess mortar. With practice, you'll learn to keep the mortar back from the edge, so it doesn't squish too far and stain the face. Strike off any excess with the trowel, but don't try to push fresh mortar back into the joint. Wait a couple of hours and go back when the mortar has stiffened. Now force it back, sliding a narrow trowel or even a wet (gloved) thumb along the joint. The excess will crumble and fall away. What's left in the joint will smooth out under the pressure of the trowel. If you've timed it right, the pressure will bring a thin slick to the surface. Smoothing is more than appearance: A well-finished joint will help keep the rain out later. For the same reason, finish off your wall with a concrete cap or a top course of wall-wide stones. This rain-shedding top will add years to the life of the wall, since moisture that freezes and expands inside the masonry will eventually destroy it.

ALLOW THE WALL TO DRY SLOWLY

In the long run, we have to keep moisture out, but when we're building the wall we have to keep it in. Mixing water with cement starts a chemical reaction that changes the cement into new, more stable compounds. When the reaction is complete and the water gone, the result is not dry cement, but an altogether different substance that binds the aggregate into a rock-like whole. What matters most is remembering that when the water is gone the reaction stops. The longer it stays damp, the stronger it gets. Shade the work, and cover it with plastic at the end of the day. Keep it covered for at least three days.

HOME FOR WAYWARD BATS

Build them a place of their own – so they don't have to live in yours! By Suzanne Kingsmill

If a large number of bats have taken up residence in your attic, it's understandable that you might want to encourage them to move elsewhere. Bat guano can really stink, and the squeaky, chattering noise from hundreds of bats can drive a person, well, batty.

However, it's a good idea to encourage these useful bug eaters to stay in the area. (A single little brown bat is capable of catching 500–1,000 mosquito-sized insects in an hour, and an amount equivalent to anywhere from one-third to almost its full body weight in food every night.) Offer them alternative housing in the form of a bat box so they'll stick around.

The bat box we've shown here has a narrow top to provide a cosy place for bats to huddle together. But research on what types of bat boxes are most successful is still underway, so feel free to experiment with the design. The exact size and shape doesn't seem to matter; what is important, though, is the width of the entry space at the bottom; the ideal width is ¾". You might want to make two types of boxes – one following the plans on the next page, and the second an upside-down version of the first, with the narrow part – as well as the ¾"-wide entry slit – at the bottom.

> ### MATERIALS & TOOLS
> Scrap or old lumber,
>   untreated, at least ¼" thick
> Handsaw or circular saw
> Hammer
> 1"–1½" common or
>   finishing nails
> Small piece tarpaper or
>   roll roofing

BUILDING THE BAT BOX

1. Cut the pieces following the dimensions given on p. 132. Use unplaned, untreated wood – old wood is great – at least ¼" thick.

2. The inner surfaces must be rough, to permit bats to climb on them. If the wood is smooth, make shallow horizontal saw cuts about ½" apart on the inner surfaces.

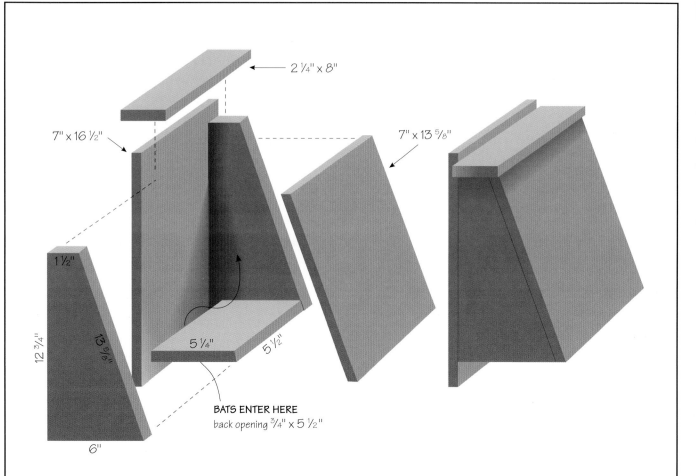

2 ¼" x 8"

7" x 16 ½"

7" x 13 ⅝"

1 ½"

12 ¾"

13 ⅝"

5 ¼"

5 ½"

6"

BATS ENTER HERE
back opening ¾" x 5 ½"

3. Nail the pieces together using 1"-1½" common or finishing nails.

4. Leave the wood unfinished. Do not use wood preservatives.

5. To extend the life of the box, cover the roof with a piece of roofing material.

6. Fasten the box securely to a building or tree trunk, as high as possible off the ground (at least 12'–15'), preferably where it will receive morning sun but will be shaded during the afternoon. Young bats grow best when the daytime temperature inside the box is 80°–90°F (26°–32°C).

Be sure to hang in a protected area – a bat house would have a better chance at the bottom of a hill than at the top, for example – and close to water.

ATTRACTING BATS TO THE BOX

Most bat colonies are found near places where insect populations are high, such as bodies of water and open meadows. The closer bat boxes are to such places, the greater the probability of their being used.

Recent reports suggest the location of the boxes may be more important than their design. After bats have been evicted from your residence, a colony may be happy to live separately but in close proximity. So if you cluster a number of boxes in one area, they can stay together if they wish. Pick a location close to the entrances the bats were using to your attic. Hanging the boxes so they face different directions will allow the bats to move between roosts as the temperature fluctuates.

Sometimes bats occupy a house within a few weeks of its being hung; often, they require a year or two to find the new house. Your chances of attracting and keeping a bat colony are boosted if you hang the boxes in the late fall or early spring, so that they are in place before migratory bats return and find their own roosts and have their young. (The boxes need to be up by the time the temperature begins to reach 50°F.) Once the bats decide where they're going to stay, that's it. They don't normally move unless they're forced out. And they return every year to the same spot.

Since the use of bat boxes is relatively new in Canada and the U.S., researchers are interested in hearing from people who have hung them. Report your experiences with your bat boxes to: Dianne Devison at the Metropolitan Toronto Zoo, Box 280, West Hill, Ont., Canada M1E 4R5; or to Bat Conservation International, Box 162603, Austin, Texas, U.S. 78716. Both organizations will also send you additional information on bats and bat boxes. Include a stamped, self-addressed envelope.

HOW TO EVICT BATS FROM YOUR PLACE NICELY

Once you've hung your bat boxes, you're ready to evict the critters from your attic. Early spring, before the young are born, or later in the summer (mid-August or early September) when the colony is dispersing, are the best times. First, locate any vents, holes, or cracks where bats can get in. Watch at dusk for a few evenings and see where the bats exit. Then start sealing the holes with mortar, wire mesh, or whatever is suitable. (Keep in mind that some bats can squeeze through a ¼" space.) Leave one or two holes unsealed for several days. The bats will get used to using these openings. Finally, hang polypropylene bird netting or a steel screening called hardware cloth – available in different sizes of mesh at hardware stores and nurseries – or even a sheet over the remaining holes, leaving the bottom edge free. This way, any stragglers can crawl down the cloth and get out, but returning bats can't get back in. When you are sure they are all evicted you can seal the last holes permanently.

IF YOU'VE GOT A BAT IN THE BEDROOM

If you find a stray bat flitting about indoors (it likely flew in through a window or chimney), stay calm – all it wants is to get back out. First, close all the doors of the room the bat's in, open all the windows, then wait and hope the bat will find its own way out. If this doesn't work, shoo it into a coffee can with a gloved hand or a broom and release it outside.

4 TOY BOATS THAT REALLY GO

Each of these nifty watercraft uses a different method of propulsion. By Russell Zeid and Steve Manley

What's a self-respecting kid to do when your parents won't let you run about in the runabout, or circumnavigate the lake solo in the dinghy? Easy. You build your own amazing boat.

Before we start, let's get a few things straight: These aren't models. These are boats that go, and they each move with a different kind of propulsion.

These boats also allow you to exercise your creativity. Once you've built one or two using our plans, you'll notice that what makes one go can also be used to make a different one go. So feel free to mix and match hull materials and different methods of propulsion. You can also make your boats bigger or smaller than the ones we've made. And with a little experimentation, we're sure you can make yours faster and meaner looking than ours, too.

We've kept the materials simple. You'll probably be able to find most of the wood you need around the cottage or in the shed. (You don't need new wood – a few dents and gouges add character.) Your recycling box will provide other materials, such as pop cans and plastic bottles. With a little scrounging and maybe a quick trip into town to the local hardware store or hobby shop, you should be able to build all of these cool boats, no sweat. So here we go. We've rated the boats in terms of complexity; the simplest one is indicated by one anchor (⚓).

TOOLING AROUND

The workshop probably has most of the tools you need. The only essential thing that might be missing is a junior hacksaw, available at hardware stores for a couple of dollars. Or you can use any similar saw capable of making thin cuts.

MATERIALS FOR WATER-STRIDER JET BOAT

- **1** small (500-ml or 16-oz.) plastic pop or water bottle, with top
- **1** plastic outer tube from a Bic pen
- **2** wire coat hangers or similar bendable wire
- **4** corks (such as those from wine bottles)
- **2** elastic bands
- **1** clothes peg
- **1** balloon (plus some spares)
- **1** empty wooden or polystyrene (hard foam) thread spool
- Acrylic paint

TOOLS

Wire cutters
Scissors
Five-minute epoxy
1 nail, about 2"-3" long

WATER-STRIDER JET BOAT ⚓

PREPARING THE HULL

1. Use scissors to cut a cockpit area out of the plastic bottle (the hull). The hole should be about 3" long and ⅓ the depth of the sides.

2. Using the nail, poke holes in the hull, as shown on drawing, next page:
  1 hole through the top, along the centre line, just behind the cutaway section;
  1 hole through the bottom, along the centre line, where the side of the bottle meets the base;
  4 holes evenly spaced along each side of the hull, about halfway down (8 holes in all; the holes on one side of the bottle must line up with those on the other).

MAKING THE CORK OUTRIGGERS

1. From the coat hangers, cut four pieces of wire, each 16"–18" long.

2. Straighten the pieces, then push one piece through each aligned pair of holes poked into the sides of the bottle. Push corks firmly onto the ends of the wires, two corks for each pair of wires, as shown. You may have to bend and twist the wires a bit to make the "feet" or "outriggers" line up correctly. (Position the front feet lower than the back ones to help point the "nose" of your boat up.)

stretch elastic bands under wire legs and over bottle to help keep legs in position

3. Stretch a couple of elastic bands around the wires, as shown on the previous page, to help keep the outriggers in place.

MOUNTING THE JET

1. Firmly push the top end of the pen tube about 1" into the hole in the spool. You may need some five-minute epoxy to keep it in place.

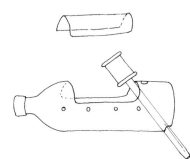

elastic band secures pen to bottle

2. Hold the spool end of the pen tube in the cockpit and push the other end through the bottom hole in the bottle. Pass one end of a small elastic band through the top hole behind the cockpit and wrap both ends snugly around the pen tube, just below the spool, to hold the pen firmly in position at the back of the cockpit. Glob epoxy around the bottom pen hole and around the wire holes to make them watertight.

3. Pull the mouth of the balloon over the top of the spool.

DECORATING THE BOAT

We painted big blue eyes on our boat, and glued a tuft of wool on top. But you can add stripes, polka dots, feathers, or anything else you like. You can even add extra corks or more legs.

Now you're ready to launch your boat. Inflate the balloon by blowing through the pen. To keep the air in, twist the balloon and clamp it off with the clothes peg or pinch with your fingers. Put your water strider in the lake and let 'er go.

EVERGLADES ALLIGATOR AIRBOAT ⚓⚓⚓

PREPARATION

1. Slit the balsa down the middle, along the grain, to end up with two 1½" x 24" lengths.

2. With an X-Acto knife or a junior hacksaw, cut from one of the lengths two 7½" pieces (the sides of the boat) and two 4" pieces (the stern and the bulkhead).

3. From the second 1½" x 24" length of balsa, cut a piece 9" long. Cut another piece 2½" long, and cut a third piece 2" long. Cut the 2" piece in half diagonally. These four pieces will be used to make the power train.

4. From the 10½" length of balsa that is left over, cut three ¼"-wide strips: one 5½" long (the middle keel) and two 5" long (the side keels).

MATERIALS

1 pc. ¼" x 3" soft balsa wood, 24" long (available from hobby shops)
Rubber-band powered airplane (available from hobby shops; we used a Guillow's "Strato Streak")
1" straight pins
1 small screw eye
Thin cardboard (e.g. Bristol board)
White glue
Five-minute epoxy
Waterproof house paint or acrylic paint
Clear plastic pop bottle (optional)

TOOLS

X-Acto knife
Small hammer
Scissors
Junior hacksaw

MAKING THE HULL

1. Make the sides of the hull: Use the saw or knife to cut one end of each 7½" piece into a curved bow shape.

2. Attach the 4" stern to the 7½" side pieces, using white glue. Push two straight pins into each joint as you go, to hold the pieces in place. A *light* tap with a hammer *may* be necessary to get the pins all the way in. In the same manner, attach the 4" bulkhead (the forward crosspiece) just behind the bow curve. (See drawing at right.) Let the hull dry.

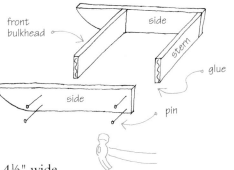

3. From the thin cardboard, cut a rectangle 12" long and 4½" wide.

Glue the cardboard to the bottom edges of the balsa wood hull, working forward from the stern, and pinning the cardboard into place as you go. Try to keep it as taut as possible. Use lots of glue and let it ooze out the edges to seal the seams. Continue to glue along the bottom, wrapping the cardboard up the bow curve and then folding it over and pinning and gluing it to the top of the front bulkhead to form a deck. Use an X-Acto knife to trim off the excess cardboard.

4. Make the keels: Lay the three ¼" keel strips of balsa along the underside of the hull, with the longer (5½") one in the middle. Space them about 1" apart and glue them into position. You might want to bevel (cut an angle on) the front of each piece first, to reduce water resistance.

SEALING THE BOAT

Smear all the cardboard-and-balsa seams and all the joints inside and outside the boat with lots of white glue. Then, generously paint all the exposed cardboard surfaces with white glue. Let the glue dry thoroughly.

ASSEMBLING THE POWER TRAIN

1. Take the propeller assembly and rubber band from the model-plane kit. Trace the rectangular shape of the back of the prop housing with a pencil onto the top edge of part C, one of the four pieces of wood that you cut for the power train. (See drawing at right.) Cut out the marked area with an X-Acto knife or junior hacksaw and epoxy the prop housing into place. Use lots of epoxy, but be careful not to get any on the mechanism.

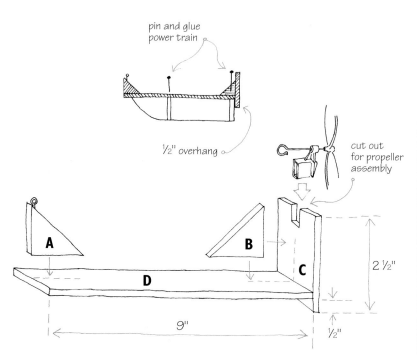

pin and glue power train

½" overhang

cut out for propeller assembly

A

B

C

D

2 ½"

9"

½"

2. Assemble the four pieces of balsa for the power train as shown in the drawing above, using pins and white glue. Gussets A and B should be on the centre line of C and D. Be sure that part C hangs ½" below D.

3. Fit the propeller: A propeller for a model plane is wound up clockwise – to pull the airplane – but we need this one to *push* our boat, so we'll be winding it *counterclockwise*. To keep the pin from slipping as you wind it, glue the pin into the prop with five-minute epoxy.

4. To provide a front attachment point for the rubber band, put a screw eye into the diagonal surface of part A, ¼"–½" down from the top. Use plenty of epoxy here to hold the wood and eye together.

5. Mount the power train on the hull: Glue and pin the power train to the stern, bulkhead, and deck. The overhang on part C should butt against the stern.

DECORATING

1. Paint your boat with waterproof house paint or acrylic paint. This will further waterproof it.

2. You can add a windshield using a piece cut from a small, clear-plastic pop bottle. Either glue it on with five-minute epoxy or attach it with straight pins. We gave our 'gator boat a ghoulish driver by gluing on the head from a plastic skeleton.

ADDING THE COWLING

1. Cut a strip of cardboard 18" long and about 2" wide. Paint it on both sides to waterproof it, and attach it to the top of the hull sides at the back, fitting it around the propeller to act as a cowling. (You may have to cut the bottom corners off at the back so the cowling isn't hit by the turning prop.) Cut two ¼" x 2" strips from your leftover balsa, and pin and glue them over the cowling where it attaches to the hull, to help hold the cowling in place. (Paint the strips the same colour as the hull.)

2. Attach the rubber band to the screw eye and the prop, wind the prop up – counterclockwise, remember – and let your 'gator boat go!

VARIATIONS

You can use the same power train to make any boat go, as long as it's not too heavy. Try mounting the power train on struts between two balsa (or small plastic pop-bottle) pontoons.

RUSTIC PADDLE WHEELER⚓⚓

MAKING THE HULL

1. The pontoons: Cut two twigs, about ¾"–1" in diameter and about 10" long. Choose a front end for each and whittle it into a rough "bow" shape.

2. The deck frame: Cut two smaller twigs, about ½" in diameter and about 6" long. Using 1" finishing nails, carefully nail them

to the pontoons, about 1" in from each end. (If your twigs are dry and split a bit, drill small holes in them first.) Using the stovepipe wire (or fishing line or twine), bind the corners in a criss-cross pattern to help keep the rough "picture frame" shape square. (See drawing, next page.)

MATERIALS
Assortment of twigs
16–20 1" finishing or common nails
2 2" common nails
1 empty plastic thread spool
1 aluminum pop can
Five-minute epoxy
5 elastic bands (plus some spares)
Stovepipe wire, fishing line, or twine
Corks (such as those from wine bottles), optional
Wooden shish kebab skewer (or thin straight stick, about 3½" long)

TOOLS
Drill
Pocketknife
Scissors and stapler
Hammer
Junior hacksaw
Pliers (if you use wire)

3. The paddle-wheel supports: Hammer in one 2" common nail, 3"–3½" from the back of each pontoon. Leave about 1½" of each nail sticking out. (They should not go all the way through the pontoons.)

BUILDING THE PADDLE WHEEL

1. The paddle blades: With scissors, carefully cut the top and bottom off a pop can. (Use a nail to poke a hole in the side of the can

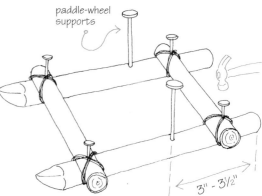

first, just under the end, to give you a place to start cutting.) Cut down one side of the "tube" and flatten out your aluminum sheet. With scissors, carefully cut six rectangles, 1" (or the length of your spool) by 1½" to form the paddle-wheel blades. Trim off the sharp corners.

2. The wheel: Using a junior hacksaw, make six slits into the plastic spool. Make your cuts between the plastic "spacers" surrounding the holes at the ends – a good guide to keep your slits evenly spaced.

WORKING WITH POP CANS

Aluminum pop cans are a great source of material for paddle wheels and rudders. They are easy to cut with scissors – and, unlike other types of cans, the metal is not extremely sharp. Of course, you still need to be careful; get assistance if you need it.

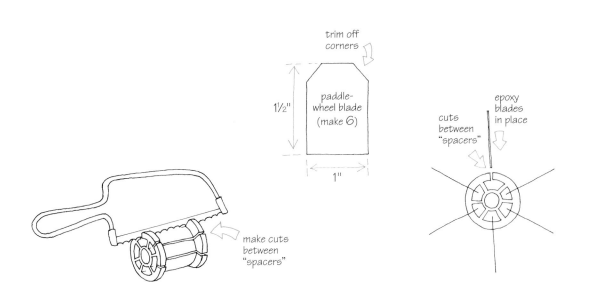

trim off corners

1½"

paddle-wheel blade (make 6)

1"

cuts between "spacers"

epoxy blades in place

make cuts between "spacers"

Insert the pop-can rectangles into the slits, and glue them in place with generous globs of five-minute epoxy.

3. Mount the paddle wheel: Push at least four elastic bands through the outer holes (not the centre) of the spool, one per hole. Your paddle wheel is now ready for mounting. Stretch the elastic bands between the two paddle-wheel supports you nailed onto the pontoons.

MAKING THE DECK

1. The deck is built of six or seven more twigs, each about 6" long and ½" in diameter, like the ones used to make the deck frame. Nail these to the pontoons *after* attaching your paddle wheel, to make sure none of them gets in the way of its

action. (We put one behind the back frame piece, and five behind the front one – but how many you use will depend on the thickness of your twigs.)

2. The mast: Drill a small hole in the centre of one of the deck twigs, whittle a point on a tall, thin twig, and jam it in the hole. Attach flags or streamers. You could even design your cottage coat of arms and paint it on a banner.

BUILDING THE RUDDER

1. For your rudderpost, use a thin straight stick or a wooden skewer, cut to about 3½" long.

2. Cut a rudder about 2¼" wide and 1½" high from your aluminum sheet. Run some epoxy down one edge, lay the rudderpost in the epoxy, and fold ¼" of aluminum over top, as shown. Staple the fold for extra strength. (See drawing next page.)

3. Drill a hole the diameter of your post in the middle of the back deck frame and insert the post from underneath. Loop an elastic band around the post just above the rudder, then stretch it behind the frame and over the top of the post. (See p. 141.) This keeps the rudder from falling out and holds it the way you turn it.

Your boat is now ready for launching. Wind up the paddle wheel and let it go. If the boat sits too low in the water (some twigs are heavier than others), improve the buoyancy by gluing corks under the decks, along the sides of the pontoons. By moving the elastics up and down the paddle-wheel supports, you can control how much of the wheel is in the water – and change the boat's speed.

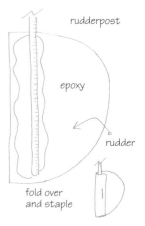

rudderpost

epoxy

rudder

fold over
and staple

HIGH-TECH TRIMARAN ⚓⚓⚓

MAKING THE DECK

1. Cut the two pieces of wood for the deck (see box below) and nail together as shown. Along the centre line of the 1" x 2", drill a ½" hole (for the mast) about 1" in from the front, and a ¼" hole (for the rudderpost) ½" from the back. In the front edge of the 1" x 4", drill a ¼" hole (for the bowsprit).

2. Paint the deck and allow it to dry.

BUILDING THE RUDDER

1. For the rudderpost, cut a piece about 7½" long from one of the wooden skewers.

2. Cut out the side of the pop can, as described in the paddle wheeler instructions on p. 140. For this boat, you'll need a larger rudder, so cut a rudder-shaped piece of aluminum, about 5" long and 3½" wide.

3. Run some five-minute epoxy down the long

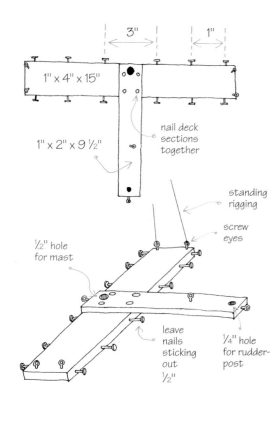

3" 1"

1" x 4" x 15"

nail deck
sections
together

1" x 2" x 9 ½"

standing
rigging

screw
eyes

½" hole
for mast

leave
nails
sticking
out
½"

¼" hole
for rudder-
post

MATERIALS
WOOD:
Deck:
1 pc. 1" x 4", about 15" long
1 pc. 1" x 2", about 9½" long

Keel:
1 pc. 1" x 3" or 1" x 4", 3½"–4"
  long (½"-thick wood is also fine)

TWIGS:
1 about ½" dia. x 25" for mast
1 about ⅜" dia. x 11" for boom
1 about ¼" dia. x 10" for bowsprit

5 pushpins
20–25 1¼" common nails
2 identical, large (1.5 or 2-litre)
  plastic pop or water bottles

2 identical, small (500-ml or 16-oz.) plastic pop or water bottles

1 aluminum pop can

14 elastic bands (but have more on hand)

1 bolt (we used a ½" hex-head bolt, about 4" long, but any heavy bolt will do)

Stovepipe wire (or similar thin flexible wire)

Wire coat hanger (or similar stiff wire, about 4" long)

Strong string, braided fishing line, or cord

8–10 ⁷/₁₆" screw eyes

3–4 thumbtacks

2 small hose clamps (½" or ¾")

2 thin wooden shish kebab skewers

Five-minute epoxy

Waterproof house paint or acrylic paint

MATERIAL FOR SAILS:

Old sheet, T-shirt, or other light cloth

TOOLS

Hammer

Junior hacksaw

Scissors and stapler

Pocketknife

Pliers

Drill

edge of the rudder, lay the rudderpost in the epoxy so that it's flush to the rudder's bottom edge, and fold the aluminum over top, making a ½" overlap. For extra strength, staple the fold behind the rudderpost. (See drawing, p. 142.)

MAKING THE KEEL

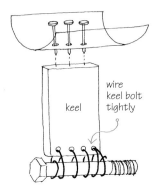

The keel will help your boat sail in a straight line.

1. First, whittle the front and back edges of your keel into curves, so your boat will sail faster.

2. Make the keel mount: Cut a curved section from one of the identical large plastic bottles. It should be at least 7" long and at least ½ the diameter of the bottle. Nail it to the top of the keel as shown at left.

3. Drill four small holes along the bottom edge of the keel and tightly wire on the heavy bolt. The bolt is the ballast that will keep your boat upright in a breeze.

ATTACHING THE DECK FITTINGS

Hammer nails into both of the long sides of the 1" x 4" as shown on p. 142, leaving about ½" of each nail sticking out. Then twist in seven screw eyes where shown.

MAKING THE MAST, BOOM, AND BOWSPRIT

1. Carefully hammer a nail (or drill a small hole, then insert a screw eye) into the tip of the twig bowsprit. Do the same thing at the back end of the twig boom.

2. With a pocketknife, whittle down the other end of the bowsprit and one end of the mast, and push each firmly into the appropriate hole in the deck.

3. Attach one of the hose clamps tightly to the mast, about 2" above the deck. Cut a 4" piece of coat-hanger wire, bend it into a "U" shape around the mast (above the first hose clamp), and then attach the boom by tightening the second hose clamp around the wire ends and the boom. Leave the wire "U" loose enough to allow the boom to swivel easily.

MAKING THE SAILS

1. Measure and cut two triangular sails to suit the size of your mast, boom, and bowsprit.

2. Attach the mainsail:

a) Tie a small knot in the top corner of the sail. Carefully hammer a nail through the tip of the sail, above the knot, into the top of the mast. Leave the head of the nail sticking out so you can attach a flag or streamers later on.

b) Attach the front edge of the mainsail to the mast using two or three thumbtacks.

c) Knot the back corner of the mainsail, and tie it to the nail (or screw eye) in the back of the boom with a short piece of string.

3. Attach the front sail, or jib: Knot, then tie the front corner of the jib with string to the nail (or screw eye) in the tip of the bowsprit. Attach only the top corner of the jib to the mast, using a pushpin.

ATTACHING THE HULLS

Align the second big bottle under the deck between the centre pairs of protruding nail-heads. Hook one end of an elastic band to one nail in one of the centre pairs, stretch it under the bottle and hook it over the second nail in the same pair. Repeat with the other centre pair of nails. Then, repeat with the

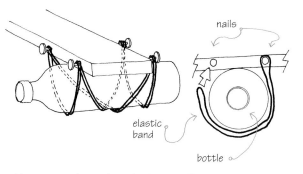

smaller bottles between the outer pairs of nails. Also cross elastic bands diagonally under the smaller bottles for extra support.

ATTACHING THE KEEL

Secure the keel under the big bottle using the centre pairs of nails and the same elastic-band technique you used to attach the bottles.

ATTACHING THE RUDDER

1. Just ahead of the hole for the rudderpost, make a friction mount (to keep the rudder from free-swivelling or falling out) with two pushpins and a few snug loops of an elastic band. (See photo at right.) Push the rudderpost up through the bottom of the hull.

2. To make a tiller, attach a 4" piece of wooden skewer to the rudder post with wire. Angle the tiller so its front end pushes under the elastic of the friction mount.

RIGGING YOUR BOAT

1. "Standing" rigging helps hold the mast upright. To make the "standing" rigging for your boat, lead four pieces of cord or braided fishing line from the four screw eyes at the outside corners of the deck to the nail at the top of the mast. Tie snugly.

2. The "running" rigging controls how far out you let your sails go.

(a) The mainsheet: Twist a screw eye into the underside of the boom, about 4" from the back. Tie a string 8"–10" long to the screw eye, run it through the screw eye on the deck, then tie it off to a push-pin lightly tacked into the deck.

(b) The jibsheet: Knot the lower back corner of the jib and tie on a string 6"–8" long; run the string through the screw eye at the front of the hull and tie it off to a pushpin lightly tacked into the deck behind the mast.

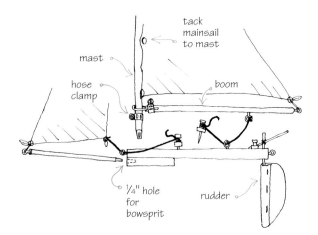

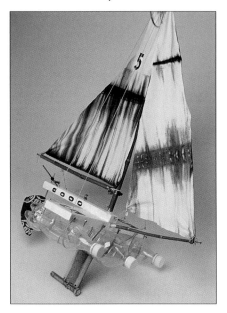

To let the sails in or out, simply move the pushpins back and forth along the deck. (As a general rule, when the mainsail is let way out, the jib should also be let out, and vice versa.)

Tie a long piece of fishing line to the screw eye at the back of the deck, or you may just watch your trimaran sail over the horizon.

NOW HOST A MINI-REGATTA

The problem with many games is they limit the number of players. Invariably, Mom will demur. "No, it's okay, I don't mind. I didn't really want to play anyway...I'll just go read on the porch." She always seems cheerful but, as she turns away, there are tears welling in her eyes.

Okay, so this is an exaggeration. Still, when a large group of people has gathered for the weekend, finding the right game to play can lead to a malady known as "martyr syndrome": Someone always ends up sitting on the sidelines. The perfect solution is the mini-regatta – a sailboat race of Lilliputian proportions.

The flexibility of the mini-regatta makes it the ideal activity. Any number of people of virtually any age can participate; nature provides the water and wind. Because competitors design and build their own boats with simple (and cheap) materials, you'll sometimes see a child genius triumph while design engineers go down with their ships.

Essentially, there are two variations of the mini-regatta. In the first, competitors get together and build their sailboats on the spot, using materials that the host provides. Creating your own guidelines for maximum hull length and mast height will preclude the possibility of Aunt Betty's 40-ft. Douglas fir dugout smashing little Egbert's 6-in. dinghy to smithereens. The ship-building, by the way, is a great activity for any rotten, rainy weather preceding the regatta.

A second variation, while more complex, is the one that leads to annual competition, grudge matches, and regatta trophies. Inform your guests about the regatta as far ahead of time as possible. To prepare for the event, they can use any materials and designs – we recommend our high-tech trimaran! – and work as hard as they wish, as long as they stick to the size guidelines. Don't worry about the adults outdoing small fry. In one mini-regatta, a modelmaker's gaff-rigged ketch with a complex autohelm system just narrowly edged out two Big Mac containers held together by Popsicle sticks, with a piece of tattered shopping bag for a sail.

In the first variation, the host has a variety of materials on hand for construction. Some handy items for hulls are meat trays, egg cartons, fast-food containers, empty plastic pop bottles, juice and pop cans, spare chunks of Styrofoam insulation and, for purists, good old pieces of wood. (Make sure everyone remembers to put a keel on his or her boat; it will prove its worth later.) For masts, straws, pencils, straight sticks, lengths of dowel, coat-hanger pieces – even broken fishing rods will do the trick. Plastic shopping bags are the generally accepted sail material, but if guests want to use cloth, let them go for it. Put the boats together with glue, tape, staples, pipe cleaners, or nails. Blobs of Plasticine are good for holding up the mast on hulls you can't drill into; they also make great ballast. A supply of multi-coloured waterproof markers will ensure your pint-sized flotilla is the swankiest on the lake.

The course can be a straight line from the diving raft to shore, around the point, or a more skill-testing triangle. You can set it up in shallow water so the captains can wade right in, but if all competitors are good swimmers, try this deep-water variation: Wearing PFDs, the captains swim along with their boats. (Swim fins, masks, and snorkels are optional.) In either case, the reason for sticking near one's entry soon becomes obvious; unless there's a crew of trained mice on board, these sailboats won't be able to tack. Gentle nudges are allowed to keep vessels on course, but judges be warned: Two common infractions are sail blowing ("Gee, why is Pat blue in the face?") and sloshing – following the boat closely using a modified breaststroke, thus creating a following wave. Spitting streams of water on opponents' sails to capsize their ships is also illegal (and vulgar). In the mini-regatta, entries that wash across the finish line as heaps of mangled wreckage still count.

With any luck, your regatta will become a regular event. Over the years, the number of competitors will grow until your neighbours will compare your cottage to Helen of Troy. The place that launched a thousand ships. —*David Zimmer*

WHITTLE A WHISTLE

*This old-fashioned slip-bark whistle makes a perfect project
for a lazy day. By Charles Long*

Decades of power lunches and competitive leisure have left us feeling guilty
about sitting by the lake doing nothing at all. It doesn't figure in the bottom
line. So whenever we aren't officially working, we paint the trim and fix the foot valve,
or work up a sweat trying to cream somebody at tennis. And we call that relaxation.

Real relaxation today requires an excuse. There's television, but that can be
even worse for the bottom line than doing nothing at all. Anyway, you can't put a
TV out on the dock at 11 o'clock in the morning. It's an image thing. The trick is
to look busy, not stupid.

Whittling offers the perfect excuse. Anyone who asks what on earth you are doing, just sitting there by the lake, lopping away at a stick of wood, can be told
you are busy "making something." What bliss.

It occurred to me recently that I hadn't really whittled anything since getting my
first wristwatch. Before then there was always enough time to whittle slingshots, bows
and arrows, hiking sticks, or whistles. When there were chores to be done, we

**Pound the stick all over to
loosen the bark**

Slip the bark off with a gentle twist

**Slide the bark back into place
and carve the mouthpiece**

could take a pocketknife to a comfy spot of shade and pare away at a stick. *What are you kids doing out there?* Making something. *Okay.* Worked every time.

Of course then, as now, you eventually had to show some result for your labours. And if the hiking stick didn't quite work out it could become a sword, or a marshmallow toaster. There was an art to the whittling business, and I don't

With the bark still on, cut a notch about ¾"–1" from the mouthpiece

Slide bark off, then slice a bit off top of wood from notch to mouthpiece

With the bark still off, hollow out an air chamber ahead of the notch

mean hang-it-on-the-wall art. It wasn't the product that mattered so much as the process. And where it was done might be as important as what was done.

Which brings us to the classic slip-bark whistle, and your role in reviving a dying art. The thing about a slip-bark whistle is that the bark has to slide off the stick on which it grew. This is whittling that requires a particular kind of tree. Fortunately, these trees grow near water, and the process works best about the time the weather turns warm.

The ideal stick is from fresh, new growth, about 4"–5" long and about ¾" in diameter. The bark should be smooth – no bumps or scars to hold it to the wood underneath. Early in the summer, just about any smooth-bark species will do: willow,

mouthpiece
end

SECTION OF FINISHED WHISTLE

maple, alder, basswood, or poplar. Willows are good, but some will have too many nodes and scars to allow the bark to slip off cleanly. Later in the summer, stick to box elder (a.k.a. Manitoba maple), or try trees growing right at the water's edge.

If you haven't whittled since your slingshot days, you'll have to sharpen the knife. If it slips, a dull blade is more likely to cut the whittler than the wood. And a dull blade might crush the soft fibres more than cut them. Any pocketknife with a small, thin blade will do.

Cut the shoot off cleanly, where it won't be missed. If you take one from a bunch of new growth, or anything from a Manitoba maple, you can call it pruning and convince yourself you really are doing something useful.

Score a ring around the stick, 1" or so from the fatter end, cutting through the bark but not the wood. We're going to leave this bit of bark on the butt end as a handle and, after soaking, slip the longer section of bark off the wood like a sleeve. If you try to slip it off the other way, the bark splits before it can pass over the fatter core.

Now the stick has to soak awhile. Are you beginning to see why this is a lazy-day project? It just doesn't work in night classes or lumber stores, and certainly not when the water's too cold. Dabble the stick in the lake for half an hour or so. Then pull it out and pound the sleeve of bark that has to be removed.

The simplest pounder is the handle of the knife. Tap the stick with the side of the handle, turning the stick as you tap it, and pound every bit of the section to be removed. Don't hit so hard as to tear the bark and, for the same reason, don't do it on a rock. Do it on the dock, or on the armrest of a comfortable wooden chair.

When you tire of pounding and the bark seems fairly loose, work the sleeve free with a gentle twist. If it refuses to budge, soak it again, pound it again, or roll it under the flat of the knife handle. If all else fails, cut another stick.

Once the bark is free, slide it back into place and whittle the tapered mouthpiece and the notch. For the notch, make a vertical cut halfway through the stick about ¾"–1" from the mouthpiece end, then slice back to it at about a 45° angle. Don't be in a hurry; make several shallow cuts rather than trying to finish in the fewest possible strokes. Save that for the golf course.

Now slide the bark off again and slice a bit off the top of the stick from the notch back to the mouthpiece end to create an air passage. Then whittle out an air chamber ahead of the notch. A chamber 1½"–2" long works best. Leave just enough solid wood at the bottom to hold the thing together. Dunk the parts occasionally as

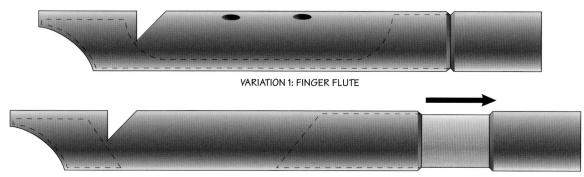

VARIATION 1: FINGER FLUTE

VARIATION 2: "SLIDE-TROMBONE" WHISTLE

you work. That keeps the bark slippery and reminds the whittler to wet the figurative whistle as well.

Put the two pieces back together and blow. Use a soft lip or you'll press the air passage closed. The note that emerges depends on the size of the air chamber: the shorter the chamber, the higher the note. If you want to get fancy, or spend some more time at this labour, use the tip of the knife blade to drill a couple of very small holes in the bark above the air chamber. Now you have a finger flute. Or cut away the connecting wood at the bottom of the chamber and slide the handle in and out like a trombone. With a bit of luck, and almost no practice, you can imitate a two-note, chickadee mating call. Any more than that is asking a lot of a lakeside whittler. Any less looks frivolous.

Back before the art was lost, author E.J. Tangerman attended a whittlers' convention and came away with pictures of elaborate chains and balls in cages. "These are difficult and tricky to make," he later wrote, "and of no practical value when finished – which gives whittling its reputation of being the loafer's pastime." Luckily, our whistle is neither tricky nor difficult, so our reputations are safe. We're just as busy as the proverbial beavers. Which raises another question: Don't beavers spend the summer loafing around the lake, lopping away at sticks?

A TRIO OF WHIRLIGIGS

A loon, a fish, and an angler that put the wind to work.
By Ron Frenette and Greg Gorgerat

Judging by the variety of flags, windsocks, and weather vanes found at lakefront places, cottagers' fascination with wind borders on obsession. In keeping with this tradition, we've come up with three whirligigs – crosses between windmills and wood sculpture. If you like to watch the wind at work, they make great roadside or dockside companions. The plans range in difficulty, with the loon being the simplest and the angler on the dock the most complex. The templates are on page 160.

FINISHING

The final paint job should reflect your own taste (and your own place, in the case of the angler), so feel free to give the fish purple spots or paint the loon lime green. We do recommend that once you've tested your whirligig to make sure all the parts fit and the mechanisms work, you disassemble it to do the finishing. Seal the wood with two coats of spar varnish thinned 30%, then lightly rub with fine steel wool, and paint using exterior oil-based paint.

TOOLS FOR ALL THREE WHIRLIGIGS

You'll need a band saw or jigsaw, jackknife, drill, twist bits, countersinking bit, dovetail saw or chisel, hammer, and screwdriver; for the angler, you'll also need Vise-grips, pliers, and tin snips.

MATERIALS FOR LOON OR FISH* WHIRLIGIG

Body:
1 piece 1½" x 4" x 23" white pine, white cedar, or basswood

Wings:
2 pieces ¼" x 3" x 11" white ash or any wood

Wing Blocks:
2 pieces 1" x 1" x 6" white ash (or use any hardwood; it holds screws best)

Hub Blocks:
2 pieces 1" x 1" x 2" hardwood

Axle:
7" of 5/16" dowel (or brass rod); 4 washers large enough for the dowel or rod to fit through

Mounting post:
15" of 5/16" steel rod
¾" #5 brass screws
¾" #5 round-head screws
1½" finishing nails
Carpenter's glue

*Fish requires modifications to wings and wing blocks; see p. 155

Illustration A

MAKE A LOON WHIRLIGIG

Our loon was cut from white cedar and carved in the round, but you could use flat pieces of exterior-grade plywood and still get a great-looking whirligig.

To avoid cursing and ruined projects, use tape to test-fit parts before you join them. If possible, use brass rod rather than wood dowel for the axle. For years of wear-free spinning, we recommend a metal sleeve inside the loon body that fits over the axle. (If you can't find material for a sleeve, your whirligig will work quite well without one.)

1. Trace loon body on 1½" wood and cut out with a band saw or jigsaw. Next, use a jackknife to round the body and make it more lifelike. Be sure to premark and leave a flat area on both sides where hub blocks are attached, as marked on the template.

2. The hub blocks can be left square, but look better if they're rounded a little. See Illustration A.

3. Mark the exact centre of both hub blocks and drill through using a $^{21}/_{64}$" drill bit (so the hole is slightly larger than the dowel).

4. Predrill pilot holes and attach a hub block to one side of the loon body, using glue and two finishing nails.

5. Next, drill a $^{21}/_{64}$" axle hole right through the loon body, using the hub block you just attached as a guide. Then attach the other hub as in Step 4.

6. Using the template as a guide, mark and drill a $^{21}/_{64}$" hole in underside of loon body for the mounting post. This will allow the bird to pivot freely on the $^{5}/_{16}$" rod. Drive a $^{3}/_{4}$" round-head screw into the bottom of the pivot-rod hole so that when the loon spins, metal will spin on metal.

7. Trace and cut out two wings; sand edges. Next, cut out two single wing blocks. The wing blocks consist of a $1^{1}/_{4}$" section of solid wood where the unit attaches to the body, with the remaining $4^{3}/_{4}$" at the end cut away on a 45° angle. See Illustration B.

8. Drill and countersink three pilot holes ($^{7}/_{64}$") along narrow end of each wing. Using glue and $^{3}/_{4}$" #5 screws, attach the wings to the wing blocks, ensuring that the longer edge of the wing is canted inward towards the loon's body.

9. Next, mark the centre of the wing block and drill through it with a $^{5}/_{16}$" bit. Tap a piece of $^{5}/_{16}$" dowel about 7" long into one wing block, securing it with a bit of glue. Slip on two washers, then slide this wing assembly through the hub blocks and through the loon body. When it comes out the other side of the loon, add two more washers and the other wing. This will be a bit difficult, and you might have to ream the hole to make the dowel fit. Glue in place. Once the wings are attached so the dowel revolves freely, trim off any excess dowel with a dovetail saw or chisel.

10. Attach the wings so their tips face in opposite directions; one pointing ahead, the other behind. To lock the wings in place, drill a tiny hole into the top of the wing block and through the axle; tap in a finishing nail to act as a cotter pin and keep the wings locked in place. If the nail protrudes on the other side of the block, snip off the excess with a wire cutter.

11. Insert the $^{5}/_{16}$" steel rod into the $^{21}/_{64}$" hole you drilled into the bottom of the loon. Drill another $^{21}/_{64}$" hole wherever you want to mount the loon and drop in the rod.

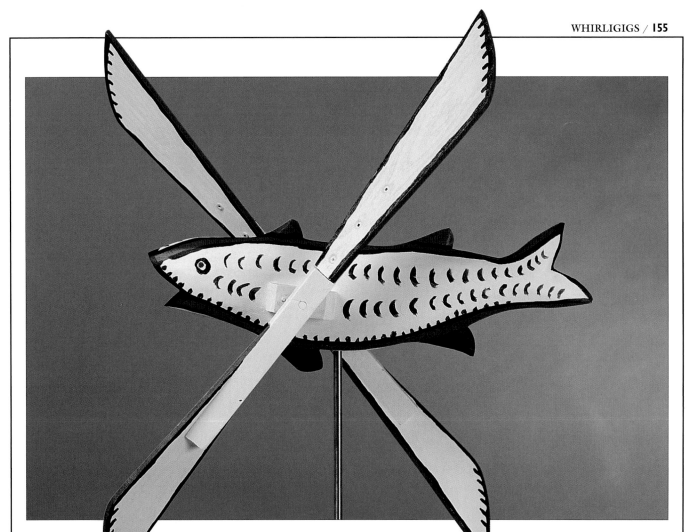

MAKE A FISH WHIRLIGIG

Follow the materials list and instructions for the loon, except for the following: Cut four wings instead of two. Double the wing blocks so that you have a 2½" section of solid wood in the centre, with 4¾" on each side of this solid section cut on opposing 45° angles. See Illustration B.

It's easy to mount these wings incorrectly, so use tape to test that they are properly assembled and aligned before drilling. The long edge of each wing (the one with the pointed tip) should be canted towards the body of the fish. Mount the double wings so they are at right angles to one another.

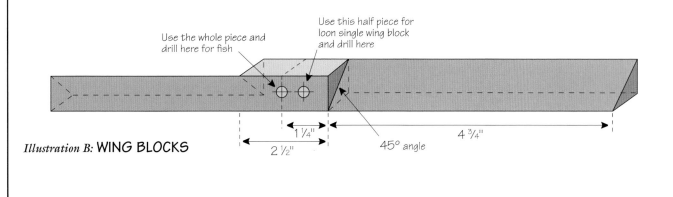

Use the whole piece and drill here for fish

Use this half piece for loon single wing block and drill here

1 ¼"

2 ½"

45° angle

4 ¾"

Illustration B: **WING BLOCKS**

MATERIALS FOR ANGLER WHIRLIGIG

Base *(total of 8 parts)*, white pine or exterior-grade plywood:
Horizontal surface ("the water"):
1 piece 1" x 5½" x 22"
Sides or "waves": **2** pieces ⅝" x 4½" x 22"
Internal supports: **5** pieces ⅝" x 2½" x 5½"

Dock *(total of 5 parts):*
Decking: **1** piece ⅝" x 4½" x 7½" white pine or exterior-grade plywood
Dock pilings: **4** 1" lengths of ¾" dowel

Fisherman *(5 parts):*
Torso and head: **1** piece 1½" x 3" x 6" white pine, white cedar, or basswood
Arms and legs: **1** piece ½" x 5" x 10" (same wood as above)
1 piece ¾" dowel, 1¾" long
1 3" flat-head stove bolt with nuts and washers.

Propeller *(6 parts):*
Propeller support arms: **2** pieces ¾" x ¾" x 13" white ash or any hardwood
Propeller blades: **4** pieces 4" x 8" thin sheet metal (roof flashing, old turpentine cans, or olive oil tins work well) or ¼" plywood

Drive mechanism:
Drive shaft: 30" of ⅛" steel rod (called key stock, and available at hardware stores)
Cam sleeve: 2" length of ¾" dowel
1 metal coat hanger
Drive shaft sleeves and prop spacer: 12½" of ¼" copper tubing

Swivel base:
1 piece ½" x 6¾" x 22" plywood
1 piece ¾" x 4" x 4" plywood
1 4" lazy Susan swivel base

Wind vane:
1 piece thin sheet metal 11" x 11" or ¼" plywood
2 pieces ½" x ½" x 6" hardwood

General:
Carpenter's glue
1" finishing nails
1½" finishing nails
½" #5 brass screws
¾" #5 brass screws
1½" #6 brass screws
¼" #8 brass screws
1½" #8 brass screws
2½" #8 brass screws
1" #8 brass screws

ANGLER

1. Make the base: Trace base templates on wood and cut out all eight pieces. Cut out the fishing hole in the large horizontal "water surface" piece.

On the two side pieces or "waves," draw horizontal lines 2½" from the bottom, as marked on template; these will guide you when joining pieces later.

Mark the centre of all five internal support pieces and drill a ¼" hole through each. Insert a 2" piece of ¼" copper tubing in each hole as a sleeve for the drive shaft.

2. Make the dock: Trace and cut out the top of the dock. Using the template, mark and cut out a hole identical to the one cut in the base section.

Next, at the end opposite to the hole, cut a narrow 2" slit in the centre of the dock. This will accept the leading edge of the wind-direction vane.

Finally, in each of the dock-piling dowels, drill a ¼" hole through the centre from end to end.

3. Make the fisherman: Use templates to cut out the five body parts. Attach the arms in a "fishing pose" with glue and 1" finishing nails. Hold or clamp the legs and torso together and drill a ³⁄₁₆" hole through all three. Bolt the legs and torso together, with one washer on either side of the torso.

After the pieces are assembled, you can use a very sharp jackknife to round the fisherman. (If you used plywood for the figure, just skip the rounding.)

4. Make the propeller: Cut the four propeller blades out of sheet metal or ¼" plywood.

Make two identical propeller-support arms with tight-fitting half-lap joints in the centre to lock the arms together.

Once you've cut the 4" angled sections at the ends of the arms, attach the metal prop blades with 12 ½" #5 screws (three in each blade); predrill and countersink ⁷⁄₆₄" pilot holes to prevent splitting the wood.

5. Build the drive mechanism: Cut a 2" length of ¾" dowel and drill a ¼" hole through it from end to end. In the middle of the dowel, cut a small notch around the outside using a knife. Twist one end of the coat-hanger wire securely around the dowel so it fits snugly in the notch, and slip the piece of dowel over the drive shaft.

For the drive shaft, use a 30" piece of ⅛" hard steel rod (key stock). Using a vise, pliers, and a steel block, bend the rod so it matches Illustration C, and the short piece of dowel rests in the bent cam section. As the propeller turns, the cam mechanism makes the fisherman bob up and down.

The coat hanger should now be perpendicular to the drive shaft: it will rise up out of the base to become the fishing rod.

6. Make the wind vane: Trace the vane onto sheet metal or ¼" plywood and cut it out with tin snips.

ASSEMBLING THE COMPONENTS

1. Place the angler so his toes are at the edge of the hole cut in the dock. Drill and countersink a ⅛" hole through the bottom of the dock and up through the bottom of the feet. Fasten with two 1½" #6 screws.

2. Place the four 1" pilings in position and set the dock/angler unit on top of them, ensuring that the two "fishing holes" are aligned. From underneath the base or water surface, mark and drill four ⁵⁄₃₂" holes through the base, through the pilings, and ¼" into the bottom of the dock. Countersink and fasten with 2½" #8 screws.

3. Attach the sides. Butt the bottom edge of the water surface piece to the lines you drew earlier on the wave pieces. Drill five ⁵⁄₃₂" holes through the sides and into the edge of the surface piece and attach the sides with 1½" #8 screws. Repeat on the other side.

4. Slide the five internal support pieces (with short sections of copper tube in each) over the ends of the drive shaft. Attach one support piece at each end of the box (keep the sleeves flush on the outside), one on either side of the cam (1" away), and the fifth roughly centred in the largest space remaining. Glue the support pieces in place and secure with 1½" finishing nails. Before nailing tight, do test turns of the drive mechanism to make sure it works smoothly.

5. Interlock the half-lap joints of the two prop arms and glue in place, making sure the blades all sit at the same 45° angle.

At the exact centre where the two arms intersect, drill a ¼" hole and insert a 2½" piece ¼" copper tubing so one end is flush to the front edge of the prop arm and the rest sticks out behind.

6. Slide the completed prop onto the drive mechanism and cut off all but 1½" of the excess rod. Drill a ⅛" hole in one of the prop arms. Using Vise-grips and pliers, bend the rod so it goes through the hole and out the other side to lock the rod in place.

7. Slide the vane into the slot cut into the rear of the dock. Attach ½" x ½" x 6" wooden brackets at the base of the vane using countersunk ¾" #5 screws. Drill vertically through the brackets and screw to the base.

8. Cut a piece of ¾" dowel to fit between the fisherman's hands. Cut a notch in this piece and wrap the coat-hanger wire (attached to the now-hidden cam) completely around it, and then forward to form the fishing rod. Clip off the excess wire. To fasten the dowel between the fisherman's hands, drill tiny holes through the sides of the hands and into the dowel ends, and attach with 1½" finishing nails.

9. Cut a fish out of scrap metal and drill a small hole in its nose to accept a snap-swivel. Tie the snap-swivel to a length of fishing line and attach to the rod with tape.

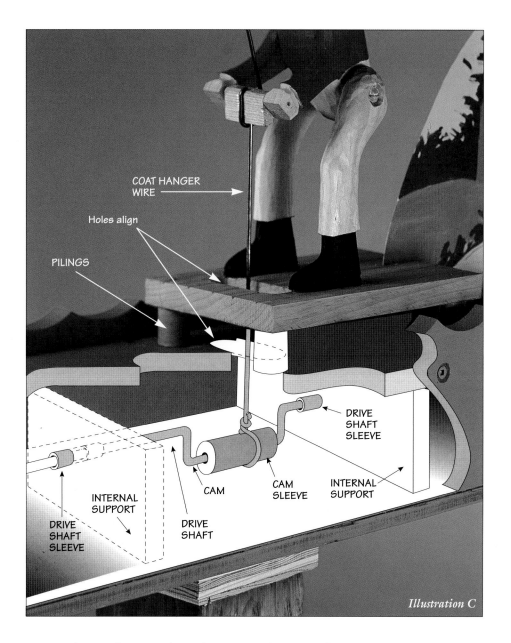

COAT HANGER
WIRE

Holes align

PILINGS

DRIVE
SHAFT
SLEEVE

CAM

CAM
SLEEVE

INTERNAL
SUPPORT

INTERNAL
SUPPORT

DRIVE
SHAFT
SLEEVE

DRIVE
SHAFT

Illustration C

10. We designed our angler to be mounted on top of a 4" x 4" post, using a lazy Susan base to let it move freely in the wind. Attach a ¾" x 4" x 4" piece of plywood to the top of a post with four 2½" #8 screws. Using ¾" #5 screws, attach the lazy Susan unit onto the piece of scrap. Mark out the centre of the base piece of ½" plywood (6¾" x 22"), and fasten it to the top of the lazy Susan using four ¾" #5 screws. Set the whirligig on the plywood base. Mark and drill pilot holes, countersink, and attach the base with six 1" #8 screws.

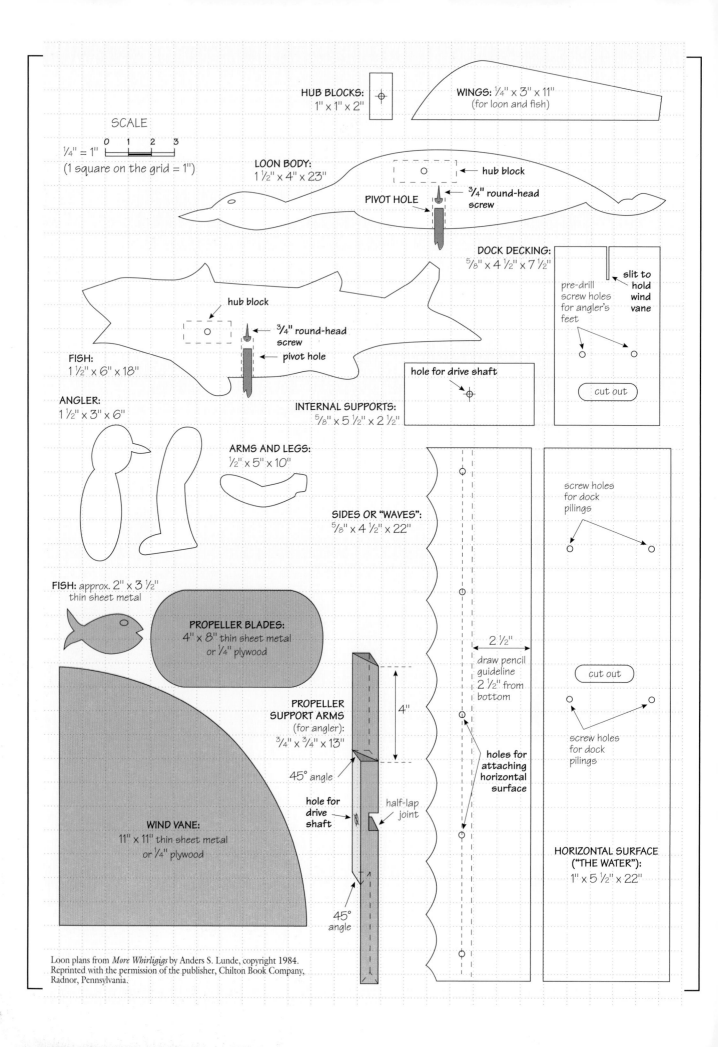

HUB BLOCKS:
1" x 1" x 2"

WINGS: ¼" x 3" x 11"
(for loon and fish)

SCALE

¼" = 1"

0 1 2 3

(1 square on the grid = 1")

LOON BODY:
1 ½" x 4" x 23"

hub block

PIVOT HOLE

¾" round-head
screw

hub block

¾" round-head
screw

pivot hole

DOCK DECKING:
⅝" x 4 ½" x 7 ½"

pre-drill
screw holes
for angler's
feet

slit to
hold
wind
vane

cut out

FISH:
1 ½" x 6" x 18"

ANGLER:
1 ½" x 3" x 6"

hole for drive shaft

INTERNAL SUPPORTS:
⅝" x 5 ½" x 2 ½"

ARMS AND LEGS:
½" x 5" x 10"

SIDES OR "WAVES":
⅝" x 4 ½" x 22"

screw holes
for dock
pilings

FISH: approx. 2" x 3 ½"
thin sheet metal

PROPELLER BLADES:
4" x 8" thin sheet metal
or ¼" plywood

2 ½"

draw pencil
guideline
2 ½" from
bottom

cut out

4"

**PROPELLER
SUPPORT ARMS**
(for angler):
¾" x ¾" x 13"

45° angle

screw holes
for dock
pilings

hole for
drive
shaft

half-lap
joint

holes for
attaching
horizontal
surface

WIND VANE:
11" x 11" thin sheet metal
or ¼" plywood

45°
angle

**HORIZONTAL SURFACE
("THE WATER"):**
1" x 5 ½" x 22"

Loon plans from *More Whirligigs* by Anders S. Lunde, copyright 1984.
Reprinted with the permission of the publisher, Chilton Book Company,
Radnor, Pennsylvania.

THE GAME OF CROKINOLE

Build a board – and impress your opponents with some playing tricks. By Michael Webster

HOW TO MAKE YOUR OWN CROKINOLE BOARD

MATERIALS

WOOD

½" No. 1 grade particle board, for a circle 30" in diameter

⅜" G1S birch plywood, for a circle 25" in diameter

⅛" G1S birch plywood, for two 1⅝" x 8' strips

OTHER

White carpenter's glue

¾" finishing nails

8 1¼" No. 8 roundhead wood screws

Latex surgical tubing

Varathane, marine-grade varnish, or lacquer

Plastic wood

TOOLS

Jigsaw or fine-toothed keyhole saw

Circular saw or table saw

Sandpaper

C-clamps (at least 8)

No. 400 emery cloth

Drill

1⅜" spade or Forstner bit

Drill press (optional)

Black felt-tip pen

Note: Exact dimensions are not critical, because there has never been an official-size crokinole board.

1. Using a jigsaw or a fine-toothed keyhole saw, cut a circle with a diameter of 30" from ½" No. 1 grade particle board. This is the back of the board.

2. To make the playing surface, cut a circle with a diameter of 25" from ⅜" good-one-side (G1S) birch plywood.

3. Sand both pieces.

4. Carefully centre the playing surface on the back and draw a pencil line around it. Remove the playing surface and apply glue to the area of the back inside the line. Clamp the playing surface in position with eight C-clamps around the perimeter, carefully protecting the

¾" lengths of
surgical tubing

⅜" good one-side
birch plywood

½" No. 1 grade
particle board

1 ⅝" x 8' strips of
⅛" birch plywood

wood with scraps of lumber. Put pressure on the centre of the board with a heavy weight and allow the assembly to dry overnight.

5. Cut two 1⅝" wide by 8' long strips of ⅛" G1S birch plywood. These will become the rim of the board. The ⅛" plywood is flexible enough to bend around the board's circumference, and the double layer offers a more comfortable handrest when taking a shot and more strength against breakage in case the board is ever dropped.

6. Glue the first strip to the edge of the back, good side facing in, and secure it with ¾" finishing nails every 3"–4". Allow the glue to dry. Beginning *opposite* the first strip's joint, glue on the outer strip, good side facing out this time. To hold the strip in place and apply even pressure while the glue dries, use as many C-clamps and self-locking pliers as you can get your hands on. (For appearance's sake, do not nail this strip except where the ends meet.)

7. Round off and smooth the edges of the rim and carefully remove any dust. Then apply a coat of clear marine-grade varnish, Varathane, or lacquer. After it dries, smooth the surface with No. 400 emery cloth.

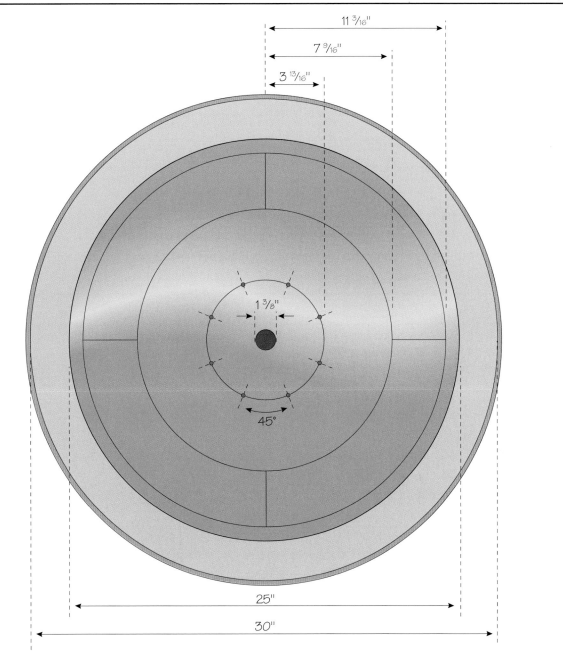

11 ³⁄₁₆"

7 ⁹⁄₁₆"

3 ¹³⁄₁₆"

1 ³⁄₈"

45°

25"

30"

8. "Paint" on the lines using a felt-tip marking pen and a series of cardboard disks held in place with a pin in the exact centre of the board. The diameters of the three circles are 7⅝", 15⅛", and 22⅜", and the four quadrant lines are set 90° apart between the outer circles.

9. To ensure a hard, lasting surface, apply four more coats of Varathane, varnish, or lacquer, sanding lightly or rubbing with very fine steel wool between coats.

10. Now add the pegs: eight of them set every 45° around the line marking the inner circle so that two are centred in each quadrant. The pegs consist of ¾" lengths of latex surgical tubing or automotive vacuum tubing over 1¼" No. 8 roundhead wood screws. Predrill the holes for the screws and insert the pegs, making sure they are straight. (A drill press is handy for this.)

11. Finally, make the "20" hole: Use a drill with a 1⅜" spade or Forstner bit to cut a hole ¼" deep in the exact centre of the board. (If you use a Forstner bit, you'll need a drill press.) Fill the small hole left by the point of the drill bit with a bit of plastic wood if you like.

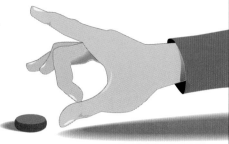

12. Your board is now ready for play. Give it an occasional coat of furniture polish to keep the playing surface fast.

Of course you need a set of disks before the game can get underway. To produce 24 perfectly round disks of identical size and consistently curved edges is a daunting task; we recommend you buy them. Proper disks have rounded edges – the better to slide into the "20" hole – and are made of hardwood (usually maple); the lightweight pine ones are a poor second choice.

A REFRESHER COURSE ON HOW TO PLAY

The game of crokinole was invented in Ontario around 1867. There's a strong element of revenge to it: If one of your opponent's disks is on the board, you are *obliged* to shoot it off. Crokinole can be played while you're carrying on a conversation, while it's pouring rain, or while you're digesting dinner. It doesn't require a great deal of physical exertion. A 6-year-old can play with a 66-year-old. About the only problem with crokinole is that too much of it can lead to "crokinole finger," a throbbing pain in one's shooting finger. (More on this in a moment.)

If you want to set up a crokinole tournament, you'll need at least one board and 24 disks. Two boards enable you to get a round robin going, with up to eight people playing at once. When there are just two players at a board, each player takes all 12 disks of one colour; when there are three, one player takes all the disks of one colour and shoots alternately after each of the other players, who play as a team and shoot six disks apiece. With four, players divide into two teams, each person shooting six disks.

Crokinole rules are by no means standardized, and variations abound. The following, however, will get you started: Using either your index or middle finger to shoot, you want your disks to knock your opponent's disks into the "ditch" around the perimeter of the board or into a lower scoring position, while at the same time leaving your disks in scoring position. As long as any of your opponent's disks are on the board, you must shoot for and hit at least one.

Players alternate shots. To shoot, you must position your disk along the line mark-

PUT A SPIN ON YOUR CROKINOLE GAME

Here's a secret known only to serious practitioners of the sport: All crokinole disks are not created equal – the high-quality ones are convex on one side and concave on the other. For a takeout shot requiring lots of power, play the disk convex side down, which will reduce friction and give it lots of carry-through. For a stop shot, increase the friction by playing the disk concave side down. Since the difference between the two sides is not easy to see, most pros spin the disk before they take their shot to determine which side is which. Convex side down, it spins a lot; concave side down, it hardly spins at all.

And it never hurts to give yourself a psychological advantage by intimidating the heck out of your opponents. To accomplish this, we recommend some whirlarama trick shooting during the pre-game warm-ups. Here's a warm-up shot that will have your opponents' jaws dropping: Stand a disk on edge on the perimeter line, about 30° to the right of centre. Assuming you're right-handed, lightly hold the top of the disk with your left index finger and flick the right side of the disk with your right shooting finger. If all goes well (and with lots of practice it will go well about 50% of the time), the disk will pirouette to the other side of the board, come back, split the posts, and spin right into the "20" hole. —*Doug Hunter*

ing the outermost circle on the board in the quadrant in front of you. If you don't hit one of your opponent's disks with your shot either directly or indirectly, your disk is removed from the board. If your opponent has no disks on the board, shoot directly for the centre hole. (Remove the disk if it makes the hole.)

At the end of each round, points are tallied for disks left on the board: Ones in the inner circle are worth 15 points; in the middle circle, 10 points; and in the outer circle, 5 points. (A disk on the line counts at the lower value. Disks on the outermost line, however, are worth 0, and should be removed from the board as they land there.) Add 20 points for each disk that made it into the centre hole. (If a disk ricochets off an opponent's disk and into the centre hole, it also counts for 20.) The difference between the scores is the winning team's tally. Games between two players are usually played to 100, between four players, to 200; round robins can continue until your finger can't take it any more.

Which brings us back to crokinole finger. The trick to avoiding it is to keep your shooting finger as close as possible to the disk, so that you are almost pushing it rather than hitting it. In other words, eliminate the air space between your finger and the disk.

And one last point: Although you can't move the board or your chair to make a shot, you can move your body – as long as part of it remains in contact with the chair. This is known, appropriately, as the "one-cheek rule." —*Ann Vanderhoof*

HORSESHOE COURT

Put in a proper pit – then follow our tips on how to play like a pro. By David Zimmer

Horseshoe pitching, believed to have originated in ancient Greece, is the ideal summertime game. It's simple, can be played by two or four people, doesn't rely on physical strength, and the level of competition can fluctuate from a friendly shoe toss to a drove-four-hours-just-to-whup-you-guys contest.

To build a proper horseshoe court, set two 1"-thick metal stakes in the ground exactly 40 ft. apart. The stakes should protrude 14 in. above the ground and lean towards each other about 3 in. Try to line them up from north to south so the sun will never be in the players' eyes.

Next, construct two 3' x 4' "sandboxes" around them, using 2" x 6" lumber, or whatever's on hand. Place the boxes so that the 4-ft. dimension follows the length of the court, and then fill them with dirt or sand. A foul line should be marked 3 ft. in front of each stake, but for casual combatants, these lines can be imaginary.

If anyone has a hard time throwing the 40-ft. distance, just mark a line 30 ft. from the stakes and throw anywhere up to that line instead. However, woe betide anyone who uses an underweight substitute to the standard 2½-lb. shoe (available in sets of four at most hardware and sporting-goods stores).

MATERIALS
2 1"-thick metal stakes
28 ft. of 2" x 6" lumber (or similar)
Sand or dirt
4 horseshoes

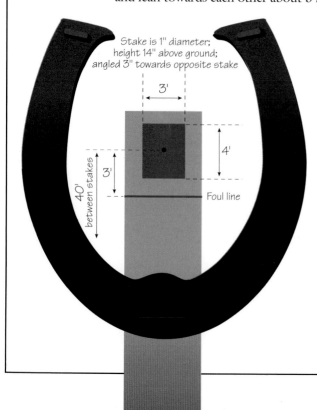

Stake is 1" diameter; height 14" above ground; angled 3" towards opposite stake

3'

4'

3'

40' between stakes

Foul line

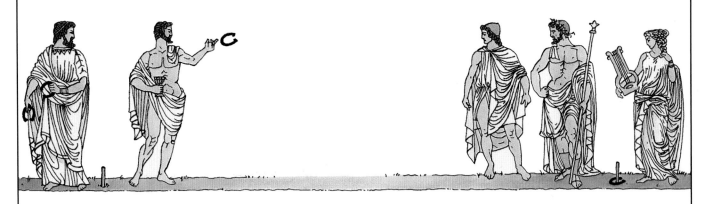

HOW TO PLAY

When two people play, each tosses two shoes in a row, and then they switch ends. When four people play, two of them stand at one end, and their partners stand at the other; the walking is eliminated. When two players have pitched both their shoes, it's called a "frame," "inning," or "end."

Since fistfights reduce family fun, here are the official scoring rules of the Horse-shoe Canada Association and the National Horseshoe Pitchers Association of America: A ringer is when the shoe encircles the stake so that a straight edge can touch the tip of each prong on the shoe without contacting the stake; it's worth three points. After ringers, the shoe(s) closest to the stake – within 6 in. – scores one point (apiece). This is where the adage, "Close only counts in horseshoes and hand grenades" comes into play.

Only one person can score in an inning; when there's a tie, shoes cancel each other out. The next closest shoe (within 6 in. of the stake) scores instead. Ultimately, a dispute over so-called "leaners" will arise. Copy this sentence and carry it with you at all times: A shoe leaning against the stake is worth *the same* as one lying on the ground – one point.

There are two ways to play a match. Under the cancellation method described above, games are played up to 21, 40, or 50 points. The count-all method is played over a predetermined number of ends, usually 20. Each player receives credit for both horseshoes thrown; thus both players can score points in the same end, and the highest score wins.

Finally, if a shoe bounces outside the box but lands in scoring position, it doesn't count. Now bring out the cooler and some lawn chairs, put on silly hats, and start pitching.

RUN RINGERS AROUND YOUR OPPONENTS

If you want to get more ringers, says expert horse-shoe pitcher Ronald Barr, you've got to break a habit that has long been a part of casual play: conversation. "If you want to be competitive, you can't be chattering. You've got to concentrate on the peg and do the proper follow-through," says Barr, who lives in Gooderham, Ontario's unofficial horseshoe capital.

Check your technique, too: As with bowling, it's important to lead with the proper foot. Generally, righties should lead with their left foot and stand on the port side of the box; lefties, vice-versa. Keep your wrist locked and your arm close to your leg, and don't release the shoe until your arm is straight out. Aiming for the top of the peg is a common mistake. "You should look at the peg right at the bottom," Barr says. "If you aim high, you'll hit the peg and the shoe will bounce back again." Your best bet is to aim for the ground 3–4 in. in front of the peg so the shoe will slide into its target. —*Laura Pratt*

TOROTORO – LET'S PLAY BULL

A raucous make-it-yourself game to test your family's nerves. By Ann Vanderhoof

You're sitting around after dinner when someone says, "Let's play a game." But what to play? Trivial Pursuit seems too taxing, Scrabble seems too slow, and all the usual card games seem too borrrrr-iiing. How about ToroToro?

We were recently introduced to this game by some friends who claim it originated in Argentina – a friend of theirs, so the story goes, learned it from some bandits sitting around a campfire. Although we can't substantiate this tale of its origins (there's even some disagreement about its name, which means "Bull Bull"), there's no doubt about how it's played. And there's no doubt it will result in a raucous good time. (The bedlam is similar to that generated by a game of Spoons.)

You need at least three people (of any age) to play, but this is clearly a game where "the more, the merrier" applies. The stuff you need to make this game is usually readily at hand: some twigs; some pieces of string; a coffee can or plastic container, such as a yoghurt tub; and one die, preferably large – but you can always simply borrow one from your Monopoly game.

Each player, except for one (the leader), should be equipped with a piece of string approximately 18"–20" long, at the end of which a twig about 2"–3" long has been securely tied. The leader is equipped with the coffee can or plastic container and the die.

The players place their twigs in the centre of the table, holding on tightly to the other end of the string. The leader shakes the die in the coffee can, then upends the can on the table with the die hidden inside. When the leader lifts the can, if the die has come up 6 or 1, the players have to pull their twigs (using the string) from the

MATERIALS
1 coffee can or large plastic yoghurt tub
1 die
Twigs
Lightweight string (such as cotton butcher's twine)

centre of the table before the leader can trap the twigs under the can. Any player whose twig is caught gets a letter: "T" the first time, "O" the second, "R" the third, and so on; when you've accumulated all the letters in "ToroToro," you're out of the game.

On the other hand, if the players are fast and the leader fails to capture *any* of the twigs, the leader gets a letter. You'll soon discover quick reactions are a definite asset in this game.

So are steady nerves. Because if the die comes up any number but 6 or 1, players are not supposed to do anything. If a player gets jumpy and pulls her twig out from the centre of the table without a 6 or 1 showing, she gets a letter. Likewise, if the leader brings the can down on the twigs without a 6 or 1 showing, he gets a letter.

After each round, the coffee can and die pass to the person on the left, who becomes the new leader. The old leader takes the new leader's twig and string and joins the play.

Soon, the room will resound with shouts of "ToroToro" and other less-printable phrases as people foul out of the game – sometimes the result of fake-outs by other players (perfectly legal, by the way, and all part of the fun). The last person left is the winner.

GINGERBREAD COTTAGE

Build this sweet retreat, then customize it with your own delicious details. By Jill Snider and Russell Zeid

What better way to show off your cottage over the holidays than to build a model of it – especially one you can eat after you've finished showing it off!

Our gingerbread cottage is a small, rustic place that sits on a stretch of rocky shoreline. It's got a big stone fireplace that chases the chill from cool evenings, a log-floored porch out front, and a sloping roof whose shingles are beginning to curl with age. A flagstone path leads down to the dock and our small runabout.

The patterns on pp. 172–174 will produce a basic cottage like ours; then it's time to be creative and customize the structure to make it your own. Patience is important. Don't try to cram the baking, assembly, and decorating all into one day; for instance, you can bake the gingerbread one day, then put the cottage together and decorate it the next. Don't rush the assembly; allow the icing "seams" to dry thoroughly before decorating. And be sure to read all the instructions, including the "Helpful Hints" and "Decorating Tips," before starting.

MAKING THE GINGERBREAD

You'll need *two* batches of dough; prepare them one at a time for easy handling.

1 cup (250 ml) shortening, golden or regular	2 tsp (10 ml) baking soda
1 cup (250 ml) lightly packed brown sugar	1½ tsp (7 ml) ground cinnamon
¼ cup (60 ml) milk	1½ tsp (7 ml) ground ginger
¼ cup (60 ml) molasses	1 tsp (5 ml) ground cloves
2¾ cups (675 ml) all-purpose flour	¼ tsp (1 ml) salt

Preheat oven to 350°F (180°C). Cream shortening, brown sugar, milk, and molasses with an electric mixer on medium speed until smooth and creamy. Combine remaining six dry ingredients. Add to the creamed mixture, mixing on low speed un-

til blended, then work with hands until a smooth, slightly soft dough forms. Add a little more milk if dough is too stiff or a little more flour if it's too soft. Cover and chill about one hour.

Working with half a batch of dough at a time, roll out dough ¼" (6 mm) thick on a well-floured surface. Cut out the pieces for the cottage, porch, dock, and boat following the patterns on pp. 172–174. (See "Helpful Hints", p. 175.)

Place pieces on greased baking sheets. Since small pieces take less time to bake, put them together on one sheet and large pieces on another.

Work leftover pieces of dough together; reroll and continue cutting. After all the pattern pieces have been cut, use leftover dough to make people, pets, etc.

Before baking, cut window from one of cottage end walls. (Reroll piece with other scraps.) Cut door from cottage front and bake with small pieces.

Bake at 350°F (180°C), 15–20 minutes for large pieces and 8–15 minutes for smaller pieces. As soon as gingerbread is removed from the oven, again place the patterns on top of the pieces and recut. *This is extremely important for easy assembly later.* Leave patterns sitting on top of gingerbread for easy identification.

After recutting the edges of the dock (piece N), cut into ½" (1-cm) "boards".

Remove all pieces to wire racks. *Cool completely before assembly.*

G. TOP OF CHIMNEY
to sit on roof (green
shaded area only):
Cut 2 pieces

E. BASE OF CHIMNEY
(to fit under roof
overhang): Cut
from lower dotted
green line to base
of chimney; cut
1 piece

**F. FULL HEIGHT OF
CHIMNEY** (solid green line):
Use entire pattern to solid
green line at top; cut 1 piece

MAKING THE ICING

The icing is used to "glue" the gingerbread pieces together, to decorate, and to landscape. You'll need about six batches to make the cottage shown here. (The quantity depends on the size of the base and the amount of decorating you do.) Prepare one icing recipe at a time so it doesn't harden.

2 egg whites
¼ tsp (1 ml) cream of tartar
2½ cups (625 ml) sifted icing sugar
Food colourings, as desired

Using an electric mixer on high speed, beat egg whites and cream of tartar together in a small bowl until frothy. *Gradually* add icing sugar. Continue beating until very stiff, about 4 minutes. (You'll need a very stiff frosting to glue the pieces together and to attach decorations, but the frosting can be softer for landscaping. Simply beat in a little water to soften it.)

Add food colouring if desired. Keep bowl covered with a damp cloth, or put icing into an airtight container to prevent hardening.

ASSEMBLING THE COTTAGE

1. Cut a base to the desired size and cover with aluminum foil. A cutting board, tray, baking sheet, heavy cardboard, and plywood all work well. We used a 16" x 22" (55-cm x 40-cm) piece of heavy cardboard. If you'd like your cottage to sit on a slope as ours does, place an 11" x 13" (28-cm x 33-cm) foil pan upside down on one corner of the base. Scrunch down the edges of the pan to make its lines less regular, and tape pan to base.

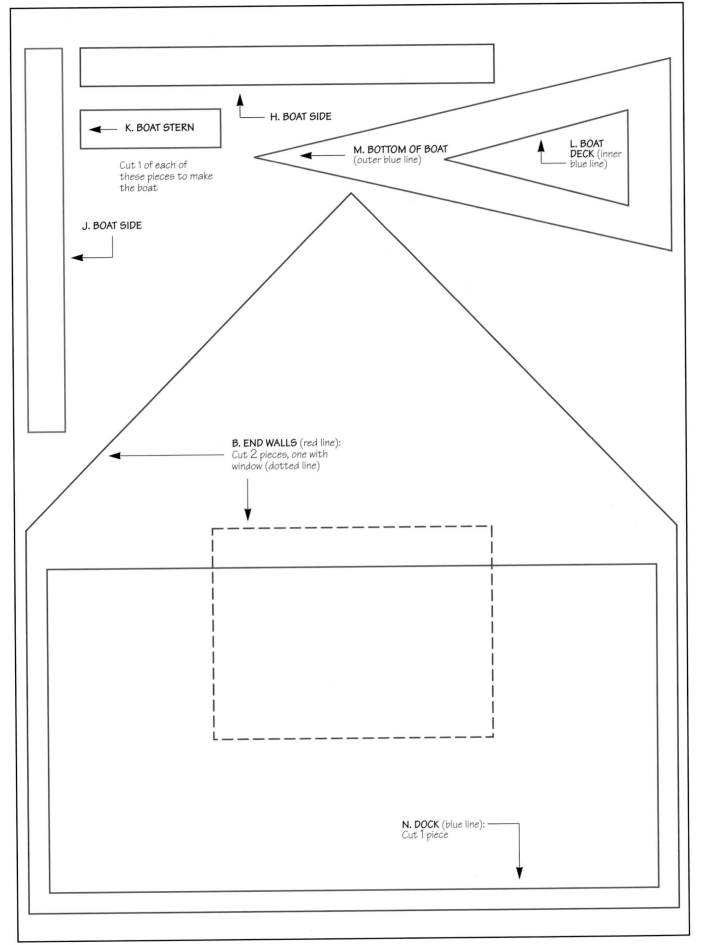

H. BOAT SIDE

K. BOAT STERN

Cut 1 of each of these pieces to make the boat

M. BOTTOM OF BOAT (outer blue line)

L. BOAT DECK (inner blue line)

J. BOAT SIDE

B. END WALLS (red line): Cut 2 pieces, one with window (dotted line)

N. DOCK (blue line): Cut 1 piece

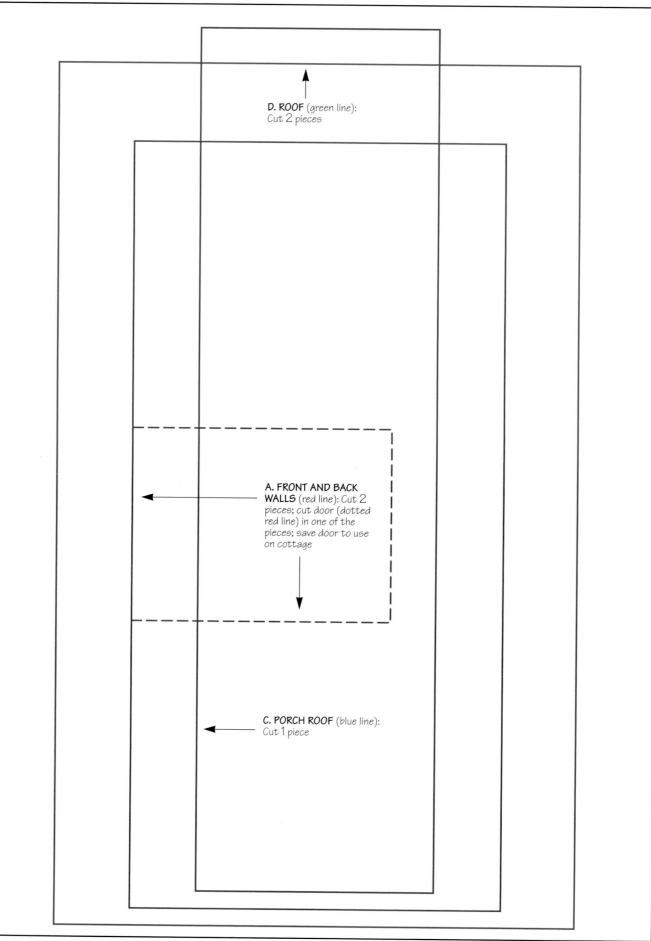

D. ROOF (green line):
Cut 2 pieces

A. FRONT AND BACK
WALLS (red line): Cut 2
pieces; cut door (dotted
red line) in one of the
pieces; save door to use
on cottage

C. PORCH ROOF (blue line):
Cut 1 piece

2. Put icing into a decorating bag with a #18 or #19 star tip, or use a small spatula or knife.

3. Apply icing along the bottom edge of the cottage back wall (piece A) and stand up on base. Support the back, or have someone hold it up.

4. Apply icing along bottom and side edges of end walls (B) and place them on *inside* of back. Support these. Repeat with front wall (piece A with door opening), placing it *outside* of side walls. Pipe a line of icing on all seams inside cottage for extra support.

5. Let cottage stand for 15 minutes to allow seams to harden before putting on the roof.

6. If you want a person in your cottage window, glue the decorated figure to the inside wall before putting on the roof.

7. To assemble the roof, apply icing along the top edges of all the cottage walls. Set one roof piece (D) in place, positioning it on the front wall so that it overhangs the end walls equally on each side. The top of the roof should be even with the top points of the end walls. Apply icing along top edge of roof. Place second roof piece (D) in position and run a line of icing along the entire edge where the two roof

HELPFUL HINTS: SMOOTHING YOUR PATH TO THE PERFECT COTTAGE

• Trace each pattern piece onto tissue paper; cut out, then trace onto stiff cardboard, label, and cut out. You may want to cut an extra set of pieces for later use, as the ones you use will get greasy.

• Keep any dough that you are not working with well wrapped and chilled.

• A pastry cloth and rolling pin cover (available in large department stores or cooking shops) make the job of rolling the dough easier.

• You'll need a long lifter (or two) to transfer large pieces such as the roof to the baking sheet. You may find it easier to roll the dough directly onto a greased and floured baking sheet, or onto greased and floured aluminum foil and then transfer the foil to the baking sheet. (Cut out the pieces and remove the scraps, leaving the cottage pieces in place on the baking sheet or foil.)

• Parchment paper is wonderful for baking gingerbread on; if you use it, there's no need to grease the baking sheets.

• When in doubt, overbake rather than underbake, as crispier cookies will be much less fragile than soft ones.

• Recutting the baked pieces as soon as they come out of the oven is one of the most important steps (see directions), as it makes assembly much easier.

• A pizza cutter works very well for cutting both the dough and the baked gingerbread pieces.

• Meringue powder (available in specialty cake-decorating shops, as well as in some kitchen shops and bulk-food stores) can be used to prepare frosting. It eliminates the nuisance of leftover egg yolks and is very easy to work with. Follow the manufacturer's directions for preparation.

• When gluing cottage pieces together, it's helpful to have an extra pair of hands to hold them in place until the frosting sets. If these aren't available – as they often aren't until the candies arrive – use other props such as spice bottles or small cans or boxes.

DECORATING TIPS

Part of the fun of making a ginger-bread cottage – especially for younger family members – is the trip to the bulk-food store to buy candy and other treats for decorating. Let the kids use their imaginations, but to get the wheels turning, here are some of our ideas:

Stone chimney – chocolate-covered raisins and candy-coated peanuts

Woodpile – pretzel sticks

Large logs – chocolate flake candy

Shutters – squares of sesame candy

Shingles – any square cereal

Porch floor – row of chocolate-covered cookie fingers

Snowpeople – two large white gum-balls (marshmallows work well too) glued together with icing and set on an icing base, wearing gummy-worm scarves and hats made of Life Savers and gumballs

Chimney cap – square of chocolate candy with gumdrop on top and a curl of icing smoke

Property – large whole nuts for rocks, chopped nuts for ground, green sprinkles for grass, gumdrops and spearmint leaves for bushes

Railings – pretzel sticks on candy-stick supports

Boat – Tootsie-Roll seat, coated-licorice fenders, Life Saver life ring; outboard made of licorice Allsorts

sections meet. Hold both pieces in position 5 minutes until set, then let stand at least 20 minutes to dry before decorating. You can use spice bottles or cans of the right height to prop the roof pieces in place while they are drying.

8. While the cottage is drying, assemble the dock and boat. For the dock, use two parallel candy sticks as a base, and glue "boards" to them. For the boat, first glue the sides (H and J) to the bottom (M), carefully trimming the ends at an angle to fit at the front. Next, glue the stern (K) and deck (L) in place. (See photo, p. 172.)

9. Glue door in halfway-open position on cottage.

10. To make the chimney, run a line of icing along chimney piece E and glue it to the end wall without the window, fitting it under the roof overhang. The purpose of this piece is to build out the wall under the overhang so it is flush with the roof edge; if necessary, apply an extra-thick layer of icing to help

do so. Then glue the longer chimney piece F to this first piece. Glue the two small chimney pieces G together, and glue them to the roof side of piece F, so their bottom edges rest on the roof. (See photo, p. 172.)

DECORATING

Be creative and plan your own design, using our "Decorating Tips" (at left) and step-by-step hints (below) as a guide.

1. Decorate the basic cottage first: Spread a layer of icing on the roof and "shingle." Outline window in end wall with icing. Draw in windows on front wall with icing and glue on shutters. Decorate door. Cover chimney with icing and add stonework.

Using the icing bag with a #18 or #19 star tip, pipe a line of decorative icing along the edges where the walls meet and along the edges of the roof. (Skip the front edge of the roof if you are going to be adding a porch.) Pipe a line of icing along the roof ridge and decorate as you like.

2. Build the porch next: "Shingle" the porch roof (piece C) and allow to dry. Cover foil base in front of cottage with icing and lay the porch floor. Cut two candy sticks to length to support porch roof – they should be just long enough to give the porch roof a gentle slope – and cement to base with icing. Put a dab of

icing on top of each support and run a line of icing along front edge of cottage roof. Put porch roof in place and hold in position for a few minutes until icing hardens. Pipe a thin row of decorative icing along edges of porch roof.

3. Create the property and the lake: Spread part of the base and the rest of the slope around the cottage with icing and fill in "ground" as desired. For water, colour some

icing blue and spread on rest of base. Use ice cream cones with pointed bottoms, placed upside down, to make trees: With the star tip, pipe frosting on cones. Decorate with coloured candy or cake decorations, then let dry. For small trees, frost only the top parts of the cones; when dry, cut off cone bottoms.

Place pieces such as dock, boat, people, woodpile, animals, and shrubbery in position while the icing is still soft.

To "winterize" your cottage, sprinkle with icing sugar put through a sieve or strainer. Add snowpeople. Oh, yes, and remove your boat from the water.

HOW TO HOST A PIG ROAST

*Put in a firepit, construct a spit, and go whole hog on your
next summer barbecue. By Charles Long*

The only problem with a family cottage is that families tend to gather there. In-laws, neighbours, and distant cousins. Even if the lake is big enough for them all, the kitchen certainly isn't, and somebody has to cook. The next time your slavering hordes of Genghis Kin descend, consider the whole-beast feast. Classic pig on a spit is a wienie roast for adults. It is cooking in another dimension. But it is more than a means to feed a multitude. It is a day-long entertainment.

Hot coals soon turn a homely porker into a juicy glaze of golden brown. It looks done hours before it really is. It smells done. With the hiss and sizzle of roasting meat, it even sounds done.

For most of the day it will be too hot to touch and too soon to taste, but with three of the five senses already down on their knees and begging, you'll have more than enough volunteers to turn the spit, feed the fire, and baste.

By the time you prop an apple between the jaws of the plat du jour and carve, your guests will burst into grateful applause. This is the only feast where the guests do most of the work and the chef gets to take a bow before anybody takes a bite.

The tricky part comes in the advance preparations, when the family tinkerer has to cobble up enough hardware to keep piglet turning over the coals. For many, the hardware is where the fun comes in. At the Canadian Pork Barbecuing Championship, held each summer in Ayr, Ontario, the tinkerers turn spits with steam gizmos and antique engines. Eating is almost an afterthought. It's as if Julia Child had married Rube Goldberg and apprenticed under Visigoths – manic fun, but more trouble than a casual weekend might warrant.

Casual roasters will be more inclined to improvise with low-tech cookery, replacing exotic machinery with guest labour and a home-built apparatus. Adapting

what's at hand takes less money, but more time. The basic requirements include: a firepit, some type of heat reflector, a turning spit on sturdy supports, and a pig.

ORDERING THE MEAT: HOW BIG A PIG?

Order the pig from a butcher or abattoir at least two weeks ahead of time. It should come gutted, scraped, and all in one piece. Be sure to stress that you'll be spit-roasting, as the abattoir would otherwise halve the carcass to speed cooling. You'll need to work with what's available, but aim for at least a pound of pig per person (more with smaller animals: a 20 pounder will feed about 10). If that seems excessive, remember there will be waste, and appetites will expand to barbarian proportions with the smell of roasting pork.

You should end up with something between 20 and 80 lbs. Anything under 20 lbs. will likely be unweaned; and while a "suckling" pig sounds exotic, the meat is rather bland. Bigger animals are more flavourful, but anything over 80 lbs. will be hard to turn on makeshift equipment. Remember, too, that the bigger the pig, the longer it will take to cook.

The hardest part may be storage, since a whole animal won't fit the fridge, much less a picnic cooler. If you can, order the pig from a butcher nearby and pick it up the night before the roast. Give it a good wash, especially inside, to remove anything the butcher left behind. Store in a cool, varmint-proof spot overnight. A few bags or blocks of ice will help keep it cold.

PLACING THE FIREPIT AND RIGGING THE SPIT

The firepit can be a simple patch of bare earth or a long metal pan to hold the coals. For safety's sake, place it away from brush and buildings, and leave lots of room for an audience of kibitzers. Bring out a table for tools, and a tarpaulin for protecting the roast and the roasters from shade or showers.

Reflectors hold the heat around the meat, like the walls of an oven. The more closely the pig is enclosed, the faster and more evenly it cooks. Old hands make closed cookers out of everything from steel drums to oil tanks. You can, however, improvise ad hoc "oven" walls with stacked concrete blocks or old roofing metal. At the very least, provide one back wall, even if it's only a bank of earth, to deflect cooling breezes.

The spit supports must be sturdy and should incorporate some means of adjusting the distance between pig and coals. One low-tech solution is to assemble two tripods using poles. You can suspend the spit in chain or wire loops hung from the tripods. And you can raise or lower the spit by splaying the legs of the tripods. Keep in mind that the spit will have to rotate steadily for many hours. However you support it, make sure that the two cradles in which it turns are as smooth as possible, and test the spit for ease of turning before you put on the pig.

The spit itself is the easy part. Cut a green, hardwood pole from the nearest stand of overgrown saplings. You'll want the straightest one you can find. A pole about 1½" in diameter and 6'–8' long will fit the average pig. Peel off all the bark and any little knots or nubs. If hardwood is hard to come by naturally, skip the sapling and buy a sturdy hardwood dowel at a building-supply store.

Now you have to fasten a handle to the fat end of the sapling or dowel in order to turn it. If you can adapt something like an old churn crank or a big wrench, fine. Or you can make your own handle using a board and a length of dowel or pole. (See drawing opposite and box below.)

BUILDING THE FIRE: START EARLY AND GO BIG

The cooking time will vary widely with the size of the pig and the placement of reflectors. Count on its taking all day and see to getting the fire going early. With an average-sized pig (30–40 lbs.) and makeshift reflectors, leave roughly six to eight hours for cooking time. This might be on the generous side, but better the pig be done too early (you can always leave it warming over a low fire) than too late. What you want to avoid is having it not ready at dinner time and succumbing to the temptation to serve it before it's done. (We'll get into how to tell when it's done in a

PUTTING ON THE HOG

To make a handle for your spit, start with a board about 3" x 16". Cut a slot about 1" x 3" in one end. Drill a round hole in the other end. Then trim the fat end of the spit with an axe or knife to make a wide, flat tongue about 1" thick. Fit the slotted end of the board over the tongue of the spit and wire or bolt it tight. The bigger the pig and the rougher the turn, the tighter this coupling has to be. Now whittle a short handle to fit the drilled hole.

minute.) Start with a big wood fire and let it burn down to red-hot coals, which will take at least a couple of hours. The bigger the bonfire, the deeper the bed of coals and the longer the heat will last. Maintain the bed of coals by adding charcoal rather than wood, for heat instead of flame. (Two bags of charcoal should see you through the day.)

READYING THE ROAST FOR THE FIRE

When the fire is down to coals, mount the entrée with an entry best accomplished before your more squeamish guests arrive. Whittle the free end of the spit to a point and push it in where the pig isn't looking. It will be a tight fit at first, and you'll be grateful you didn't start with too big a sapling. Lift the tail and press on. A twist will help, as will a dollop of lard. Guide the point of the spit out through the mouth until the pig is centred on the pole.

It's a tight fit now, but as the day wears on piggy is bound to loosen up – and, unless you've taken precautions, the spit will begin to turn freely, leaving the meat flopping burned side down. The trick is to fasten beast to pole to keep them turning together. There are skewers and fancy clamps designed for this, but the crudest, simplest solution is to drive two long roofing nails through the back and into the pole – one at the back of the neck and the other just ahead of the hams. Stretch the feet out fore and aft and wire them tightly to the spit.

The body cavity is still open at this point and will soon become floppy chops if you don't sew it shut. First (why waste the space?), stuff it as you would a fowl. Bread, onions, apples, garlic, nuts, anything. Pack it tightly – we once used too few apples and they rattled around in the rib cage like bingo balls – then sew it shut with heavy twine. Finally, dress the ears and tail with aluminum foil so they don't burn.

The pig is now ready to set over the fire and turn. Suspend it at least a foot above the coals and watch closely, adjusting the height as necessary; you want to cook it as close to the heat as possible without burning it. The skin will soon brown, then crack. By the time the pig is done, some parts of the outside will be almost black. Not to worry – that's just skin. What you don't want to do is burn the skin completely off and expose the succulent meat beneath to direct heat. It's far better to hold the heat close with reflectors than to lower the meat too close to the coals. Some whole-hoggers baste with herbed oils, honey, and secret stuff. Others just splash on some beer now and then. In either case, the basting has more to do with keeping the skin intact than with adding to the flavour of the meat. What really keeps things juicy is the melt of fat from inside the meat. Porky is a natural butterball. But there's a downside to this too: Dripping fat can flare on the coals and burn the beast. Which brings us to your three assistants, recruited from among the early arrivals. You'll need a stoker, a turner, and a water person.

GET THE PARTY COOKING: LINE UP YOUR HELPERS

The turner is supposed to crank the spit at a steady 4 rpm. Speed isn't critical, but stress the number anyway just to give the task some technical panache. Provide a chair and a heat shield for bare knees. Despite appearances, this is not the most important job. Assign the crank to those guests who would otherwise be in the way. And substitute freely – this is Participaction for carnivores.

The stoker keeps the fire at an even glow with a scatter of charcoal now and then. Too much charcoal at once will first cool the fire and then overheat it. The ideal is to keep it right where it was when the last flame died.

The water person stands at alert, armed with a squirt gun to extinguish flares from dripping fat. That's the official job description. Unofficially, the water person ensures that stoker, turner, and chef don't suffer thirst from working too near the fire.

As chef, your duties are to adjust the height of the spit and rake the coals under

PIGGING OUT: HOW TO MAKE CHAMPIONSHIP STUFFING

Bill Hillis of St. Thomas, Ontario leads the "Galavanting Gourmets," past champs at the Canadian Pork Barbecuing Championship in Ayr, Ont. The Galavanters turn their custom-made cooker with a motor salvaged from a milk cooler. Bill attributes their success, however, to the Galavanters' special fuel. "We used dried corn cobs – about two feed bags full. People said it gave the meat a sweeter taste."

The Hillis crew eschews basting, but did stuff their prize-winning 86-pounder with five loaves of bread. The fine points, according to Mary Hillis, included: four whole-wheat to one white loaf, one and a half cans of cream of mushroom soup, onions, apples, sage, salt, and pepper. They ran the bread and onions through a food processor and combined this mixture with the remaining ingredients in a large garbage bag. They lined the pig's cavity with a crib-sized cotton sheet and then put in the stuffing. The sheet absorbed some of the grease and allowed a tidier presentation at judging time.

the parts that need the most cooking. In practice, this means an hourglass-shaped bed of coals, with hot spots under the thick hams and shoulders, and a cooler middle under the much-thinner abdominal section. If you're at all uncertain, check the hams and shoulders occasionally with a quick-read meat thermometer and adjust the coals accordingly. Finally, the chef has to settle all claims as to whose turn it is to do what, and to hold back the hungry mob until the main course is truly done.

SLICING AND SERVING IT UP

"Done" has little to do with number of hours cooked. "Done" is determined by sticking the quick-read thermometer deep into the thickest part, the ham. And do make sure it's really done. Undercooking is about the only way to spoil this feast. (Well … maybe a collapsing spit is an even worse disaster.) When the internal temperature of the ham reaches 176°F, or 80°C, you can hoist piggy – spit and all – onto the table. Extract the nails and the spit, prop the customary apple in the jaws, and carve.

The skin should peel off in strips. Set it aside for those who like that sort of thing. Likewise the trotters and tail. Scoop out the stuffing and stack it on a platter. Most of the meat is at the shoulders and the hams. Take that off in slices, right to the bone. If forks don't suit the crowd, slice the meat directly into sandwich buns. The choice pieces – the loins – lie on either side of the spine, between the hips and the ribs. Pull each loin off in one piece and slice it up for those special guests who helped. The rest of the meat will come off the carcass in juicy, barbarian chunks. Let the hordes help themselves to seconds.

The omnivores will expect something else on their plates. There's the stuffing, of course, but potato salad, applesauce, sauerkraut, and beans also all go well with barbecued pork. The best part is that all these accompaniments can be prepared ahead of time and not distract the chef's attention. Once you've got the fire and the spit under control, try setting an iron kettle of baking beans right into the coals, under piggy's middle. The kettle helps block the heat from overcooking the thinner rib section. Better yet, hot fat drips off the ribs and into the bubbling beans.

Be prepared for the vegetarians and the squeamish with meatless wieners and sausages and a bundle of sticks. Once the spit is out of the way, distribute sticks and sausages. Assure the vegetarians that your wieners contain no meat. Assure the squeamish that, no, the little piggies at the sausage plant weren't as cute as this one.

If spit-roasting appeals but pork is a problem for religious or dietary reasons, there are alternatives. Goat and lamb are small enough to be roasted whole. Neither, however, is naturally fat enough to be self-basting. Goat, especially, is lean and prone to drying out over the coals. Even lamb requires the chef to be more attentive with the basting. Whole beef is out of the question with makeshift equipment. A side or a quarter might be light enough for the improvised spit, but at that point you might as well barbecue the thing on a grill and forget the spit. Your guests will still eat well. They just won't be able to play with their food while it's cooking. ◢

GINGERBREAD LOON COOKIES

Make and decorate some treats that will remind you of life at the lake. By Jane Rodmell

Stars, trees, reindeer, and gingerbread people are the traditional shapes of the Christmas season – but we think our gingerbread loon is a cut above the rest. Hanging on the tree, these loon cookies will bring back memories of summer at the lake, and children will love decorating them. In fact, a batch of undecorated loon cookies makes a great gift for lakeside friends with kids; pack them in a tin with little bags of candies for decorating, a copy of the icing recipe, and ribbon for hanging the finished cookies.

To make a loon cookie "cutter," just trace the pattern on page 186 onto a piece of poster board or lightweight cardboard and cut it out.

GINGERBREAD:

3½ cups (875 ml) flour
2 tsp (10 ml) ginger
1 tsp (5 ml) cinnamon
1 tsp (5 ml) ground cloves

½ tsp (2 ml) baking soda
1 cup (250 ml) soft butter or margarine
1 cup (250 ml) brown sugar
½ cup (125 ml) molasses

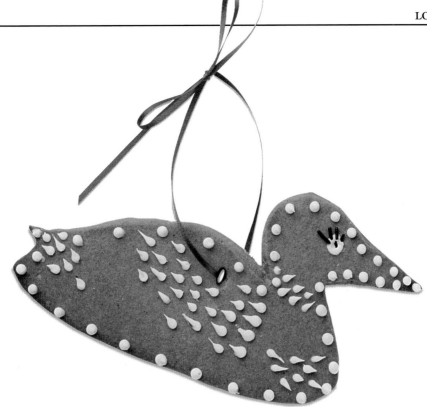

Sift flour, spices, and soda together. Set aside. Cream butter or margarine with sugar until light. Beat in molasses until smooth. Stir in dry ingredients a cup at a time, blending well to make a soft dough. (You may not need all the flour.)

The dough can be used immediately, or refrigerated or frozen until needed.

Flour a counter top or pastry board and a rolling pin. Roll out gingerbread to a thin, even layer about ³⁄₁₆" (0.5 cm) thick; don't let dough get any thinner or it will be hard to handle. It's easier for kids to work with the dough if you first divide it into several pieces.

Lay your cardboard loon cutout on top of the dough; cut around it with the tip of a sharp knife. Have some smaller cookie cutters on hand to fill in the spaces on the dough between the loons. Carefully transfer the cutouts to lightly greased and floured baking sheets using a spatula or lifter, being sure to support the loon's head and bill while doing so. If the cookies are to be hung on the Christmas tree, use the end of a drinking straw to cut a hole on the loon's back before baking.

Bake in a preheated 350°F (180°C) oven for about 10 minutes until cookies are firm to the touch and an even medium brown. Transfer to racks to cool.

Makes about 1½–2 dozen loons.

ICING:

3 egg whites
½ tsp (2 ml) cream of tartar

3–4 cups (750 ml–1 L) sifted icing sugar
Food colouring

Beat egg whites with cream of tartar until frothy. Gradually add icing sugar and beat until smooth and shiny.

Spoon some of the icing into several small containers and add a dab of food-

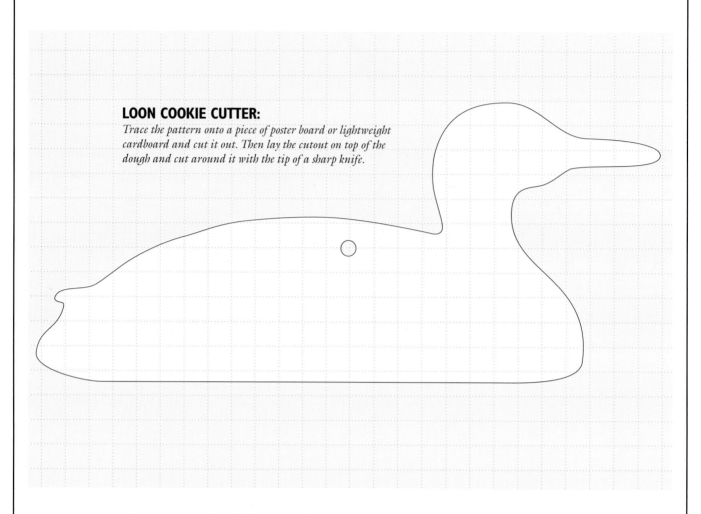

LOON COOKIE CUTTER:
Trace the pattern onto a piece of poster board or lightweight cardboard and cut it out. Then lay the cutout on top of the dough and cut around it with the tip of a sharp knife.

colouring paste (available at specialty stores) or a drop or two of liquid food colouring to each. Keep the containers covered with plastic wrap since the icing hardens quickly. If necessary, add a few drops of water to return icing to working consistency. When you're ready to decorate, fill several small icing bags fitted with writing tips. Have an assortment of small colourful candies, jellies, sprinkles, and silver balls on hand. After the icing hardens, tie ribbons through the loons if they are to be used as tree ornaments.

MAKING MAPLE SYRUP

Even if you have just a few sugar maples, you can tap into the sweet taste of spring. By Charles Long

Maple syrup is nature's cure for those summer's-never-comin' blues. Just as that drift of grit and mitten by the curb approaches a state of permafrost, the sweetest sap begins to rise unseen. For those who have a few sugar maples on their property, it's worth a preseason visit just to take this first pulse of spring.

To embark on a syrup-making expedition, you'll need a ½" auger, your biggest boiling pan plus a smaller one, cheesecloth, a small sieve, and an egg. And don't forget the pancake mix. Stop at a farm-supply store en route for pails and spiles, the proper name for the inexpensive aluminum spigots or taps.

How many? You'll need about 40 litres (40 qts.) of sap to make 1 L (1 qt.) of syrup. On a good day, a single tap can fill a standard 8-L pail. On a bad day, the drip's too slow to even wet the bottom. So strike when the weather is right – a warm sunny day following a freezing night. Under those conditions, half a dozen taps can catch enough for a ravenous family's brunch.

Use big healthy sugar maples – nothing less than 12" in diameter – and remember that sap, like *sapiens,* prefers the sunny side of the tree. The largest trees can take more than one tap, spaced around the trunk; but if you have enough trees, stick to one tap each and spare the extra stress of multiple taps.

Drill about 1½" into the wood, at a slightly upward angle. There's instant gratification if you've caught the weather right; the first gurgle of sap will follow the auger out of the hole. Tap in the spile with your fist and hang the pail on the hook. (Be careful not to split the bark or you won't get any sap.) The first *plip plip plip* will tell you you've done it correctly. If the sap drib-

MATERIALS

Auger with ½" bit
Spiles
Pails
2 pans for boiling (one, the largest you can manage; the other, somewhat smaller)
Outdoor grill
Candy thermometer (optional)
Cheesecloth
Small sieve
Egg

bles down the tree instead of into the pail, the spile is not in tightly enough. Rap it again, or drill a little deeper in case the spile is hitting the back of the hole.

While the buckets are filling, improvise an outdoor evaporator with a grill propped up on bricks or the barbecue. Anything but the kitchen stove will do – this much indoor boiling would peel the paper off the wall.

Gather a reserve of sap before you start the fire. You don't want the pan to boil dry if the trees aren't dripping fast enough to keep up with the evaporator. On the other hand, stored sap soon starts to ferment (as quickly as milk sours), and will produce a darker, lower-grade syrup or no syrup at all. One compromise is to make a weekend of it, gathering one day and boiling the next.

Boiling time depends on the surface area of the pan. With kitchen-sized equipment, you may need most of a day, but if the crew gets impatient, you can always cook weiners in the would-be syrup and pass out drinks of pure, icy sap.

Keep the evaporator at full boil, and top it up regularly as the level drops. Be careful around the pot: Boiling sap is hotter than boiling water. Monitor the quantity of added sap, and stop when you've reduced the liquid by about 20 to 1 – when 40 L of sap, for example, has boiled down to 2 L of dark bubbly stuff. Another indicator is to measure the temperature with a candy thermometer: When it reaches 220°F (104°C), you've got syrup. If it starts to foam and rise in the pan, you've gone too far; add more sap or take it off the fire immediately.

Now pour the hot liquid into the smaller pan, using damp cheesecloth to filter out any bits of bark or bug.

When it has cooled, break in an egg, shell and all. Whip it around with a fork and put it back on the heat. As it nears the boiling point, the egg will collect any guck the cheesecloth missed and bring it to the surface in a vile-looking scum. Scoop this off quickly with a tea-strainer or sieve. Then boil the syrup just a little more to thicken, and take it off as soon as it starts to foam.

May your summer be as sweet.

QUINJE OR SNOW HUT

Pile up a mound of snow, hollow it out, and you've got a cosy winter retreat. By David Zimmer

In summer, the tree fort is the answer to every parent's prayers. It keeps the kids entertained all day, allowing adults time to pursue more serious endeavours like Scrabble, hors d'oeuvres, and snoozing in the hammock. In winter, however, the tree fort has about as much appeal to a kid as going into town for a haircut.

The solution, of course, is to have the kids build a snow hut – easy to do, fun to play in, and actually quite toasty inside. We're not talking about an igloo, which is built of blocks and requires a type of snow rarely found south of Moose Factory. The snow hut – what the Canadian Outward Bound Wilderness School calls a quinje (pronounced kwin-jee; also spelled quincee) – is made by piling up the snow and digging out a hollow in the middle. Quinjes are very strong because the weight of the snow in the mound packs down the pile and makes it dense. Also, as you move the flakes around when piling up the snow, the molecules are jiggled enough to heat up and melt a bit. When the flakes cool down again, they freeze and lock together. Call it cold fusion.

The ideal quinje-making temperature is around -10°F (-23°C), but any temperature, from below freezing right down to -40°F (-40°C), will work just fine as long as the snow is nice and fluffy.

Begin by piling up snow

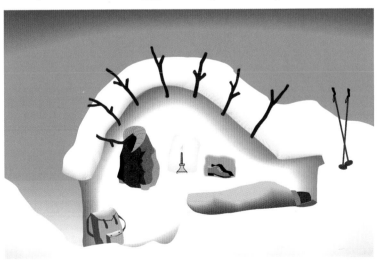

in a large mound. You want to end up with a total snow depth of about 9 ft., so if you're already standing in 3 ft. of snow, add another 6 ft. on top of that. Once the snow is piled, jab about 15 12"-long sticks into the dome of the pile, as you would into a pincushion, so that only the tip is showing. These will be used as depth gauges when you're hollowing out the pile. (You want the walls of the quinje to be about 12" thick.) At this point, let the quinje "cure." After about an hour, the surface might still look soft, but the interior will be fairly solid. Start digging.

It's helpful to think like a groundhog. You want to remove snow from the inside and move it outside – the same way a groundhog hollows out a burrow. Dig down first, and then head for the middle of the mound. This will give you more space on the inside, and keep wind from howling right in the front door. Keep an eye out for the depth-gauge sticks you pushed in: When you get to the tips of the sticks, you know the dome is approximately the right thickness.

Once the quinje is hollowed out, start the interior decorating. Using snow, build raised platforms for sitting (or sleeping). The snow keeps your body off the cold ground, or lake ice, and adds a measure of insulation. Small niches or shelves can be carved into the walls to hold any gear – a candle, for instance, which will elevate the temperature inside the snow hut and, thanks to the reflecting ability of snow, provide a wonderful light that you can actually read by – even in the dead of night. With a single candle burning and a couple of bodies inside, the temperature inside the quinje will rise 8°F–10°F (5°C–6°C). And at night, from outside, that lone candle gives the snow hut a warm, luminescent glow.

Because of its thick snow walls, it's almost impossible to hear any outside noises when you're inside a quinje. So it's a good idea to mark your area off with flags or skis stuck in the snow, because to a snowmobiler your cosy nook will simply look like an inviting launch ramp.

Finally, be assured that after a night of use a quinje is very strong, and the roof will support the weight of several adults. Besides, even if the whole shebang comes tumbling down, it's easy to stand up, crawl out, and start digging again. 🦆